Preview 2001+

Preview 2001+
Popular Culture Studies in the Future

edited by

Ray B. Browne

and

Marshall Fishwick

Bowling Green State University Popular Press
Bowling Green, OH 43403

Library of Congress Cataloging-in-Publication Data
Preview 2001+ : popular culture studies in the future / edited by Ray B.
   Browne and Marshall Fishwick.
        p.   cm.
   Includes bibliographical references.
   ISBN 0-87972-689-X (cloth). -- ISBN 0-87972-690-3 (pbk.)
   1. Twenty-first century--Forecasts. 2. Popular culture--Forecasting.
3. Popular culture--Study and teaching. I. Browne, Ray Broadus. II. Fishwick,
Marshall William.
CB161.P74   1995
303.49'09'05--dc20   95-46247
                                                                         CIP

Cover design by Laura Darnell-Dumm

Contents

Introduction

We have been slouching, with ambivalence—anticipation and dread—toward 2001 for a long time—indeed since the last millennium, a thousand years ago. Who since then could imagine a year on our Western calendar that didn't start with a 1? Slouch no more—start sprinting. Its imminence hovers over us. Ready or not, we confront the next millennium—2001 A.D.

In our lifetime, references to the 21st century used to conjure up science fiction—images of Buck Rogers and his helmeted cowboys in spaceships built like Buicks. No more. Technology has moved on, bringing new hardware and new software. The President we elect in 1996 will take us to the new dawn of the new century and the new millennium. The world we shape today will move us into a new one—brave or cowardly, successful or disastrous. What will the new world be like when we are networked, digitized, downloaded and soaring into cyberspace, when everybody lives alongside the Information Highway?

This much we know: we already live in a culture of impermanence. Paperbacks disintegrate, Polaroids fade, computers crash, pop groups are out before we know they are in. Transitional technology—like CD-ROMs, Unixtapes, diskettes, Betamax and eight-track tapes come and go with the season, or sooner. The first hypertext novel—Rob Swigart's *Portal* (1986)—was designed for that year's Apple Macintosh. A few months later the new model (Macintosh SE) appeared, and Swigert couldn't even run his novel. Ted Nelson, the computer pioneer, summed the problem up: "The so-called Information Age may be the Age of Information Lost." For sure Paradise has not yet been regained.

But far more than information has been lost. Much certainly has changed. Society seems no longer to sustain itself. The old American morality on which we built the "American Way of Life," the hope of the world, has melted away. Our sense of purpose and of ourselves has become warped. Instead of a nation we have become factions of self-interest, putting clan and tribe, ethnopietistic and nationalistic interests before the common good. Our changing attitudes have rewritten our vocabulary, and our new language has directed our lives. We no longer have the words *personal responsibility* and *shame* in our language and we no longer have personal responsibility and shame in our lives. We are

1

wrenched into warring parts. And the real question before us is whether violent assertion of what we claim as individual rights will not destroy us all individually and collectively.

Instead of the global village that it was supposed to collect us into, TV—and especially CNN—has driven us into hundreds of battling camps. The real question is how long the world's peoples—and the earth—divided among ourselves can survive. No wonder our scientists direct their radio beams toward space, searching for intelligence, and our ordinary people see spaceships and little creatures visiting them, leaving messages everywhere, especially on the wheat fields of England. (Apparently the superior intelligences find what they respect in rural England.) All of us are reaching out to find intelligent beings, realizing, however, that intelligent beings are not going to live long with the civilizations of *Homo sapiens*, since there is little sapience among us. Some of us suspect that those intelligences have already paid us a visit and hurriedly departed. If so, we may as well turn off the switch on our radio probings and save our money. Those intelligences out there already know too much to answer our call. Arthur C. Clarke's novel *2001* clued us into that world.

So we approach the new century and the new millennium (as our ancestors did earlier millennia) with fear and trembling. We think we may see T.S. Eliot's "eternal Footman" holding our coats, and we are afraid. Our fear is shaded with anarchy, and anarchy reaches out to its opposite, prophecy, and the voices in the Bible and the most enigmatic portion of that Bible, the Book of Revelation. The Book—regardless of what religious belief it codifies—has always been the Source, the Rock of Ages and the Seer of the future, the tea leaves of our past and the future. The fear of the day is that of the Apocalypse—as outlined by a recent highly influential movie called *Apocalypse Now.* Fundamentalism—the fiery voice of immediate fear—has rushed out of the churches and into the streets, into politics and popular culture. Fear of the imminence of the apocalypse is not new. In the early 17th century, British poet John Donne anatomized the unease and disquiet that new forces in life brought:

> And new philosophy calls all in doubt,
> The element of fire is quite put out;
> The sun is lost, and the earth, and no man's wit
> Can well direct him where to look for it.
> And freely men confess that this world's spent,
> When in the planets, and the firmament
> They seek so many new; then see that this

Is crumbled out again to his atomies.
'Tis all in pieces, all coherence gone. . . .

*(An Anatomie of the World. The first Anniversary
of the Death of Mistress Elizabeth Drury*, 1611)

More recently, the celebrated poet William Butler Yeats wrote "The Second Coming," with a stark prophetic passage which has echoed throughout culture ever since:

Things fall apart; the centre cannot hold;
Mere anarchy is loosed upon the world. . . .
The best lack all conviction, while the worst
Are full of passionate intensity.

Yeats predicts a Second Coming, when a strange creature will emerge from the sands of the desert:

And what rough beast, its hour come round at last,
Slouches towards Bethlehem to be born?

Joan Didion used Yeats's phrase in the title of her popular 1968 book, *Slouching Towards Bethlehem*, and we recall it now as we approach the millennium once again. Yeats's fears and powerful poetic language seem to apply to our times. We cannot identify the "rough beast" nor the time of its coming but we know it will arrive on the Information Superhighway.

So how are we to cope with all the rough beasts out in cyberspace, with our warring factions, our overheated and overambitious media, our complex popular culture? As usual, a truism rings true: an informed public is a responsible public. The best way to make the public informed is through education and a thorough knowledge of the popular culture in which we live. Without that knowledge we are like fish swimming in polluted water until they detect the menace and escape or perish. The waters in which we swim rush fast.

All around us the showers of gloom and doom threaten us. They turn up in talk shows, tabloids, and TV miniseries. They are the theme of blockbuster movies, like *Terminator II* and *Natural Born Killers*, and in terrorists' acts worldwide. One can easily believe that things are falling apart.

Even our spectacular technological advances and headlong dashing down the Information Superhighway toward perfection have raised much apprehension. The alarm was sounded in 1986 by

4 Preview 2001+

Theodore Roszak in *The Cult of Information: The Folklore of Computers and the True Art of Thinking.* He warned that we are lost in a jungle of undigested facts, beset by statistical blizzards that numb and befuddle. He reminded us that Big Brother in George Orwell's *1984* controlled by sending out endless statements on production and consumption. When Roszak's book was published there were 2,200 data bases on the market. We do not know how many there are now. But we do know that they have different codes, protocols, and command languages, creating our electronic Tower of Babel. Experts estimate that the data being coded doubles every 20 months. Where will this land us in the 21st century?

Many believe we shall be much better off, and much happier, than we are now. The popular consensus is that we are creating a new Utopia, even a new Eden. *Time* magazine reflected this view in its special spring 1995 issue with the front cover banner: WELCOME TO CYBERSPACE!

Certainly the corporations that get rich from the new technology (and advertise in magazines like *Time*) are enthusiastic. Others are not so sure. Have we made a Faustian bargain? Do we get great power but give up our humanity? Has technopoly replaced technology?

Just what is technopoly? The first explicit principles were laid out in Frederick Taylor's *The Principles of Scientific Management* (1911). The primary goal of human labor and thought is efficiency; technical calculation is superior to human judgment; and the world should be guided by experts. These principles, designed for the industrial workplace, eventually seeped into all aspects of American culture, and the "corporate lifestyle." It turns workers into "hands," then robots, becoming, in Neil Postman's words, totalitarian technology; and its chief support comes from computers.

Computers don't work; they direct work. They have little value without something to control. Bureaucrats use computers to create the illusion that decisions are not under their control. "Computers have determined. . . ." Has anyone in or out of the university not met this mandate? In Postman's words: "A bureaucrat armed with a computer is the unacknowledged legislator of our age, and a terrible burden to bear."

Postman traces the rise of technopoly in his recent and provocative book with that title (New York, Vintage, 1993). He builds on the work of Lewis Mumford, Herbert Read, and Jacques Ellul. All cultures, he contends, fall into three types: tool-using, technocracy, and technopoly. Humans devised tools over the centuries to meet immediate and specific survival needs: the arrow, club, spear, and even more complex items like temples and cathedrals. Until the 17th century, all cultures were tool-users. In *The Advancement of Learning* Francis Bacon, the first technocrat, outlined the foundation of a college for invention, anticipating the mentality of the modern world. He saw science as a source of power and progress; new inventions would be devised because they were powerful, not just because they were required. Bacon died in 1626 and it was years before his "colleges for invention" appeared. The 19th century invented inventing and mechanization took command. The best American example is Thomas Alva Edison, "The Wizard of Menlo Park," who spent most of his life thinking of things to invent. The idea was that if something could be done, it should be done. Progress became our watchword and our expectation.

All this altered the way we thought, talked, and acted and what we meant by "knowledge" and "truth." Every tool conceals an ideological bias. As Postman points out, to a person with a hammer, everything looks like a nail; to one with a pencil, everything looks like a list; to one with a camera, everything looks like a picture; to one with a computer, everything looks like data. Clearly computer culture is in ascendancy. What human skills, personal contacts, and traditions are in danger of disappearing? This from the legendary hacker Clifford Stoll, now a leader in the cyberspace backlash: "The computer community is impoverished. . . . Without a church, cafe, art gallery, theater, or tavern. No birds, rivers, or sky. Plenty of human contact, but no humanity."

All this indicates that the upcoming millennium is gripping and disturbing. Nothing is more fascinating, more addictive, than "looking into the future." Locked in the present, with little understanding of what today (let alone tomorrow) really is or means, we create our own mirage of wish-dreams. This book is, in this sense, part of the mirage. Popular Culture Studies joins the endless line of those trying to fathom "what it all means," what new challenges await us, and how we can meet them. Caught up in events that confuse us, given clues we can't comprehend, we proceed with fear and trembling. But proceed we must. There is no turning back.

America's near-domination of global popular culture may come to an end, as other world-dominant cultures of the past have. The sun now sets on the British Empire, Rome is no longer the capital of the world; that is Washington, D.C. Those world-dominant cultures were washed away by the seas of time. We are now witnessing a kind of new cultural fusion, in which portions of our popular culture (entertainment) are reworked, recast, and then replayed with a regional or national spin. Frank Brown, head of MTV Europe, sums it up about one element: "America still provides aspirational models, but now it's a two-way flow. The fusion has resulted in a much more diverse and varied youth culture."

Britain's A. Robert Lee sees our popular culture as *A Permanent Etcetera*, while Henry A. Giroux finds it among *Disturbing Pleasures*. Giroux thinks our popular culture is linked not only to commercialism and consumerism but to forms of pleasure, possibility and struggle.

In the 21st century, the great world divisions will be not so much ideological as economic and cultural. The terms "first-" and "third-world" will blur and fade. Popular culture will be recognized as not merely a form of entertainment but as a crucial key to survival since it is the voice of democracy and equality. It is everyday culture, and everybody has everyday culture.

So one of the great problems of the 21st century will be to understand the dynamics of the great force of popular culture unleased in a world of disparate peoples. We will have to look beneath the surface of society, of technology, of human behavior. We must identify old and new wellsprings of energy, technique and faith. This means clearing not only the junkyards from our highways and cities but also the bric-a-brac from our intellectual attics and universities. This will be a gargantuan task. The need is urgent. This study tries to move us in that direction.

The essays in this book are divided into five sections: Parameters and Dynamics of Popular Culture Studies; Leisure and Recreation; Sense of Community; Marketing Cultures; and Extension or Circularity.

In the first section, the initial essay, by Gerald Graff, may surprise many of us. His contention is that instead of the usual concept of the university and college as an Ivory Tower, the institutions of higher education are now properly institutions of popular culture and must become even more so in the next century.

Next Ray Browne discusses in general the cautions we need in future successful studies in popular culture, then tries to set parameters, or eliminate them, for such studies.

Then Ray Browne and Richard Gid Powers turn to a favorite approach to reality in the form of a dialectic over where Popular Culture Studies are and how they should develop in the next century and millennium. Next Marshall Fishwick turns to one of the great forces of our time—religious fervor—and charts its course now and its implications for the future. In the next essay, John Hague speculates over the questions of American civilization and ways of studying it in the future.

The second general section contains four essays. In the first, "The Play World of the New Millennium," James Combs, a highly respected political scientist, outlines the future world of *Homo ludens* and hopes that "the play-force of popular culture helps transform it beyond the wretched present into a garden of earthly delights." Next, two essays take up the present and future place of tourism and travel in the next millennium. Though slower than the electronic media, the airplane has been almost as powerful a force in shaping the present societies of the world, and this force will only grow in the future. A major ingredient of leisure time—and with many people far more than leisure recreation—is, of course, sports. The very nature of sports is at this moment undergoing a profound change. No longer is it a collective, game activity but instead it is an activity in which people compete to become stars and then to cash in on the stardom. When a professional football team will pay a running back $14 million a year for three years merely to run up and down the field trying to escape being tackled, then the concept of sports, and what they are doing to society, must be re-examined.

In the third section we present two essays taking up opposite attitudes toward the developing place and role of community in society. There can be no doubt that most of the forces unleashed in contemporary society address themselves to what kind of community people live in and seek. Clans, tribes, nationalist groups grip the problem of individual rights and community rights. Which are paramount and which must be sacrificed, and to what degree? These problems energize the two essays "Cultural Fragmentation in the 21st Century" by Arthur G. Neal, and "Community, Boundaries, Social Trauma and Impact in the 21st Century" by H. Theodore Groat.

In the fourth section, we turn to selling and marketing, the great thrust that drives all human activity. In the first essay, "The Big Chiliasm, or, Julian West, Meet the Genitorturers," Jack Moore studies one of the remarkable phenomena of our time and concludes, in the words of one of the participants, "We like our pain. And we're selling it." As we approach the end of the book and the promise of the end of time, "Marketing the Apocalypse: The Direct-Mail Ministry of Jack Van Impe," by Stephen J. Stein, and "Jock Evangelism," by Ken Baker, suggest a particularization of the great American hustle.

Finally, we have in the last section what could be an apparent paradox in "Internet 2001 and the Future," by Richard Jensen, and "Millennium" by Winfred Barton. But the speed and comprehensiveness possible on the Information Superhighway might be no more than that, comprehensiveness and speed, accelerated *déjà vu*, as we say, all over again.

Perhaps unclouded sunshine is not the correct forecast for the future. But if, as we suggested earlier, an informed public is a less vulnerable public, then we may be able to avert or postpone doomsday through an intelligent study of the problems. These essays, we hope, are the proverbial windows of opportunity.

Works Cited

Bacon, Francis. *The Advancement of Learning*. Oxford: Clarendon, 1926.

Didion, Joan. *Slouching Towards Bethlehem*. New York: Farrar, 1968.

Giroux, Henry A. *Disturbing Pleasures: Learning Popular Culture*. New York: Routledge, 1994.

Kowinski, William S. *The Malling of America: An Inside Look at the Great Consumer Paradise*. New York: Morrow, 1985.

Lee, A. Robert, ed. *A Permanent Etcetera: Cross-Cultural Perspectives on Post-war America*. Boulder, ⊾O: Pluto, 1994.

Max, D.T. "The End of the Book?" *Atlantic Monthly* Sept. 1994: 61.

Postman, Neil. *Amusing Ourselves to Death: Public Discourse in the Age of Show Business*. New York: Viking, 1985.

Roszak, Theodore. *The Cult of Information: The Folklore of Computers and the True Art of Thinking*. New York: Pantheon, 1986.

Rushkoff, Douglas. *Media Virus!: Hidden Agendas in Popular Culture*. New York: Ballantine, 1994.

Swigart, Rob. *Portal*. New York: St. Martin's, 1988.

Taylor, Frederick. *The Principles of Scientific Management*. New York, London: Harper, 1911.

I

Parameters and Dynamics
of Popular Culture Studies

The parameters and dynamics of Popular Culture Studies are not absolutely clear in everyone's eyes. That there has been a great upsurge in such studies in the last ten years is evident. A decade ago most of the interest in such studies came from scholars who were not mainline, those who were in some way affiliated with the general Popular Culture Studies movement, and those who, more or less from a Marxist point of view, studied mass culture, with which they may or may not have equated popular culture.

Now the scene has changed dramatically. Conventional scholars in conventional disciplines—such as sociology, history, literature, religion, etc., etc.—are recognizing the necessity for making the everyday culture associated with their disciplines at least a dimension of their study. The result has been a great widening-out of interest and inclusion of the field in general studies. The result has been the discovery of much material in scholarship and an enrichment of that scholarship. The material of study has been broadened, the result more nearly a complete and analytical investigation. As a consequence, scholarship has improved in every way.

The University *Is* Popular Culture

Gerald Graff

Like most academics, I was surprised that the recent attack on "political correctness" in the humanities has been so persuasive to such a wide audience. Not that I don't think political correctness is real and something to worry about. PC *is* a real problem, I think, even if Roger Kimball and Dinesh D'Souza say it's a problem. But the allegations by these and other conservatives of the takeover of the entire American university by activist radicals have been so phantasmagorically exaggerated that I was amazed and dismayed that so many unsuspecting nonacademics have seemingly bought it. The more I think about the matter, however, the more I wonder why I should have been amazed. Given the remarkably nebulous picture of the academic humanities that has existed in the public mind, why shouldn't the public have found the PC horror stories completely convincing? And what is likely to unconvince that public if these attacks continue into the next century, as they figure to do?

The fact is that the recent anti-PC attack would never have been so successful if it had not been overlaid on uncertainties about the humanities that have existed ever since they first became academic departments a hundred years ago. If academic humanists have proved to be sitting ducks for the most exaggerated misrepresentations, surely one reason is that few people outside universities and not many inside have been able to form a clear idea of just what it is an "academic humanist" does. Three anecdotes to illustrate my point:

1. Several years ago, on my way to a conference at the National Humanities Center in North Carolina, I and several other conference participants find ourselves at the Raleigh/Durham airport looking for the courtesy vans that are to drive us out to Research Triangle. Just then an announcement comes over the intercom: "Will the parties going to the National *Humanitarian* Center please meet your buses at the baggage claim area."

2. The national Humanities Alliance recently commissions a public relations firm to survey public perceptions of the humanities. Though the great majority of those interviewed claim to have a favorable image of

This essay appeared previously in Democratic Culture 3, no. 1 (Spring 1994), *the newsletter of Teachers for a Democratic Culture.*

the humanities, like the airport pager a substantial number associate the term with "humanitarian" activities such as prevention of cruelty to animals. Others who answer yes to the question of whether they themselves participate in the humanities list "singing in the shower" as an example of humanistic activity.

3. A college dean confesses that he has always had difficulty understanding why the humanities should have become a department and research field. "What I don't see," he says, "is why there need to be whole departments to cover the books that I read going to work on the train every day."

These cases are not surprising, for we humanists have done little to address—or even recognize—the widespread public incomprehension about what it is we do, what our research is all about, and why it should be supported by institutions devoted to educating undergraduates. And when we *have* recognized the public's incomprehension of our activities, we have tended to treat it as an inevitability rather than something we might be able to change. In fact, we have come up with all sorts of reasons either why we cannot represent ourselves to a broader public or why we should not.

In the olden days, this disdain for public representation justified itself as a refusal to lower ourselves to the level of the philistines. In today's more politically enlightened times, the disdain is justified as a refusal to be co-opted by the dominant structures of discourse. Whereas popularization was once seen as vulgar, it is now seen as politically complicit. But the resulting ineptitude at representing ourselves to a broader public ends up being the same in either case.

It is odd that an institution that has recently generated such an unprecedented degree of sophistication about the workings of *representation* should remain arrested at so primitive a level when it comes to thinking about its own representations. But having treated mere image-making as beneath our dignity, we have left it to our enemies to construct our public image for us.

To put it another way, the humanities have yet to come to terms with the fact that, once the university became a mass institution, it perforce became an agent of cultural popularization. I wonder if we have ever really believed that mass education is possible—that is, that it is possible to reach most students, not just the top 15 or 20 percent. One might think that it would be easy for teachers who work in a *mass* education system to think of themselves as popularizers, and that it would be easier still now that many humanists are more receptive than we once were to the study of popular culture. American popular culture and the American professional university emerged at the same moment historically, and they have followed similar lines of development and expansion. Yet we still tend to think of popular culture as something we may *study* but not as something that we *are.*

Of course it is the competitive relation between academic and non-academic forms of popular culture that makes it difficult to see their points of commonality. It has long been a commonplace—heard equally on the Right and the Left—that academic intellectual culture has been in a losing competition with the media for the attention and allegiance of students. How can the culture of the book possibly compete with the culture of TV? How can Immanuel Kant and Henry James hold their own against the Super Bowl, Wrestlemania, and Madonna?

The oppositions are deceptive, however, in more ways than one. For if there is a real gulf here, it is no longer between Madonna and Henry James, now that both have become objects of academic analysis, but between Madonna on the one hand and academic discourse about Madonna *and* Henry James on the other. The real opposition is not between media culture and high culture, but between media culture, which has popularized itself successfully, and the culture of academic intellectuality and analysis, which has hardly begun to imagine that it may have possibilities of popularization, or which remains deeply ambivalent about popularization.

There are signs that the present culture war may be altering this attitude, shaking humanists out of our traditional complacency and forcing us to recognize that we too are part of the culture industry and are engaged in a critical struggle for survival in it. If recent anti-PC attacks force us to become more aware of our responsibilities for public representation, it may eventually be possible to look back at even the most ill-informed and malicious attacks and say, "Thanks, we needed that." Whatever one may say about them, the success of these attacks has exposed something that we cannot afford to ignore, namely, how poorly we humanists have performed our role as popularizers—that is, as teachers.

The very hostility that has been expressed toward academic humanists in the culture war is a sign that the distance has decreased between those humanists and the nonacademic public, who a generation ago would not have cared enough about their doings to make bestsellers of books like *The Closing of the American Mind* and *Illiberal Education.* Then, too, not all the curiosity has been negative. During the same period when attacks on "the rising hegemony of the politically correct" were crowding the *New York Times* op-ed pages, the *New York Times Magazine* was running picture stories glamorizing academic trend-setters like Richard Rorty, Elaine Showalter, Henry Louis Gates, Stanley Fish, Cornel West, and Stephen Greenblatt. The anti-PC attack represents only the nasty side of America's highly ambivalent and often worshipful fascination with the academy. We have only just concluded the first generation in American history during which a majority of eligible Americans went to college, creating a large sector of the middle class that wants to keep in touch with what is going on on campus, if only to know what its tuition money is buying for its sons and daughters.

Let us return to my earlier comparison between the popular media and the academy in their notoriously unequal competition for the minds of the young and the culture at large. The point I would now add is that the media did not achieve their enormous influence without elaborately thought-out efforts at collective organization. Everyone knows that the awesome effort of organization that goes into the making of even the slightest television commercial is in many ways a more impressive creative feat than the resulting product. To be sure, a television commercial has cultural influence because it has the backing both of money and ideological hegemony. Even so, the commercial would not achieve such ideological potency without a tremendous amount of teamwork involving writers, directors, actors, photographers, station managers, and innumerable other participants in a division of labor that is integrated to a staggering degree.

What I want to suggest is that it is foolish to think that academic culture can compete with the television commercial or the rock concert unless it is willing to think seriously about how it organizes its own representations. It is not foolish, however, to believe that academic culture has a potential that has gone untapped because it has failed to think seriously about how it organizes its representations.

This is not to say that American teenagers would drop Beavis and Butthead or *Wayne's World* for *PMLA* if only we organized the MLA convention more effectively. I am saying, however, that some of the intellectual concerns even of the MLA convention (which is bound to have a panel on Beavis and Butthead one of these days, if it has not already) have a potential interest for young people that won't be discovered or tapped without an effort at organization.

If we academics are willing to study the media we should also be willing to learn from them. To be sure, there are vast differences: organizing a Madonna concert or a Miller Lite commercial is clearly something quite different from organizing the history of literature, much less the history of culture, or the discourse of anthropology or literary criticism. Quite apart from their enormous advantage in the amounts of money available to them, the organizers of concerts and commercials also enjoy a degree of consensus about the ends and means of their representations that academics do not and cannot have or even desire. We have an idea what it means to organize a rock concert, but what does it mean to "organize" the history of culture or the discourse of the humanities? And who will decide who gets to be the organizers and the organized?

Neither the cultural left nor the cultural right have the power to superimpose a privileged agenda on the entire curriculum—that is the limitation of all the schemes for a "radical curriculum" or a "pedagogy of the oppressed." Nor is a monolithic leftist or rightist curriculum even desirable, since neither the left nor the right agenda can become intelligible to students unless they are taught in relation to one another. However at odds they may be ideologically, the cultural left and the right are cognitively interdependent—they need one another in order to become comprehensible to those students and others for whom terms like "cultural left" and "right" are now nebulous.

It will not do, however, to disdain the idea of "organizing" academic and intellectual representations because such an idea is ideologically problematic—what idea would not be?—or because it sounds ominously like social engineering. The history of culture and the discourse of the humanities are *already* elaborately organized in innumerable complex ways, by departments, journals, fields, curricula, courses, and programs. The choice is never between organizing institutional representations or not organizing them, for by definition *some* form of organization of institutional representations is inevitably always in place. To pretend that it is possible to occupy an autonomous space that is not already organized is only to make it more likely that the existing mode of organization will not change.

I have argued elsewhere that as academic culture has become more ideologically diverse and conflicted, it is increasingly impossible to organize departments and curricula around a consensus on what should be taught and why. My argument that the best response the academy can make to the conflicts over culture is to "teach the conflicts" themselves has been an organizational argument, an argument about how difference and controversy can replace consensus as a means of giving coherence to the curriculum.

Critics who have called this proposal impractical, or too radical, or not radical enough, have missed the central point, which is that the academy is *already* teaching the conflicts now and has been for some time. The academy teaches the conflicts, in effect, every time a student goes from a science class to a humanities class or from a class taught by a traditionalist to a class taught by a feminist.

The academy is already teaching the conflicts now, but it is doing so in a poorly organized way, representing disparate positions and assumptions to students as a series of isolated monologues rather than in their engagement and relationship with one another. When this disconnected mode of representation does not simply conceal the major cultural conflicts from students—they are becoming too hard to conceal—it prevents students from gaining control of the intellectual discourses in which the conflicts are fought out.

A student today can go from one literature teacher who assumes that "the Western humanistic tradition" is uncontroversially above criticism to another teacher who refers uncontroversially to that tradition as an instance of the "hegemonic ideology of the dominant order." Since the hypothetical student never sees these two teachers in dialogue with one another, he or she may fail to recognize that they are referring to the same thing—that is, that they are in disagreement. Such a student is likely to be confused about the nature of both teachers' positions, which make sense only in relation to and in dialogue with one another. These two teachers need one another in order to become intelligible to their students—and to others outside the academic orbit.

In conclusion, then, I am suggesting that there is a connection between the academy's unintelligibility to students and other non-professionals and the fact that we tend to teach in isolation from our colleagues, effacing the dialogical relations between our positions that our intelligibility depends on. But I am also suggesting that there is a connection between this nondialogical mode of organization and our notorious unintelligibility to the general public. A conflicted institution like ours can explain itself only by making its differences coherent. This we have not done, and we cannot do, as long as we fail to organize ourselves and our curriculum more dialogically.

That is why clarifying to outsiders what we do has to be a collective, not an individual, project, and why we need to start applying to the curriculum the sophisticated analysis of representation that we are accustomed to applying to film and television. But beyond such analyses, we need to come to terms with the inevitable task of popularization that has been given to us whether we are comfortable with it or not. In other words, we need to come to terms with the fact that we are teachers—not teachers as opposed to researchers but teachers and popularizers of our research. The media did not achieve its vast influence without effective organization. Neither can the academy.

As we move into the next century, the task gets ever larger, and how we attempt to deal with it becomes ever more urgent. Just as in the past the coming of a new century has stimulated new ways of thinking, the dawn of the 21st century should free us from long-ingrained assumptions and enable us to see the vital connection between higher education and popular culture studies.

Coping with Success:
Homo empatheia and Popular Culture Studies in the 21st Century

Ray B. Browne

In thinking of coping with the success of Popular Culture Studies we should remember that all phenomena of life are fields of enquiry in such studies. Success in the study of popular culture is inevitable and imminent.

It is prudent at this time to address the issue of what the future holds. Many people see ahead in the calendar the Great C, the birth of a new century, and the much greater M, the next millennium, and they realize the trauma of such an occasion and the opportunities a new century—and a new thousand years—seems to offer. We need to think seriously of what lies in store for Popular Culture Studies in the 21st century.

Judging from the throbs and pulsations currently emanating from the field, I would say that the new century holds great promise. The advances in the immediate past—say the last five years—have been almost staggering. With this success we need to think about our proper moves for building on that success. How should we approach Popular Culture Studies as we move toward the 21st century?

First, where are we now? Some peripheral but important signs. In the broadest sense, the term, over which we have shed so much sweat and blood, is now the language of the land. It occurs in all the media, and without any self-consciousness: people no longer put quotation marks around it, or even explain what it means. Generally, except for journalistic brevity the term *pop* is giving way to the more dignified word *popular*. Interestingly, it is now the language of Wall Street. *USA Today* recently reported, for example, that "popular culture" stocks are hot property. One stock (Timberland) soared 338 percent (Nov. 11, 1993).

Essentially the same essay is published concurrently in American Popular Culture at Home and Abroad, *edited by Lew Carlson, Western Michigan University's New Issues Press, 1995.*

Second, Popular Culture Studies is the red button in academia these days. It is a growth industry. Although there is still, as far as I know, only one Department of Popular Culture in the world, other academic departments are developing scholars and courses in popular culture in such traditional fields as anthropology, architecture, art, English, ethnic studies, journalism, law, radio-film-TV, religion, sociology and women's studies. There are many free-lancing individuals throughout the country teaching one or more courses. We estimate that at least a million students in the United States take a course in popular culture under one name or another every year. Departments which a few years ago did not see any place for popular culture studies are now welcoming them. At M.I.T. a professor of Literature, Film and Media Studies, who has never worked with the Popular Culture Association, offered for the second time in June 1994 an expensive seminar entitled: "Ninja Turtles, the Macho King and Madonna's Navel: Taking Popular Culture Seriously." The course served a need: "Responding to growing public interest, this seminar is designed for teachers who hope to address issues of popular culture in their classrooms, for scholars who want a good overview of basic work in Cultural Studies, and for laypersons who desire a better grasp of the roles that popular culture plays in our everyday lives." The course is further justified: "No longer seen as trivial, popular culture has found its way into the academy and scholars are adopting new approaches for analyzing and evaluating films, television, comic books, rock music and other forms of commercial entertainment." One of the features of the course is a "major exhibition," by the Museum of Modern Art "considering the relationship between modern art and popular culture." Some of us may cringe at the naivete of the instructor's approach, but he demonstrates how everybody is getting into the study-popular-culture act.

Well, not everybody yet. The literati cling to the old ballasts like swimmers afraid to test the gentle currents of change. But not without some challenge. One academic who has turned to the literary extreme in her criticism is D.J.H. Jones, a pseudonym for a critic who according to the blurb on her dust jacket "has served as department chair at seven of the eight Ivy League schools, six of the Seven Sisters, and one institution in the Atlantic Coast Conference. He/she has been the recipient of significant and insignificant grants," continues the blurb, "from every major and minor granting agency. A reconstructed New Critic, Jones has had brief incarnations as a deconstructionist, Marxist-feminist, postmodernist, and poststructuralist but now firmly denies any critical allegiance. He/she currently teaches courses in the literature of catering while pursuing a graduate degree in deviant psychology."

In her criticism of the ways of modern academics, Jones turns to crime fiction, in her delightfully acerbic novel *Murder at the MLA*. Nancy Cook, a bright and promising assistant professor of English at Yale, in explaining academia to the homicide detective in charge of the case is asked what she would do to reform the academic system if she were given the power. In her ideal system, she explains, "work will have something to do with the real world. Right now, the real world exists about once a year at Yale, when they have their United Way drive. It's the same at a lot of places. The March of Dimes is the most innovative thing the department chairs can think of" (121). Later she explains how *power* in academia is everything: the power to withhold knowledge, to deny advancement, to shroud recognition, to protect turf, to prevent equality. All these immoral acts performed while professing the power of literature to advance the humanities in life.

There is a lovely double entendre in Jones's title, for indeed, there are two kinds of murder at MLA. In addition to the acts of homicide, which she pictures, all too often, to paraphrase *Macbeth*, academia does murder learning, or at least twists and stunts its growth. But murder will out, and there is an increasing recognition of the need for the everyday world—the study of popular culture—in academia.

History especially is turning to the study both directly and as an enrichment of other major topics. "Popular culture is a mainstream field in American history now," says David Thelen, editor of *The Journal of American History*. "It's at the center of a lot of interpretive issues in the humanities" (qtd. in *Chronicle of Higher Education*, 16 Feb. 1994).

An excellent example of the way the scales are falling from the eyes of the defensive self-righteous is an account given in the acknowledgments of Robert C. Davis's *The War of the Fists*:

A few years ago, shortly after I had discovered the pleasures and challenges of the Chronicle of the *pugni* in Venice's Museo Correr, I mentioned to a more experienced colleague how much I would enjoy the chance to write my own history of the city's *battagliole*. His immediate response was, in so many words: Why? Who would ever want to read about such a tasteless topic? . . . Happily, as I have explored and worked out the principal themes of the *War of the Fists*, I discovered that my colleagues in Venetian history, and indeed in social history generally, were as likely to be as fascinated and attracted as I was by this cult of popular violence and public disorder that flourished for so many centuries in the heart of the world's Most Serene Republic. It is largely due to their constant encouragement, support and criticism—their understanding of the central role of popular culture in an absolutist society— that this book has been possible. (vi)

A more direct approach is found in the manuscript currently being prepared by Robert W. Rydell, *Popular Culture in America, 1865-1920*, in a series generally edited by historians John Hope Franklin and A.S. Eisenstadt, and a chapter in another book in the same series, *Home Front U.S.A.: America During World War II*, titled "Campaigns and Popular Culture," by Allan M. Winkler.

Most American journals in the humanities and social sciences gladly publish articles on popular culture. The Popular Culture Association has ten regional chapters, and four of them have journals.

Nearly all the presses in the country, which 20 years ago would not have touched the subject, have been stimulated to start publishing in the field. There are at least five books on Walt Disney currently in preparation, which should be published within a year. Some presses, like Routledge and University of Manchester Press, seem to be publishing more books in various fields of popular culture than in any other; though nearly all have a leftist political bias, they are nevertheless studies in everyday culture. Presses like the University of Chicago, University of California—and Columbia University—are developing strong publication records in the area. Greenwood has its popular culture .series, as does the Press of the State of New York. Let me illustrate the range of publications from perhaps some unexpected presses:

Bodylore (edited by Katharine Young, 1993); *Halloween and Other Festivals of Death and Life* (edited by Jack Santino, 1994); *Personal Discipline and Material Culture: An Archaeology of Annapolis, Maryland, 1695-1870* (by Paul Shackel, University of Tennessee Press, 1993) *Great and Noble Jar: Traditional Stoneware of South Carolina* (by Cinda K. Baldwin, 1993); *Images of the South: Constructing a Regional Culture on Film and Video* (edited by Karl G. Heider, 1993); *Singing Cowboys and Musical Mountaineers: Southern Culture and the Roots of Country Music* (Bill C. Malone, 1993); *Reading Football: How the Popular Press Created an American Spectacle* (by Michael Oriard, 1993), *Subduing Satan: Religion, Recreation, and Manhood in the Rural South, 1865-1920* (by Ted Ownby, University of North Carolina Press, 1993); *We Gather Together: Food and Festival in American Life* (edited by Theodore C. Humphrey and Lin T. Humphrey, 1991), *Cemeteries and Gravemarkers: Voices of American Culture* (edited by Richard E. Meyer, Utah State University Press, 1989).

I could go on and on through virtually every university press in America: *Poor Whites of the Antebellum South: Tenants and Laborers in Central North Carolina and Northeast Mississippi* (Charles C. Bolton, Duke, 1994); *Citizen Worker: The Experience of Workers in the United States and Democracy and the Free Market During the Nineteenth*

Century (David Montgomery, Cambridge, 1994); and *The Hunt for Willie Boy: Indian Hating and Popular Culture* (James A. Sandos & Larry E. Burgess, University of Oklahoma Press, 1994); and from small presses: *Outwrite: Lesbianism and Popular Culture* (Gabriele Griffin, Pluto Press, Boulder, 1993).

In teaching and research in the traditional fields in academia, Popular Culture Studies are saturating most schools. In English Departments, and the whole Modern Language Association, for example, perhaps the movement is most revealing. Members of English Departments have been traditionally both the bitterest foes to the study of popular culture and the most enthusiastic supporters, and the source of the largest number of participants in the Popular Culture Association and publishers in the *Journal of Popular Culture*, about 50 percent. Other fields within the MLA have always participated though to a lesser extent. For at least ten years the Popular Culture Association has had two sessions at the annual Modern Language Association meeting, and for about the same period Popular Culture has been one of the official fields of study in the MLA. So we have had a foot in the door for some time. Now, however, the door seems to be opening wider because of pressures from various other sources. At the annual meeting of the MLA in 1992, 10 percent of the sessions were in popular culture subjects; in 1993 the number had almost doubled, to 19 percent. Let me give you some examples:

380. *The West German Discourse on Terrorism since the 1970s*
 1. "Kluge's *Strongman Ferdinand* and the Discourse of Terrorism," Kent Casper, University of Colorado, Denver.
 2. "Heinrich Böll and Terrorism," Erhard Friedrichsmeyer, University of Cincinnati.
 3. "A German Nightmare: The R.A.F. and the Return of the Repressed," Matthew Grant, Cornell University.

413. *German Television: Politics and Aesthetics*
 1. "Foreigners on German Television" Multiculturalism and Gender in Hark Bohm's film *Yasemin*, Sabine Von Dirke, University of Pittsburgh.
 2. "'Tartort': The Generation of Public Identity in a German Crime Series," Michelle Mattson, Columbia.
 3. "From Building Blocks to Radical Construction: (West) German Media Theory since 1970," Michael Gisler, Middlebury College.

459. *Healing Narratives*
 1. "Quilting: Postmodern Performance as a Celebration of Mourning," Marcia Blumberg, York University.

2. "Alcoholism and the Epistemological Cure," Rosemarie Johnstone, University of Minnesota.

3. "Frida Kahlo's Therapeutic Art," Susan Taylor, University of Tampa.

4. "Coming Out with Secrets: Lesbians and Incest Narratives," Ann Cvetkovich, University of Texas, Austin.

In sociology and the American Sociological Association perhaps the proportion of people working in Popular Culture Studies is even higher. In the 88th annual meeting of the American Sociological Association (1993), for example, 23 percent of the sessions were clearly on such subjects. Let me give you a few examples. Two were listed as "Popular Culture."

315. *Regular Session. Popular Culture.*

1. "Recreational Terror: Audience and Textual Strategies," Isabel Pinedo, Fairleigh Dickinson University.

2. "Popular Culture and Emotional Experiences: Rituals of Filmgoing and the Reception of Emotional Culture," Steve Derne, St. John Fisher College.

3. "New York Jews and Chinese Food: The Social Construction of an Ethnic Pattern." Gaye Tuchman, University of Connecticut; Harry Gene Levine, Queens College, City University of New York.

4. "The Pursuit of Wellness," Peter Conrad, Brandeis University.

251. *Regular Session. Visual Sociology*

1. "Artists' Views of New Jersey," Judith J. Friedman, Rutgers University.

2. "'Wish You Were Here,' Asylum Postcards," Robert Bogdan, Syracuse University.

3. "Biography and History as Negotiated Order: The Visual Construction of a Presidency," Diana Papademas, State University of New York, Old Westbury.

4. "From Illustration to Integration: The Presentation of Photographs as Sociological Research," Steven J. Gold, Whittier College; Charles S. Suchar, DePaul University.

Even nearer to home, the percentage of presentations in the latest American Anthropological Association program was a reassuring 75.7 percent. Though the researchers there differ somewhat in their approach, their eyes are on the same subjects as ours. For example: "Trail, Distress and Torture: Violence and Justice in the Andes, Raquel Ackerman; "Martial Gods and Magic Swords: History, Myth and Violence in Chinese Popular Religion," by Avron A. Boretz, Cornell University;

"His and Hers: Gender and Garage Sales," by Gretchen M. Herrmann, SUNY Cortland; "Spirituality, Religious Experience, and American Country Dancing," by Juliana Flinn, University of Arkansas at Little Rock; "Rituals of Resettlement: Identity and Resistance among Maya Refugees," Nancy Wellmeier, Arizona State University; "Surveilling Cirque Archaos: Transgression and the Space of Power in Popular Entertainment," by Kenneth Little, York University; "Yes, It's True: Zimbabweans Love Dolly Parton," by Jonathan Zilbert, University of Illinois.

Closer to home, of course, are the people working in American Studies. According to the 1993 international meeting program, 126 of 176 sessions, over 70 percent, were on popular culture subjects. For example:

1. "Narrative and Power in the Documentary Film: Agee, Levitt, and Meyers' *The Quiet One*," by Maren Stange, Cooper Union.
2. "The Romance of Social Change: Documentary and the American South," by Jane Gaines, Duke University.
3. "Documentary Film and the Power of Interrogation: Kopple's *American Dream*, Moore's *Roger and Me*," by Miles Orvell, Temple University.

The Laugh of the Medusa: Women, Performance, and the Question of Hierarchy (97):
1. "Topsy's Sister: 'Bad' Women and Performance Tradition," by Lillian Schlissel, Brooklyn College.
2. "Art Against Patriarchy: The Transgressive Acts of Jenny Holzer and the Guerilla Girls," by David Brody, Boston University.
3. "Native American Identity Issues and Spiderwoman Theater's Counter-Mimicry," by Rebecca Schneider, New York University.
4. "Comic Interventions: Women's Stage Humor at the Turn of the Century," by Susan Glenn, University of Washington.
5. "Comedy and Cultural Hierarchy: The Elinore Sisters in Vaudeville and Musical Comedy," by M. Alison Kibler, University of Iowa.

Closest to home of all are the people working in folklore. The 1993 program of the American Folklore Society demonstrates that virtually every session and paper was in the field of pre-electronic or electronic-age popular culture:

42. *Folklore and Film*
1. "Dance for a Chicken: The Cajun Mardi Gras" (a film), Pat Mire.

2. "Collaboration Between Folklorists and Filmmakers: Roles and Responsibilities," Maida Owens.

3. "The Present and the Past in Cajun Mardi Gras," Carl Lindahl.

4. "On the Edge of Chaos: The Relationship Between the Mardi Gras and Its Observers," Barry Ancelet.

71. *Final Addresses*

1. "Gone Home: Family Plots in an Indiana Graveyard," Suzanne Waldenberger.

2. "The Quick and the Dead: Graveyards as Reflections of Social Attitudes Towards Death," Peter G. Harle.

3. "'The Little Graveyard Where My People Are': Family Cemeteries in Southwest Louisiana," Marcia Gaudet.

4. "Decoration Day: Alabama's Day of the Dead," Joey Brackner.

What do all these statistics and examples demonstrate? They show how widely popular culture subjects are being studied in academia. I assume the trend will continue, and in the immediate future at a fast clip. Some of the efforts are traditional, some are new. Other academic disciplines are holding binoculars on the future and trying to read the winds. Undoubtedly some will be partially correct and useful, for to paraphrase a U.S. president, some prognosticators can be wrong (or silent) all the time, all can be wrong (or silent) some of the time, but not all can be wrong (or silent) all the time. One of the most vigorous prognosticators is Cultural Studies, which is trying to establish its parameters.

One of these people, Fred Inglis—who dedicated his latest book, *Cultural Studies* (Blackwell 1994), to cultural analyst Clifford Geertz— for example, seems to have some insight. He believes that "the study of culture is a moral activity." He thinks that cultural studies must be "in *opposition* to the dominant politics and culture of the day." He wants to find an "inclusive description-plus-explanation" that "may only be explained in a narrative," which should be "the common, Cultural Studies" (x-xi). Inglis believes that "the study of culture is a moral activity." As you might expect, he carries this assumption into a quasi-religious conclusion: "Backing art as the best evidence we have of human potential *and* achievement commits me," he says, "to reaffirming that the origins of art lie only in ordinary experience, in all its extra-ordinariness" (xi). So though his fervor seems to reach back to Matthew Arnold, which he denies and whom he does not care for, Inglis in effect seems to be searching for a useful driving force. Most of us, I believe, would differ sharply with his moral purpose and with all his effort to narrow explanation of phenomena to narrative.

All the evidence about the current and future state of Popular Culture Studies indicates that the approach to culture is being co-opted by and integrated into all other fields as a legitimate discipline and approach. The question then follows, can we and should we remain an entity or have our goals been achieved in the larger success of having popular culture become the legitimate study of all fields in the humanities and social sciences? In this day of increased blending of fields into broad thrusts, should we gracefully bow out? I think the answer to all questions is that we should definitely stay the course. We can and should remain a well-defined field—and approach—to the study of culture.

There are several reasons we in fact must make our contributions. Literature people and others are going to delegate Popular Culture Studies to the usual multiple and transitory ideologies and theories. Many historians, and virtually all cultural studies people are going to talk about Popular Culture Studies in Marxist terms and as "mass" culture. For example, in a recent publication two Australian cultural studies scholars insist that people read in their field "the political dimensions of knowledge," and insist that "the intellectual project of cultural studies is always at some level marked . . . by a discourse of social *involvement*" (xviii). People in Popular Culture Studies will not appreciate the bias here. Besides, one cannot totally accept a point of view which calls the shopping mall "banal" but then follows up with two pages of directions on how to study it (*Australian Cultural Studies: A Reader* xv-xvii).

Anthropologists, sociologists, American Studies people, communication experts—all are going to direct the study through their particular lenses. Those efforts are going to be informative to a certain extent. So we can claim that we in Popular Culture Studies have pioneered the way and opened up the territory to a vast new field of necessary understanding. But we must persevere in our own way.

We must, for example, redouble our efforts to try to make studies in the humanities internationalized and comparative. So far we have had limited success. There is a Popular Culture Association of Japan that meets every year and publishes a journal. There is a tremendous upsurge of interest in the field in China, where six of my works have been translated and published and where we have in one of the provinces a Center for Popular Culture Studies. Every two years we have a meeting in Europe, which so far has always been in England. I am working on a conference in Mexico. We have these twin meetings with the German American Studies Association, which I find very promising. At Aristall University in Thessaloniki, Department of English, one can do Ph.D. work in popular culture.

We have always attracted some 200-300 scholars from outside the U.S. to our annual—and regional—meetings. They come from Germany, The Netherlands, France, England, Portugal, Canada, New Zealand, Australia, Mexico, Central America, India, and other countries. But because of local conditions or attitudes of participants, and local peer pressures, we have not been able to establish any kind of organization in these countries. I would hope that the time is ripe and that some individuals are going to start coming forward to establish Popular Culture Associations to study their own cultures, not American, or at least their own vis-à-vis American. Favorable signs crop up everywhere.

In *Comics in Australia and New Zealand: The Collections, the Collectors, the Creators*, the editors comment on the growing importance of popular culture studies in those countries: "Popular culture and its many forms of expression are becoming the object of serious scrutiny, and libraries are endeavoring to form archival collections of such materials" (3).

As the field grows we need to realize that Popular Culture Studies is more important than individual fields and to incorporate all of them. Popular Culture Studies are the new humanities, the overriding arch that covers all the activities of human nature and softens the sharp edges into understanding, compassion, empathy and, we hope, preservation of the human race. We in Popular Culture Studies are needed to continue to urge this understanding. Popular Culture Studies should be, as it were, the mainframe of the computer system of human understanding which receives, coordinates and redistributes all efforts and accomplishments. To reach this end, we need to keep our identity and to redouble our efforts. Reclaiming democracy for all in a democratic society is a task that requires constant effort and vigilance.

It is assumed that we understand that studying popular culture carries no approval or disapproval, no endorsement or condemnation. It is shortsighted for one to try to understand only what he or she "loves." The point is to analyze and understand. Only then can one intelligently approve or disapprove, if that is the point. Those who blindly despise popular culture do so because they do not understand and therefore feel threatened by it; their attitudes and lifestyles seem in jeopardy, as indeed sometimes they are, and such people will perish before yielding a merit point to everyday culture. Those people should remember that the most effective way to challenge an attitude or movement is first to understand it. Still they want to maintain an acadarchy, variant of "Father Knows Best," best called "Teacher Knows Best," or those in authority know how to maintain their authority. To perpetuate their positions they invest in all kinds of evolving critjarg (critical jargon) to keep the professor's ascendant position secure. This obfuscation is bound to continue for it is a mainstay of academia. The task of the Popular Culture scholar is to bring clarity to such attitudes and expressions.

Undoubtedly as the new century develops, new ideas and methods of studying popular culture will come to us. Meanwhile, I have three suggestions of how we might cope with our success.

1. We need to make up our minds that Popular Culture Studies is a recognized legitimate field of inquiry, though there are certain unenlightened minds that still refuse to recognize it. But then some schools are denying the validity of sociology, have never recognized anthropology, accept folklore marginally, are closing out American Studies programs and are even suggesting that literature is no longer a proper field of inquiry. Those attitudes, where possible, should be countered and reversed.

2. We need to settle among ourselves a working definition, or definitions. Perhaps we don't want or can't find a definition suitable to all; that may be a strength. But it is time we quit nit-picking and examining our navel while everybody else is playing around with the rest of our body. If we cannot decide positively on a definition, we should at least recognize that there are certain modes of thinking that cannot prevail—a kind of excluding definition. For example, we should not act as though we believe that entertainment, especially the media— film, TV, music, radio, MTV, etc.—constitute a nation's popular culture. They are the most obvious and to some people outside academia seem to be the totality. But there are obviously hundreds of other aspects of culture that make up a civilization. I suggest that we be as comprehensive and inclusive as the most effective anthropologists are.

In looking for a model we might pause for a moment at the motto of the *New York Times*, "All the news that's fit to print," and broaden it to, "All the news *is* fit to print," though trying to read the Sunday edition of that newspaper might lead us at times to think the contrary. Everything is of interest to someone at some time. Cable news which tries to cover every aspect of life provides a better model because everything, both great and small, seems important, to one degree or another, to someone. Perhaps National Public Radio provides us with a proper model in its program *All Things Considered*. In Popular Culture Studies all things should be considered and each given its proper weight and importance. Some people might argue that such a definition is too broad and comprehensive. I would suggest, however, that we might at times be too close to the information highway of culture to determine which sparks are hot enough to set a fire. For example, who recognized that the early Elvis Presley would completely transform American popular music? It is prudent for the student of Popular Culture Studies to be inclusive rather than exclusive, to cast the net for all fishes at least for examination, for on the cultural food chain, everything is important to someone.

3. Having decided upon at least some parameters of definition, we need to resolve to wring the full meaning, not a level or direction of meaning, not a partial meaning—as far as we can—from the society around us, and in so doing try to properly direct it. I have urged us to look upon popular culture as the New Humanities and Popular Culture Studies as probings in humanistic studies. This means every area of the humanities. We need to remember that the humanities are if not the skeleton of human existence then at least the life's blood, the elements that distinguish us, as far as we now know, from other animals. The New Humanities—that is Popular Culture—mark us as *Homo empatheia*, people who empathize with one another and represent if not an achievement at least a goal for all to seek to reach. In our troubled and threatening times, the only home of safety and comfort lies in understanding and affection. We need to strive more and more to go beyond *Homo sapiens* because sapience has not achieved our desired results, and beyond faith, which often does not bother to see, and become *Homo empatheia*. The human race deserves and must have better than it has had in the past or has at this time.

Works Cited

American Anthropological Association Program, 1993.

American Folklore Society Annual Program, 1993.

American Sociological Association Program, 1993.

American Studies Association Annual Program, 1993.

Burrows, Toby, and Grant Stone, eds. *Comics in Australia and New Zealand: The Collections, the Collectors, the Creators.* New York: Haworth, 1994.

Davis, Robert C. *The War of the Fists: Popular Culture and Public Violence in Late Renaissance Venice.* New York: Oxford UP, 1994.

Frow, John, and Meaghan Morris. *Australian Cultural Studies: A Reader.* Urbana: U of Illinois P, 1993.

Inglis, Fred. *Cultural Studies.* Oxford UK: Blackwell, 1993.

Jones, D.J.H. *Murder at the MLA.* Athens: U of Georgia P, 1993.

Modern Language Association Annual Program, 1993.

Rydell, Robert W. *Popular Culture in America, 1865–1920.* Arlington Heights, IL: Davidson, forthcoming.

Winkler, Allan M. *Home Front U.S.A.: America during World War II.* Arlington Heights, IL: Davidson, 1986.

A Rejoinder to R.B.B.

Richard Gid Powers

As always, Ray Browne has given us plenty to think about.

Always, when Ray writes about popular culture studies, he writes with passion, knowledge and—obviously—with authority. This time is no different. But I want to challenge him to do more to help us understand not just the fact that popular culture studies are closing in on their "immanent" triumph, but why.

What did he just give us? A Whitman catalog of recent pop culture studies: books, articles, and lectures. We learned not only that there are such things as asylum postcards, but that there is a learned fellow out there somewhere in the vast stretches of the Republic studying them and coughing up his knowledge into scholarly missives that bear, if I got this right, the MLA's stamp of approval. It was an arresting list: provocative, many would say, even outrageous. But the stuff is there. It exists.

But do popular culture studies *need* to exist? Did that stuff have to be written? What need did it fill? Why, to phrase this as a question capable of being investigated, did popular culture suddenly become so interesting in the last four decades of the 20th century? And why have popular culture studies prospered even though there are phalanxes of poobahs who would have, if they could have, consigned popular culture and everyone involved with it to perdition? There are probably more of them than of us, we who agree with Ray that Ted Williams and Tennessee Williams, the Ten Commandments and the Ten Little Indians are all part of the same culture and are all equally worthy of attention; that in the next millennium the only ticket that will be needed for cultural studies will be a 35-buck membership in the PCA.

Ray has called our attention to the fact—pleasing to him, and, I would venture, to most of us—that popular culture studies have flourished like the green bay tree, but he has not explained why: whether in its oddity our work is not just a reminder that there are things no philosophy can explain; or, as Art Linkletter used to say, popular studies just prove that "people are funny."

Here is the question—according to me. If there were no MLA paper on asylum postcards, would a tiny chunk of the foundation of the

29

universe be torn away, leaving the whole cosmos teetering on the edge of the void to be sucked into the incomprehensible abyss from which we all emerged and to which we all will return when our time has come? Was the whole course of history directed to one single goal—to produce that paper on asylum postcards? Was it for this that Adam delved and Eve span, the slaves of the Pharaoh labored, Attila smote the Christians and was baffled by the cross, that the swamps of Holland were drained, Africa despoiled of diamonds, and astronauts sent to the moon?

Well, in a way.

My argument is this: for the Popular Culture Association and its hangers-on (like me) to have prospered, there must have been more behind that success than the beaming countenance and devilish intellect of Ray Browne.

I will endeavor to elucidate. First, let me indicate one important difference between Ray and me on the dynamics of popular culture studies. In his paper, Ray laments the generally leftist political bias of "nearly all" the books on popular culture recently released by presses— other than his own, I would assume. The reason for his unhappiness, I suppose, is that he rejects (as do all decent citizens) the Clauswitzian notion of scholarship as politics by other means. Nevertheless, whether Ray and I like it or not, the uncomfortable fact is that popular culture studies' growth has been fertilized by the idealism of the left. It is radical scholarship's vision—that all human beings are equally entitled to their place in the sun—that has produced the popular culture explosion. It is only by looking at scholarship on the left that we see why popular culture studies have become necessary.

I will explicate, with a little less generality, by focusing on one historian whose work exhibits the democratic tendency of the best popular culture studies.

Those of us who have read Patricia Nelson Limerick's *Legacy of Conquest* know that her book is not simply a synthesis of the newest scholarship of the new Western historians. She also implicitly provides a vision of the way a democratic culture ought to work.

Legacy is a work filled with arresting metaphors. Here are two. As a mental map of the new Western history, Limerick replaces Frederick Jackson Turner's linear, east-west march of progress with a diagram of an imaginary subway system—a somewhat unexpected metaphor for a leading Western historian, by the way. (Only someone who doesn't have to ride the subways is going to find thinking about them particularly edifying.) Her point is that in a subway system, no station is the center of the system, no station the beginning, none the end. Where you are seems the center, where you start seems the beginning, where you are going seems the goal of the system, but only for you, and only for this trip. To shift from the metaphorical subway to the history of the West, there are any number of starting points, any number of centers, all interconnected, all equally important, and all equally capable of introducing debilitating gaps into the system if they are forgotten.

Another of Limerick's metaphors: erasures. For her, the hierarchical notion of culture and the myth of historical progress "erase" the memory of all those who are judged inferior by the gatekeepers of cultural taste, or who are buried by the surge of manifest destiny. She argues that traditional Western historians, by concentrating on the political extension of the American national state, have erased the history of all those races and groups who do not fit the stereotype of settler, rancher, pioneer or Indian-fighter. The task of the new Western historian is to erase the erasures made by the historians who told the story of the winning of the West. By analogy, the task of the popular culture historian is to recover what was demolished during the construction of the cultural canon, what was forgotten during the triumph of the Arnoldian idea of culture, and to fight against any more willful forgetfulness in the future.

The Legacy of Conquest and other good popular culture studies are energized by their enthusiasm for democracy as the most stimulating of human experiences. *Experience*, and not *idea*. Thinking of democracy as an idea can lead to the dismaying post-modernist conclusion (I spotted it in an essay by Jean-Francois Lyotard) that dismisses democracy as just another cultural fiction somewhat less coherent than the ideas of monarchy or even totalitarianism, and no more legitimate.

Democracy in popular studies is evolutionary. Popular studies hold that a hierarchal notion of culture is sterile, constraining, and lifeless; that high culture produces, for the most part, works of the secondary imagination: the combination and recombination of past works as described in postmodernist explications of literary texts. Popular culture studies are moved by an excitement over the unrealized and inexhaustible potential of the human race released for the first time in history by the immanent universal participation of all peoples in the human enterprise. Popular studies find it more fruitful to search for culture within the vast expanse of the democracy than within the bailiwicks of acknowledged and approved high cultural excellence. Consider—if we put Stephen Sondheim, Tom Stoppard, and Peter Martins together in a room, something fairly good is likely to come out, but we can easily imagine what it will be like, something like what those artists and other trained professionals like them have done before. The result is unlikely to be the "Life has begun again" sensation of a great rock concert, or to have the mind-bending impact of one of Tom Wolfe's early "Here comes everybody" renditions like *The Pump House Gang*—the amazing result of taking the mute, inglorious Miltons of history, shipping them to California to frolic in the sun and surf and play with cars, paint, dope, and dollars.

One more digression, before wrapping this up. In his vision of the pop culture millennium, Ray foresees the collapse of the old cultural unity into a chaos of personal tastes and different and individualized aesthetic theories; that is, everything that is, is good, because somebody thinks it is good, and there the matter rests—so says Ray. Everyman his own Bernard Berenson.

That seems to me to be a rather serious philosophical mistake, and so I appeal to Ray to draw back before it is too late and he plunges into a foul and black Gehenna of diabolic moral anarchy and squalid artistic nihilism. Every philosopher since David Hume has held that Ray's notion of a purely subjective aesthetic (or morality) is untenable; ideas of the good and the beautiful are not spawned within the isolated heart, but are intersubjective; individuals have as little control over their artistic tastes as they have over the rules of grammar. Aesthetics is learned like language, not individually spawned; there are hard, invariable rules underlying both language and aesthetics (though nobody can exactly figure them out).

It is unlikely that there ever will be a universal aesthetic in popular culture, anymore than there is agreement in this area in the high arts; but it is only by means of philosophical and self-reflective analysis on the social construction of our preferences for some things over others that we can recognize how popular culture corresponds to the forces that hold democracy together.

The thoughts of classic aestheticians like Schopenhauer are just as valuable for understanding Beavis and Butthead as they are for gauging the appeal of Beethoven. Schopenhauer, if I understand him correctly, measures a work's artistic excellence by its ability to release us from our subjectivity to achieve a dispassionate, disinterested perspective on reality. Carried to the ultimate extreme, art allows us to escape the tyranny of the will and achieve the point of view of the divinity. But wait! This would mean that for God to appreciate the beauty of anything, this argument for instance, He would have to move to a perspective outside of Himself, which is impossible. We then have a paradox: either nothing is beautiful to God, or there is no God.

That is why Schopenhauer should be kept out of the hands of grammar school children, who by virtue of their tender ages and philosophical naivete are liable to lose their faith in the face of philosophical conundrums. (To the best of my knowledge, American education is doing a commendable job of shielding school-age children from Schopenhauer, but I want to raise the alarm in case William Bennett's "back to basics" movement ever tries to cram Germanic philosophy down the craws of babes who would be better off learning the rudiments of condoms and seat belts.) But perhaps Ray proposes his doctrine of laissez faire aesthetics to save the souls of American youths from the Germanic skepticism that has problematized the existence of Santa Claus and the Easter bunny and has banished God from the classroom.

And that—really, this time—brings me to my conclusion. If I have not misremembered Ray's bibliography of his own writings, which I misplaced somewhere—I usually keep a thick copy next to my heart both as inspiration and as protection against assassins' bullets—one of his first projects was a study of Abraham Lincoln.

Lincoln historians have spent more than a century studying his life and words to understand his complex vision of democracy, one that evidently could not be fully expressed in the words of his age or of ours, though Lincoln had a better command of the English language than the average president. Ray, as a scholar trained in Lincoln lore, is well fitted to the task of excavating the democratic foundations of popular culture studies, and my challenge to him is to do just that. Honest Ray is the man for the job.

So as not to abdicate completely my responsibility to propose a solution to the problem of popular culture's unexplained vigor, I would leave Lincoln to Ray and propose Walt Whitman as the patron saint of the Popular Culture Studies movement (and of the Internet: recall Whitman's lines, "Seest thou not God's purpose from the first? / The earth to be spann'd connected by network").

"The secret shall be told," Whitman promised, "All these separations and gaps shall be taken up and hook'd and link'd together." Here is the program of the Popular Culture Association: "Program" literally, because the programs of the PCA's national meetings, in their astounding and wacky diversity, seem themselves Whitman catalogs. Let Whitman himself explain that the secret of the popular culture explosion is "in things best known to you finding the best, or as good as the best. . . . The popular tastes and employments taking precedence in poems or anywhere." What justifies studies of asylum postcards is Whitman's justification for his poetic catalogs, a democracy so radical that it makes the humblest human occupations equal to the most exalted, and raises human obscurity to divinity:

I swear I begin to see the meaning of these things,
It is not the earth, it is not America who is so great,
It is I who am great or to be great, it is You up there, or any one,
It is to walk rapidly through civilizations, governments, theories,
Through poems, pageants, shows, to form individuals.
Underneath all, individuals, I swear nothing is good to me now
  that ignores individuals,
The American compact is altogether with individuals,
The only government is that which makes minute of individuals,
The whole theory of the universe is directed unerringly to one
  single individual—namely to you.

There is the future of popular culture studies, now and in the next millennium.

Work Cited

Limerick, Patricia Nelson. *Legacy of Conquest: The Unbroken Past of the American West*. New York: Norton, 1987.

Replying to a Rejoinder

Ray B. Browne

Dick Powers and I, though with our eyes on the same star, seem to be separated by a common academic curse. I failed to make my position clear (or he refuses to see it!) and he teases my argument by pulling on a string of particulars that does not lead to the core of my position (or I think he does!). So we smile at each other over my chasm of insufficient development while he wanders around through his swamp of a different agenda.

In my essay I tried to heed Lincoln's observation that if we know where we are and where we are going we might get to our goal more quickly. So I described our present launching pad to our Society of Heart's Desire and suggested that if we keep our determination up and our minds open we can move toward our goal. I suggested that (my point three) after all our stepping from rock to rock on our trip through the swamp of human existence perhaps our realization that empathy among all peoples is a large platform on which we might catch some breathing time before slogging on to peace and happiness. I tried to be no more precise because I did not want to rest on smaller particular stones that will soon sink in the mire of changed theories or will be quarantined because they will be covered with deadly academic gases.

It is the academic gases that I know and fear, not the intellectual or seeming nonintellectual inquiring mind, and I want more inquiry by all kinds of minds. Contrary to the monster Dick thinks I see in all "leftist" political bias, I pride myself on being of such persuasion. But I do have trouble with Marxist doctrinaire thinkers who ride on Marx's coattails without at all thinking about his thinking. One does not need years in the British Museum to realize that capitalism, organized religion and academia—but less so than all forms of totalitarian governments and the hierarchies in other animal societies—exploit the poor and weak by withholding the power of equal knowledge, equal rights and equal opportunity. In human society the name of the game is *power*, and forcing its release through access to knowledge and understanding is ultimately the goal of Popular Culture Studies. But that goal can hardly be achieved as long as intellectuals have their feet caught in the underwater netting of doctrinaire ideologies. Experience in scholarship teaches us that nearly all theories are mere milestones leading down the highway around which are piled numerous skeletons of abandoned theories. All too frequently these mounds become shrines for scholars who cannot or will not abandon them.

Democracy is the dynamic of movement on that highway of scholarly development; as Dick correctly puts it, "Democracy in popular culture is evolutionary." I believe society is always *becoming*, is gradually moving, never is finished. That is the democratic process. The immediately present dynamic in the democratic movement—with the explosive surges of tribalism, ethnopiety, regionalism, nationalism and individual definitions of personal rights—is a powder keg that takes us to a new mixture of folk and popular cultures, where the drive for immediate development from the former to a sophisticated version of the latter may create unbearable tensions and actions that test whether the center or the edges of human existence can hold. Surely the dynamic in its convulsions of development is going to remake the body of world society.

These convulsions will demonstrate that society is far more than aesthetics, the union of perfection in God. In fact it can demonstrably be charged that aesthetics is another artificial standard imposed by those in power. Beauty is largely in the eye of the possessor. I would not want to be caught in bed with Romantic nonsense that a medium of artistic expression—like, say, a slab of marble—has its aesthetic statement enfolded in its nature and the aesthetician's role is merely to allow the marble to speak. Nor would I subscribe to countless other ways of describing quality, perfection or privilege. In the world of collectible art I would agree with the perceptive de-canonizing remarks of art historian Jon Huer, "Never has there been a greater mixture of comedy and insanity in an institution than that displayed in the Art Establishment" (2), in which at least half of the so-called masterpieces are hoaxes and apparently just as effective as the genuine until proven to be inauthentic. Then they become worthless, having been stripped of the cachet of being by one of the masters. There must be more to life than so-called beauty, at least as defended by those who claim to have a special appreciation of it. How about justice, or self or societal development? It may be that after equity, equality and justice have been achieved, then beauty— genuine beauty, not that declared by the elitists—becomes life's object. So far, however, such theory is largely a mote in the aesthetician's eye that he is trying to use to blur the public's vision.

So, not to get impaled on Dick's paradox of God's sense of beauty, I would think that if God is not interested in more than beauty then we don't want to waste our time on Him or on the question of whether She exists. The urge is to try to allow human society to survive and develop. I believe that it can—perhaps only—if human existence grows more democratic and I think that Popular Culture Studies properly driven are a great academic agent for that development, if those studies are considered to be the humanities.

Academia is hardly in the driver's seat in the world today. "Things are in the saddle / And ride mankind," observed Emerson over a hundred years ago. These things are generally electronic or their spinoffs. But academia can still play a role in society's development in the humanities if academicians can keep up with the real world rather than the ones they create or perpetuate in their own heads. Popular culture studies are a major link to that real world.

Work Cited

Huer, Jon. *The Great Art Hoax: Essays in the Comedy and Insanity of Collectible Art.* Bowling Green, OH: Bowling Green State University Popular Press, 1990.

Scorched by a Browned-off Browne

Richard Gid Powers

Hmm! I seem to be in a somewhat awkward position. After dancing around in front of Ray Browne's lair, screaming insults and daring him to come out and rumble, he has made an appearance—and I have more of a fight on my hands than I expected. Not only that: he got in his protest against my cheap debating ploys even before I could point out *his* own crooked tricks (which I am sure all readers can see through).

I was going to compliment Ray on his rejoinder's refusal to kowtow to vulgar prejudices against mixed metaphors, but I now stand forewarned that he is going to denounce as diversionary tactics any of the polite conventions used by all civilized essayists to elevate their discourse above the level of sheer mayhem. I had better come right to the point.

In my original rejoinder—that is, missive two in this series—I challenged Ray to do more than congratulate us all on the evident prosperity of popular studies, to explain why they have done so well. I made a bet that if Ray were to play the hand he dealt himself, he would have to draw a connection between the growth of popular studies and the evolution of democracy towards the universal participation of all in the political and cultural life of the human species.

I was right. In his short, eloquent, but comprehensive statement of principles, Ray calls my bet and raises the stakes. I said, "Popular culture studies are moved by an excitement over the unrealized and inexhaustible potential of the human race released for the first time in history by the immanent universal participation of all peoples in the human enterprise." Ray agrees, and goes me one better. He sees in what pessimists decry as the collapse of civilization—"explosive surges of tribalism, ethnopiety" and the like—a "powder keg" that "is going to remake the body of world society."

As was clear from my evocation of Lincoln and Whitman, I am with him so far. Where I thought I had him was when he moved from democracy to aesthetics. Surely, I jested, he was not trying to lead us into a morass of moral and aesthetic anarchy with his belief, in my paraphrase, that "everything that is, is good, because somebody thinks it is good, and there the matter rests."

Well, shut my mouth! That's just what he thinks, and he makes no apologies.

The popular culture studies movement is not merely a symptom of the contemporary explosion of democracy, he says. It is one of the causes. The goal of popular culture studies is to challenge the power that withholds "equal knowledge, equal rights, and equal opportunity" from all, particularly the "poor and weak." Even more provocatively, he charges that "aesthetics is another artificial standard imposed by those in power." To buttress his position, he points to the museum world, where "at least half of the so-called masterpieces are hoaxes" that are valuable until proven inauthentic, at which moment they are immediately rendered worthless. All aesthetic judgments, he implies, are tainted by the same species of fraud.

Anticipating objections, Ray raises the stakes even higher: "There must be more to life than so-called beauty, at least as defended by those who claim to have a special appreciation of it. How about justice, or self or societal development?"

I have to declare that I am well satisfied by the political thrust of Ray's response to my challenge. But in even the strongest argument some points are stronger than others. And some that are, let us say, less strong.

I am particularly pleased by Ray's evocation of the spirit of democracy as the soul of popular culture studies, and his statement that the dynamic of democracy is an evolutionary one. But I am compelled to point out that there is democracy and then there is *real* democracy. Even Whitman and Lincoln held that democracy by, for, and of the people could flourish only within a constitutional framework: for both Lincoln and Whitman the Civil War came to be a test of whether the constitutional forms that made a just democracy possible could survive; or whether there would be a return to the rule of the strong over the weak, which then as now some could justify as more democratic than mere liberal democracy. Whitman, one critic claimed long ago, even used the Constitution as a metaphor for the creative tension between the individual and the cosmos in his poetic evocation of man's spiritual evolution.

Where in Ray's original essay or in his counter-rejoinder does he give recognition to the need for rules (by whatever name) to preserve individual liberties within the explosive evolution of democracy that he and I both applaud? Stated in that way, the question may be unfair, since I have defined the terms. Put another way: where in Ray's theory is the functional equivalent of the constitutional forms that try to ensure that the liberal part of liberal democracy will survive today's political powder keg? Ray's answer—which I admittedly neglected to deal with in my rejoinder—is "empathy."

Is this suggestion adequate to the task at hand? Surprisingly, I think it might be—not in its present form of "insufficient development" (as Ray characterizes his argument)—but potentially. It might even answer my qualms about Ray's sweeping away all aesthetic standards as roadblocks on the way to equity, equality and justice.

By "empathy" I take Ray to mean the reflexive tendency to imagine oneself in another's place, to feel and think as another might, and therefore weigh one's actions in terms of their consequences for others. If I have stated matters correctly, Ray's "empathy" is the same as David Hume's "sympathy," which the Scottish sage makes the bedrock of the moral sense. (Empathy, sympathy—you say "Tomato," I'll say "Tomahto.") It takes a mere moment's reflection to see that if empathy is made the categorical imperative of the democratic and the popular studies movements, then a set of limitations on the power of the majority is immediately called for since groups as such (majorities most emphatically included) only rarely feel empathy for an individual; indeed, groups most characteristically define themselves by their *lack* of empathy for outcast individuals—the "other," whether criminal, foreigner, or prophet. Maybe when we reach the Society of Heart's Desire things will be better, but we better protect our assets along the way. I put it to Ray: will not the forms of liberal democracy (which are the bulwarks of "capitalism, organized religion and academia" and bear down hard on the "poor and weak") be as necessary to safeguard "empathy" as they were to safeguard "liberty" for Madison, Hamilton, Jay, and Tocqueville—and for much the same reasons?

To make a final point: fixing on "empathy" as the core value of popular cultural studies also raises the possibility of a democratic aesthetic equally applicable to all levels of culture. It is particularly useful in isolating what is wrong with the purely commercial products of the entertainment industry that exploit passions without exploring them: catharsis without enlightenment Aristotle called works like these that deny the possibility of empathy with the characters or between members of the audience.

In concluding, I congratulate Ray for his forceful answer to my rejoinder. Now that I have been crushed to the earth, my clothes reduced to tatters and flesh to steak tartar, I inform my opponent that on the point in dispute, my honor has been fully satisfied. I am singed, not to say scorched, but I am satisfied by Ray's reply, and await with anticipation his final words on this question of such grave import to all of us who drag our little cultural studies talents to the word processor every day to do our bit to break the chains that keep humanity from romping in the "Society of Heart's Desire."

Looking to the Millennium

Marshall Fishwick

Have you been feeling nervous lately? Does all the news seem like bad news? Is your hair beginning to fall out? Do you keep losing your keys and your kids? Is your best friend unemployed?

Do you feel traumatized? Maybe it's the millennium.

Everyone likes to talk about the future, but nobody ever knows what it will bring. This is especially true when we find ourselves approaching the end of an era, a century, or a millennium. We will reach such a magic moment on January 1, 2001 A.D.—the beginning of *both* a century and a millennium. One thing is sure: no one living will be around to see such a double whammy again.

No wonder we've begun to get the jitters; to see bad omens and ominous portents; to hear things go bump in the night. Didn't Nostradamus, the 16th-century French astrologer and Prince of Predictors, say the end of the world would take place on July 30, 1999?

Looking back to January 1, 1001 A.D.—the last time we faced a double whammy—we see what we might expect. No less a figure than Saint Augustine had chosen that date for the appearance of the Anti-Christ. Strange events plagued every community and region. Farmers refused to plant for the next year's crops, since Armageddon was near. Others left their homes and waited in the streets for the end. Mass hysteria and suicides were widespread.

Already we can predict, on the basis of hard evidence, that our century and millennium will end not with a whimper (as T.S. Eliot predicted) but with a bang. No one knows how many atomic bombs are concealed out there, and how many unfriendly nations (our list includes North Korea, China, Iraq, Libya, and who knows what others?) can and will procure one. Empires crumble, alliances weaken, holes puncture the ozone layer, warlords defy the U.N., AIDS spreads—it is the only epidemic on record in which not a single victim has survived. What does it all mean? Where and when will it all end?

Already we can see what lies ahead: hysterical songs and poems, collections of the last this-or-that, cults popping up like wildflowers. Already economists predict collapse, preachers the Second Coming, ecologists the end of nature, intellectuals the end of modernism. But wait, there is more. History is about to end, so we must confront endism.

This idea, put forth first by Francis Fukuyama, says we are in for very sad times. There will be neither art nor philosophy—just the perpetual caretaking of the museum of human history. Endism isn't entirely new—both Hegel and Marx advanced the idea, and Daniel Bell published *The End of Ideology* a generation ago—it has picked up a new popular audience in the 1990s, just as Orson Wells's 1938 radio broadcast called "The War of the Worlds" caught our mood on the eve of World War II. Popular culture always holds the mirror up to the times.

Certainly despair has dominated recent art and politics. Our theaters are full of three-handkerchief movies. Michael Keaton's *My Life* takes us into the world of inoperable cancer, Stephen Spielberg's *Schindler's List* to the holocaust. In *Philadelphia* the young Tom Hanks character dies of AIDS and in *Shadowlands* the cancer-doomed wife says, "I'm going to die. The pain then is part of the happiness now. That's the deal." Some deal.

On every side, we hear that standards have decayed, schools declined, foreign policy fizzled. The love affair with high tech is over. Robots, nuclear power, and computers promised to make us free—but have instead tyrannized us to a degree unparalleled in history. Law and order are vanishing. We thought we were creating a brave new world. Instead, we seem to be smearing it with oil and getting ready to blow it up. William Pfaff hits all these dour notes in *Barbarian Sentiments: How the American Century Ends.*[1]

We have been slouching toward it for a long time—indeed, since the last millennium, a thousand years ago. Who since then could imagine a year on our Western calendar that didn't start with a 1? Slouch no more—start sprinting. We will very soon confront the next millennium.

Religion has always been a major force in our culture, and shows no sign of abating.[2] The first European settlers believed so strongly in God's guidance that they sailed over uncharted seas and challenged a "howling wilderness" full of savage beasts and beastly savages. Puritanism is still a potent force in America, supported by a standard body of literature and thundering sermons. Emphasized for centuries, the strong "Chosen People" idea gained credibility and importance. This conviction of God-elected uniqueness was part of the colonies' survival apparatus. The kind of government established violated most traditional accepted European rules for successful governments. If they *were* to succeed, the Founding Fathers realized, they had to preserve the myth of God's guidance.

Names of saints and martyrs dot maps of North and South America. America was the safety valve, missionary field, haven for every religious group. No nation has ever received such a bewildering variety in such numbers: dissidents from all the Protestant sects, Judaism, and Catholicism. They were Shakers and Quakers, Pentecostals and Penitentials, Baptists and Anabaptists; Dunkers, Mennonites, and Hutterites; all kinds of Anglicans, "low and lazy, middle and hazy, high and crazy." The colonies housed the radical religious sentiments of English groups like the Ranters, Ravers, and Diggers. Turn on your television: the ranting and raving still goes on. It is the American way. It comes with the territory.[3]

The millennium topic is hot; and where hot topics are, there popular culture is also. Count on the Millennium Blues. Expect a strong dose of hysteria and trauma.

Nothing is more fascinating, more addictive, more controversial than "looking into the future" and telling what you see. Locked in the present, with little understanding of what today (let alone tomorrow) really is or means, we create our own version of reality, our mirage of wish-dreams. This lets us substitute speculation for information, rumor for reality. It opens the gate to endless sloganeering and sentimentality.

Pop culture joins the endless line of those who try to fathom "what it all means"; what new challenges await us; and how we can meet them. Caught up in events we cannot decipher, clues we cannot comprehend, we proceed with fear and trembling. We've got the Millennium Blues. We face a unique and terrifying factor. What is "new" is the prevalence of newness—the changing scope of change itself. What is unprecedented in today's world is that most things we see, buy, wear, and use are more short-lived than we are. We purchase, plunder, pave, and rush forward. But where are we going?

To hell, say a whole group of terrified Christians, convinced that the Apocalypse is at hand. Do you have a fatal case of the Millennium Blues? Have they good reasons for their gloomy prognosis? Will this be a major theme of popular culture in the century that is close at hand.

Why is the religious right so frightened?[4] The answer is obvious: we live in frightening times; everything nailed down is coming loose; the world we inherited has been turned upside down. The unthinkable is featured every night on the 6:30 news or in our leadings newspapers and magazines. Here's an example: "Brace yourself—plagues are stalking the planet." That's the theme of Richard Preston's 1994 season's roller coaster bestseller, *The Hot Zone* and in the same year Laurie Garrett's *The Coming Plague*.

In both books the argument is both terrifying and persuasive. Amidst the degradation of the envionment and the population explosion, we all face not only the advance of old diseases (tuberculosis, malaria, and cholera) but also such new ones such as AIDS and Ebola. Ebola Zaire kills nine out of ten of its victims. It is in Richard Preston's phrase, a "slate wiper." And guess what? In 1989 a building full of Ebola-stricken monkeys in Reston, Virginia—a few miles outside of Washington!

Another new disease called Marburg is so infectious that in a few days a Level 4 virus literally dissolves the body. All these seem to make a mockery of the science of immunology. Is the wrath of God being visited upon us, as fiery preachers insist?

Nothing new here. The most popular book in 17th-century New England was Michael Wigglesworth's terrifying epic poem, "The Day of Doom." Children memorized portions of the poem, including the part about doomed unbaptized children. Wigglesworth offered a slight concession: they could enter "the easiest room of hell."[5]

This same sense of doom motivated Jonathan Edwards in the 1740s, when our first Great Awakening took place. His famous 1741 sermon, "Sinners in the Hands of an Angry God," brought people to their knees. He insisted that emotion, not intellect, is central. God must enter, since passions untransformed are bad. The original sin is selfishness. That is the theme of our 20th-century televangelists.[6]

Times change but not people, not basic themes of popular culture. One of them is religion, and the awakenings and revivals that descend upon us about every 50 years. What we need, as our century ends, is a new map of religion, based not only on beliefs but also on social behavior and mass communication. Martin Marty suggests a map in *A Nation of Behaves* (Chicago: University of Chicago, 1976). He posits six religious clusters: mainline, evangelical/fundamental, Pentecostal/charismatic, new religions, ethnic religions, and exotic cults. One thing is clear: we are not at ease in Zion, where work is the means and play the end, entertainment the addiction and religion the expedient. Our new Generation X, which will lead us into the 21st century, spends much of its time not in the church pew but the TV room. That is the center of modern American ritual. Are we entertaining ourselves to death?

Marty posits six clusters: six cyclical Great Awakenings, the fifth ending in our century, the sixth stretching into the next. The five are: The Colonial Awakening, the Frontier Awakening, the Urban Awakening, the Modernist Awakening, and the Evangelical/Fundamentalist Awakening.[7]

"Evangelical," from the Greek word evangelion (the evangel, or good news) spreads the good news that the original apostles proclaimed and the gospel writers (or Evangelists) recorded. Evangelists accept the absolute authority of the Bible, are converted (or "born again") to Christ, and share their faith with others.

If we think of "right" as being a more rigid and literal position, then fundamentalists are to the right of evangelists. They are the "strict constructionists" of evangelism. In popular culture and politics, we speak of the religious right with this group in mind, centered on dogmatic Protestant fundamentalism. The two colorful fundamentalists who first achieved national status were William Jennings Bryan (1860–1925) and Billy Sunday (1863–1935).

Willie and Billy, as they were called, dominated popular religion. Billy said he knew no more about theology than a jack rabbit knew about Ping-Pong: but this "Calliope of Zion" was great on the platform. A baseball player turned preacher, Sunday hit home runs and slid into home plate for Jesus.

Willie, "The Great Commoner," was rooted in rural America—Bible thumping and Bible pumping. He was a perennial Democratic candidate for the presidency, his party's standard-bearer for 20 years.[8]

But the greatest evangelist of the 20th century, Billy Graham, came out of the South. (So did major African-American preachers—Martin Luther King, Jesse Jackson, Father Divine, and many others.) Graham has been heard by more people (live and through mass media) than any preacher who ever lived. He blessed the inaugurations of every president from Dwight Eisenhower to Bill Clinton. No one can predict the arrival of such an evangelist and say if the 21st century will produce another. It seems more likely, viewing the scene in the 1990s, that we shall have to be content with show-biz televangelism.

Billy Graham might have only one God, but he has two faiths: Christian fundamentalism and Christian Americanism. His message is so direct and simple that no one (not even presidents) can miss it. Admit your sins, repent, turn to Christ. You will be forgiven and saved.

His "crusades" are masterpieces of organization and inspiration. Special provisions are made for the deaf, handicapped, elderly. Message boards, ground crews, lost-and-found booths, ushers, concessions and parking lots are fully staffed. Fill out a convenient form and you get *Decision* (Graham's monthly magazine) for a whole year free. All this worked well in countries around the world—especially Russia, where the crusades have been enormously successful. His faith, charm, and Southern accent have endeared him around the world.[9]

The American center of popular religion in the 21st century may well remain where it has been for generations: in the American South. The Great Frontier Revival which swept through that region in the 18th century has never really abated. Religious revivals, full of sweat and sanctity, have never gone out of style, even though the nation has become increasingly secular. Especially in the Deep South, in the period when cotton has been picked and tobacco laid by, the Spirit is apt to strike. Many a soul is saved by prayer, promises, and fried chicken. It's Amazing Grace.

It has long been fashionable to ridicule what H.L. Mencken called the Bible Belt, but that does not deter Southerners. That shows no signs of abating as we approach a new century and a new millennium. I predict that the sixth Great Awakening will see the Sun Belt and the Bible Belt linked, and much religious conversion and fervor. For those who like labels, the new one might read: Turn Right.

The South has risen again. In the 1990s it is the fastest-growing American region, able to outbid both Athens and Beijing for the 1996 World Olympics. There is new money, new energy, new capital in Dixie.[10] And a significant portion of it might go to a new religion. Look at what some of the evangelists of our generation have achieved.

Jimmy Swaggart's JSM Operation Center outside Baton Rouge was built on land worth $2.8 million and with a $5 million TV station, a $30 million worship center, and other expensive buildings. On the North-South Carolina border Jim and Tammy Bakker built a huge theme park, Heritage USA, which set out to rival Disney World.[11]

Swaggart and the Bakkers were discredited, but they did what Southerners expected—they repented, cried, paid their penalties, and came back praising the Lord. Their tried-and-true formula should work for years to come. But the two most influential models, it seems to me, will be Jerry Falwell and Pat Robertson. By mixing religion and politics, and working hard for influence within the Republican party, they crossed the line between church and state. Falwell's Moral Majority and Robertson's Christian Broadcast Network (CBN) set a new agenda for popular religion and popular culture.

In the late 20th century Jerry Falwell became the leading spokesman for the religious right. His empire is centered in Lynchburg, Virginia, where his Liberty Baptist Church teems with life. Complete with classical columns, the octagonal high-tech building is flanked by acres of parking space for hundreds of cars. Far off one sees 30 or 40 yellow school buses waiting to bring in the sheep to heed the shepherd. This is where the action is: the Bible-believing Thomas Road Baptist Church. When not on the road, Jerry might be in the pulpit, cultivating the down-home look and grass-roots connections that are his secret weapon. People like Jerry "real good." And they pay for the privilege. He is pious, prosperous, and popular.[12]

"Has Don recovered from his fall off the ladder, Joe?" he asks. (Not even a sparrow falls without Jerry's noticing.) When a red-headed lad named Stephen comes forward with the American flag, Jerry recalls that he was at the hospital when Stephen was born, ill with spinal meningitis. "We joined hands around his bed and prayed. He passed through the crisis. That's when his hair turned red." Bursts of laughter. Jerry's not just a preacher—he's a standup comic.

While praising the Lord, he gets in a few good words for his own institution, Liberty Baptist College. Their football team, the Flames, has one of the state's best ends. The girls' volleyball team has won first place in a tournament. That's enough to make the ushers pass the collection plate. The Lord loveth a cheerful giver.

Falwell uses friendly, easy-to-remember gimme-gimmicks: Stake Your Claim, Silver Anniversary, and Memorial Brick families. When you join Jerry you become a Faith Partner; the computer does the rest.

Falwell exudes confidence. His blue tailored suit has an expensive look; his gold rings and quartz watch sparkle underneath television lights. He has beads of sweat on his forehead, and a large comfortable grin on his face. He is a pro. Cables from multiple TV cameras snake up and down the aisles. Fluorescent lights bathe the church in an eerie glow that lights up the dandruff on men's shoulders. Behind the pastor is a choir of 60 photogenic people in powder blue robes. Clean-shaven men smile brightly at the cameras and the crowds. Women have elaborate hairdos, glossy red lipstick and ten-tooth smiles. Everyone knows that the real congregation is "out there," where the tube must stand in for the body of Christ.

Behind this casual, almost chummy, service is a clearcut goal: saturation evangelism, which will deliver the gospel to every available person at every available time by every available means. That's why Falwell travels over half a million miles a year. And when he preaches in Lynchburg, radio and film tapes go out to over 500 radio stations and 400 television stations. The church operation requires $60 million a year.

How significant are the Faith Partners, centered here but spread over the land? What impact will they have not just on the Thomas Road Baptist Church but on the American Republic? How good are God hucksters as vote getters? Whom can a person believe when rating their political clout?

One can study the latest available numbers; but let no one forget that the Partners' power far exceeds mere numbers. They have changed the *tone* of political life in America; their passionate loyalty (especially that of the young and the converted) cannot be discounted. They remind us of eighth-century Muslims, who conquered half the area of Christendom in less than century.

For fundamentalists, the future of their church and the future of their country are inseparable. They are involved not only with a theology but an ideology—a picture of the world to guide and inspire them. The essentials of the good and godly life are being threatened by various "enemies of the Lord" who control much of the world today. Rather than change the message of the Gospel to meet the ever-changing needs of society, the fundamentalists believe the secular world and modern ways must be changed to fit the Gospel. They lament the runaway divorce rate, pornography plague, banning of God from the schoolhouse, spread of homosexuality—all tied to the rise of "secular humanism." The answers to the problems facing the world today lie in the revealed truth of the Bible. This translates to what Falwell likes to call the "old-time" traditional American values—including monogamy, law and order, and free-enterprise capitalism. How would this come about? Through a renewed emphasis—a more apt word might be crusade—on the divine destiny of the American democracy of the Founding Fathers. It's time to go home again.

Three dominant social attitudes characterize his church: (1) an overriding social and political conservatism, (2) a strong individualism and bourgeois mentality, and (3) acceptance of traditional American values. Evangelists who championed these attitudes in the '70s became the vote getters of the '80s. To "make it on TV" they put frosting on the cake—glamour, pageantry, exaggeration, sensationalism. But the cake itself was baked from a time-tested American recipe.

Falwell has built a coalition of fundamentalists and evangelists to "reshape the forces of conservative Christianity," and "return our nation to its spiritual and moral roots." Such statements give Jerry both credibility and publicity. He, if anyone, has moved Fundamentalism from the underground to the foreground. Over 200,000 students are preparing for Christian vocations in conservative schools. The Christian school movement is estimated to have 15,000 schools with over 2 million students.

The figures are inflated, critics say. The fear of blacks, not of the Lord, inspires many of those private schools. Perhaps; but we err if we downgrade the figures, then walk away. Fundamentalist preachers, Falwell in particular, have clearly demonstrated—on all levels, in all regions—that they have appeal and know how to use it. Jesse Jackson popularized the term Rainbow Coalition. But it was Jerry Falwell who made one.

Millions who want school prayer, strong families, and "decent communities" free of hippies, oddballs, and porn have heard Falwell and said, "Now *there's* our man!" Mainline churches waffled. Jerry said it straight.

Hence his "new" following confirms a standard media axiom: attitude change is most effective when the "new" attitudes are merely extensions of old existing ones. This is how Jerry builds. As the number of discarded, disfranchised, and lonely grows, so will his church.

Most Americans identify Jerry Falwell with the Moral Majority. Founded earlier by Richard Viguerie, a Roman Catholic layman, the group sought aid from Falwell's computer lists of "Old Time Gospel Hour" donors in 1979. Gradually Falwell became the spokesman, and most visible symbol, of the group that combines patriotism, politics, and fundamentalism. As part of the strategy, Falwell held "I Love America" rallies in 50 states, setting up para-church organizations and regional offices. Membership figures are disputed. Falwell claimed 800,000 in 1980, a figure which was said to include 70,000 ministers. The majority were from the Baptist Bible Fellowship and Southwide Baptist Fellowship. Many nonreligious groups joined in, attracted by the fight to "Preserve the traditional American way of life." Their influence on the 1980 and 1984 elections gave the Moral Majority new hope and greatly expanded its program.

Not all Americans were pleased with attitudes and interventions of the Moral Majority. New bumper stickers turned up on cars: "Member of the Immoral Minority," "The Moral Majority is *Neither*." Media writers formed a group to oppose the Moral Majority—"People for the American Way." Its leader, Norman Lear, had produced such innovative television series as *All in the Family, Maud,* and *The Jeffersons.* In a letter to President Reagan, Lear pointed to the President's growing allegiance to the new Christian right and the seeming inability of Reagan and proponents of a stricter separation of church and state to reach agreement.

The President, defending his position, said in one letter: "I am not using this office as a pulpit for one religion over all the others, but I do subscribe to George Washington's remark regarding high moral standards, decency, etc., and their importance to civilization and his conclusion that to think we could have these without religion as a base was to ask for the impossible."

"Obviously," he continued, "when I'm addressing an audience who share my own religious beliefs—indeed, a religious group—I see nothing wrong with talking of our mutual interests. I can recall no instance where I have ever tried to proselytize others or impose my beliefs on those of other faiths."

Lear, responding that the correspondence had been "enlightening, but alas, not encouraging," concluded: "Perhaps we must simply agree to disagree."

Those following the controversy noted that 20 years earlier Jerry Falwell had held a totally different view. In a 1965 sermon called "Ministers and Marchers" he had said:

Believing in the Bible as I do, I would find it impossible to stop preaching the pure saving gospel of Jesus Christ and begin doing anything else, including fighting Communism, or participating in civil rights reforms. Preachers are not called on to be politicians but to be soul winners. Nowhere are we commissioned to reform the externals.

By then the mainstream Protestant churches—Methodists, Episcopalians, Congregationalists, Presbyterians and the like—had turned away from trying to make the nation "a Christian commonwealth" to supporting civil rights, opposing the Vietnam War and making active efforts on social issues, usually on the side of political liberals.

At the same time, the political system was undergoing a basic change. The major political parties, which once assimilated and assigned priority to issues, were being replaced by a host of individual interest groups that competed directly for government assistance and recognition. For years fundamentalists stayed out of politics. Then, on short notice, they jumped in with both feet. They found common cause with the Republicans; picked winners and made winners. Their day had come.

While the fundamentalist churches have been gaining members and resources, partly through television broadcasts, mainstream churches have had no such growth. They have been involved in internal disputes over their positions on political issues: how far they should go, for example, in condemning foreign policy and in criticizing the practices of capitalism and nuclear expansion.

Indeed, the whole religious scene has become bewildering to the average churchgoer. New groups, communes, crusades, sects, and "freaks" have become so jumbled that many critics ended up condemning them all. Especially in the '60s, when there was a new Eleventh Commandment (Do Your Own Thing!), confusion reigned and sympathy waned. Even participants and apologists had trouble sorting things out. A plastic-wrapped, shine-and-glow, show-and-tell society mixed cynicism with hope, means with extremes, sense with nonsense. The path the '60s took was a whirlwind of high moral purpose combined with the centrifugal forces generated by creating new directions in an atmosphere of terrifying freedom.

So bring on your flower children, love-ins, lock-outs, group encounters, and gang bangs; the assassination of leaders, race riots, unwanted wars, and ecology's dance of death. Take the magical mystical tour through strawberry fields and marmalade skies of psychedelia. Try astrology, kinky sex, Ouija boards, Tarot cards, and I Ching. *Do your own thing!*[13]

Jesus People roamed the land, headed for places like the Areopagus House in California, the Lighter Side of Darkness House in Illinois, or the Love Inn in New York. By 1967 there were more than 800 "Christian Houses" functioning, 200 in California alone, and an up-to-date "Jesus People Directory." One convert, Arthur Blessitt, dragged a cross 3,500 miles from California to Washington, D.C., preaching along the way. That's a hard act to follow.

Members of the Process Church of the Final Judgment wore three-horned goathead symbols and silver crosses. They worshipped three Gods—Jehovah, Pan, and Satan. The Holy Order of MANS chose an acronym for mystic terms which the group would not reveal; but they stressed reincarnation and extrasensory perception. The Children of God preached complete disregard for authority and for all laws. In their communes mail from home went into a bag marked "Egypt," the synonym for bondage. The days of "Home Sweet Home" on the living room wall seemed over. At that point Jerry Falwell and the fundamentalists emerged. Liberalism seemed bankrupt. It was time to get out the Bible.

There is little that distinguishes Falwell as a theologian. He is a fundamental Southern Baptist, using the phrases and clichés of his faith. His God is a righteous ruler who demands vengeance. His prophet is Elijah, who wants to see the chaff burned with unquenchable fire. One of Jerry's favorite gestures is the forefinger pointed at the sinner. He seems not to notice that three fingers are directed back at him.

He excels as a promoter-salesman. He knows God is in the details; that lots of little items bring in big bucks. Any edition of his *Moral Majority Report*, for which he claims a million subscriptions, confirms this.

Look at the ads. Buy a comfortable slipper ("It won't slip out from under you!"), lower your blood pressure without prescription drugs, stand or sit without help in a "cushion lifting chair." Help yourself to sleep better, with an "inflatable sleep incliner wedge—" only $4.88. Or buy a pair of professional toenail clippers for $2.99. Try a new Electronic Pain Killer, which relieves muscular backache, headache, even pain of tennis elbow, arthritis, and bursitis! (It's on sale for $29.95).

Perhaps you'd rather have "The Complete Words of Francis A. Schaeffer," or the old-time records of Kate Smith or Nelson Eddy.

Of course, there is a large assortment of Bibles and plastic relics —to say nothing of a religious quartz clock. Patriots can buy the "Double Eagle" Ronald Reagan commemorative coin ($10 plus $3 for mailing). For fishermen there is a spinning reel for only $4, and for health buffs a book entitled *Vitamin Side Effects Revealed*. Get-rich quick schemes abound: "Retire before fifty—Clean with Duraclean!" "Sell part-time, make full-time income!" "Make $1,000 a month with just a hacksaw."

But the main thing that Jerry sells, after salvation, is education. The centerpiece is his Liberty Baptist College, founded in 1971 with 141 students to "train champions for Christ." Growth was phenomenal. Falwell was soon urging the flock to watch the Macy's Thanksgiving Day parade on TV and see the band "from America's fastest growing college"—his, of course. True enough, there was the Marching Flames Band from LBC. At first, classes were held at the church, with church staff serving as faculty. By 1982 the college had 4,000 students and plans to develop 200 acres of the 4,200-acre tract Falwell bought on hills outside Lynchburg. Most of the funding came from monthly contributions of $15 to $20, solicited through Falwell's church and television audience. Operating expenses for 1982 exceeded $21 million. In 1985, with an enrollment of over 5,000, the college officially changed its name to Liberty Baptist University.

By then the buildings on Falwell's tract had 75 academic majors, including schools of religion, education, arts and sciences, communications, and business. Projecting an enrollment of 50,000 by the end of the century (including master's and doctoral programs), his university, said Falwell, would be "the Fundamentalist Harvard in academics and the Fundamentalist Notre Dame in athletics." The University was also challenging its graduates to start 5,000 new churches in North America by the end of the century.

All this gives the faithful reason to rejoice, but the atmosphere on campus is far from festive. The tone is Puritanical. The motto might well be "Resist the sins of the flesh." Only born-again students are accepted. They may not dance or attend movies; girls must wear modest dresses; boys, coats and ties. Proctors tell students when to study, when to pray, when to go to bed. Church and chapel attendance is mandatory. No beards or mustaches. Sideburns cannot go below the earlobes. Hair must not touch the shirt collar. No country or rock music (not even Christian rock), no smoking or drinking, and a daily room check. Married male students must, "as heads of the household, see that wives dress with appropriate Christian modesty." Dating is permitted—but freshmen and sophomores must double date. Most of the students I interviewed said they liked the campus and the codes. They feared they "couldn't handle" the freedom (they prefer to call it license) of "worldly universities." Jerry knows what is best. We remember George Orwell.

Those who shudder and see in all this a new form of mind control, perhaps even Big Brother, should realize that Fundamentalism has positive appeal. It champions strong marriages, clean living, moral responsibility. That all are in short supply provides Falwell with wonderful targets. He gives Southern paranoia full license, combining theater and technology with masterful effect. He has learned much from his political mentor, Ronald Reagan, but Falwell always looks out for Falwell. Noting the rising tide against Reagan's visit to a German military cemetery in 1985, Falwell spoke out against it. He makes a point of knowing where his sheep are, and how they think. Then he can lead them.

Gradually Falwell has attained international attention. In 1984 he was chosen to "represent" America's policy in a debate at England's Oxford University. In 1985 he visited South Africa, during a period of racial unrest and crisis, to get first hand information on the problem. Returning to the United States, he appeared on national television and denounced Bishop Desmond Tutu, who is black and a Nobel Peace–prize winner, as a "phony." He even pledged the support of the Moral Majority for the white South African government. Twenty years earlier Falwell had chastised white American preachers for joining civil rights marches. Then, too, thousands rallied to his side.

The Rev. Jerry Falwell is a perceptive, ambitious man, and he saw a new target in liberal Bill Clinton. Anyone who favored abortion and gays in the military had to be attacked, and attack Falwell did. Some of his claims were in poor taste, and embarrassed even his supporters. But as Clinton's ratings fell, Falwell's attacks mounted. Still, it seemed to some that Jerry had begun to fade in the new national climate.

Pat Robertson, Falwell's evangelical Virginia neighbor, fared better. He had a more substantial and credible background and education; and he grasped, better than anyone else, the power of television. He could boast of a series of "firsts"—first religious TV station, first religious network, first to use a talk-show format. Perhaps most impressive of all, he was the first to have worldwide connections (through the American Forces Radio and Television Services) and to run for the presidency. He was prominent at the 1992 Houston convention of the Republican Party, and seems to have the most promising future of all the major televangelists.

Son of a U.S. senator, Phi Beta Kappa, graduate of the Yale Law School, Pat Robertson presides over the "Video Vatican" at Virginia Beach. Trained as a minister, anxious to serve the poor, he fled a Pentecostal parsonage in Brooklyn, purchased a defunct television studio, and launched the nation's first Christian television station (WYAN) in 1961. To rally the faithful under the banner of the "700 Club," Robertson used telethon and telephone volunteers with the goal of getting 700 people to pledge $10 a month. And lo, the hundreds became thousands. Viewers enjoy his "celebrity meets celebrity format," as Robertson interviews fascinating people who write best-sellers, lead the place among the Top Ten, roam the corridors of power. All have one common denominator: they are born-again Christians, who make their pitch and thus bolster Robertson's Christian Broadcasting Network.

This multi-million-dollar operation involves four television stations, a recording company, a 24-hour-a-day programming service available to more than 3,000 cable systems, a complete news network, a university, and satellite earth stations. Its daily audience is estimated at over 7 million. How well does it all work? In a single 1985 short telephone campaign, CBN raised over $77 million. Robertson's appeal was typically low-key but persuasive. "I'd like us to get all that's ours in the Kingdom," he said night after night. Apparently he got it.[14]

He also got the urge to be the President of the United States. In 1988 he announced that he would run if 3 million people urged him by signing petitions. He got the signatures and $10 million and had raised over $27 million by April 1988 before suspending his campaign. He had also got over 40 percent of the vote in three state caucuses and over 18 percent in five state primaries. All this won new attention and respect for the religious right.

Robertson's 1992 campaign faltered after a short trial run, but Robertson and his allies were not daunted. They had distributed 40 million copies of a voter guide, and had a major influence on the Republican Party Platform. Working diligently with Republicans at the grass-roots level in 1994, they won many nominations and were largely responsible for the choice of Ollie North to run for the Senate from Virginia. He got campaign funds from all over the nation. With a Republican landslide a distinct possibility, there was already talk of Pat Robertson's being a candidate for the White House in 1996.

That popular religion will be a major factor in 21st-century America there can be no doubt. In an article aptly titled "Bibles, Ballots, and Beatific Vision," Gary R. Pettey notes that "the trigger has been pulled, and fundamentalism has been propelled into the 'Social Unrest' phase."

How much unrest, and how soon? These are questions which future popular culture historians will have to answer.

But the big gift for the Religious Right came in 1994, when the American voters gave the Republicans control of both the House of Representatives and the Senate—for the first time in 40 years. Of the 60 Republican first-year members of the House, two-thirds were supported and championed by the Christian Coalition, the powerful right wing of the Republican Party.[15]

Particularly noteworthy were the number of Southern Baptists who had positions of great power. In addition to Jerry Falwell and Pat Robertson, there were the President and Vice President of the United States, and the powerful new Speaker of the House, Newt Gingrich. So far as politics are concerned, we deal not only with the "winds of change" but a tornado, changing the way we live and govern. That this will have an enormous effect and influence on 21st-century America, there can be no doubt.

Notes

1. Pfaff's book, published by Hill and Wang in 1989, lists a number of other books that favor the barbarians. For more sympathetic views, see Randall Balmer, *Mine Eyes Have Seen the Glory: A Journey into the Evangelical Subculture in America* (New York: Oxford UP, 1989); and Harold Bloom, *The American Religion: The Emergence of the Post-Christian Nation* (New York: Simon & Schuster, 1992).

2. The best overview is Sydney A. Ahlstrom, *A Religious History of the American People*, 2 vols. (New York: Doubleday, 1975). Two other helpful studies are Robin Attfield, *God and the Secular: A Philosophical Assessment of Secular Reasoning from Bacon to Kant* (Cardiff, Wales: U College P, 1978) and George M. Thomas, *Revivalism and Cultural Change: Christianity. Nation-building and the Market in the Nineteenth-Century United States* (Chicago: U of Chicago P, 1989).

3. For a development of this point of view, see Marshall W. Fishwick, *Common Culture and the Great Tradition: The Case for Renewal* (Westport: Greenwood, 1988).

4. See Robert Liebman and Robert Wuthnow, eds. *The New Christian Right: Mobilization and Legitimation* (Hawthorne, NY: Aldine, 1983). Since then, the Christian Coalition has assumed a major role in the politics of the 1990s.

5. Leonard I. Sweet, ed. *The Evangelical Tradition in America* (Macon, GA, Mercer UP, 1984) and Alan Heimert, *Religion and the American Mind, from the Great Awakening to the Revolution* (Cambridge: Harvard UP, 1966).

6. The best summary of Puritanism is still the anthology of Perry Miller and Thomas H. Johnson, *The Puritans* (New York: American Book, 1938). Also valuable are E.S. Morgan, *The Puritan Dilemma: The Story of John Winthrop* (Boston: Little, Brown, 1958), Darrett B. Rutman, *American Puritanism* (Philadelphia: Lippincott, 1970), and Sacvan Bercovitch, *The Puritan Origins of the American Self* (New Haven: Yale UP, 1975).

7. Marshall W. Fishwick, *Popular Religion and Popular Culture* (New York: Haworth, 1994). See also William G. McLoughlin, *Revivals, Awakenings, and Reform: An Essay on Religion and Social Change in America, 1607–1977* (Chicago, U of Chicago P, 1978).

8. William Jennings Bryan, *The Memoirs of William Jennings Bryan by Himself and His Wife Mary Baird Bryan* (Port Washington, NY: Kennikat Press, 1971). See also George M. Marsden, ed. *Evangelism and Modern America* (Grand Rapids Eerdmans, 1988).

9. A well rounded but somewhat rosy account is John Pollock's *Billy Graham: The Authorized Biography* (New York: McGraw, 1966). Two more useful biographies from which my account is drawn are William G. McLoughlin, Jr., *Billy Graham: Revivalist in a Secular Age* (New York: Ronald Press, 1960) and Joe E. Barnhart, *The Billy Graham Religion* (Philadelphia, United Church Press, 1972). All three have bibliographies.

10. Richard G. Peterson, "Electric Sisters," *The God Pumpers: Religion in an Electronic Age*, ed. Ray B. Browne and Marshall W. Fishwick (Bowling Green, OH: Bowling Green State University Popular Press, 1987) 116-40.

11. Quentin J. Schultze, *American Evangelicals and the Mass Media* (Grand Rapids, MI: Academic Books, 1990): 81-88. See also Clyde Wilcox, *God's Warriors: The Christian Right in Twentieth-Century America* (Baltimore: Johns Hopkins UP, 1992).

12. Jerry Falwell, *The Fundamentalist Phenomenon* (Garden City: Doubleday, 1981).

13. Theodore Roszak, *The Making of a Counterculture* (New York: Doubleday, 1969).

14. Steve Bruce, *Pray TV: Televangelism in America* (London, New York: Routledge, 1990) 24-53. See also Robert Abelman and Stewart Hoover, eds., *Religious Television: Controversies and Conclusions* (Norwood, NJ: Ablex, 1990).

15. Marshall Fishwick, "That Old-Time Religion May be Mainline," *Roanoke Times* 20 Mar. 1995: 34.

Whither American Civilization Studies after 2001?

John A. Hague

In the aftermath of the 1994 fall elections, it is not only members of the Democratic Party who need to reassess the health of American society and their strategies for curing the ills of that society. Every thoughtful student of American culture and civilization needs to address major questions about the present and future health of American society in order to chart the course of the culture and to prepare means of dealing with it.

The election made it crystal clear that, despite an increasing number of jobs and indications of substantial economic growth, and despite the absence of battlefield casualties in the last two years, there are, among the present electorate, a large number of very unhappy campers. The first question to be addressed is "Who are these unhappy campers?" and the second is "Why are they so unhappy?" The third is "What does their unhappiness portend for the future?"

The unhappy campers are, I believe, spread across every income, ethnic, racial, religious and social grouping in American society. Many are poor, without adequate housing, without the security which comes from various forms of insurance, and without hope that things will get much better. These are people surrounded by affluence which taunts but does not touch their lives. Many, perhaps most, struggle day in and day out to make ends meet, but they have nothing extra to meet emergencies or to indulge in activities which most Americans associate with leisure. Some, admittedly, have given up, and have turned to drugs and violence to escape the monotony of threadbare lives, but those who think that most of America's poor are lazy, ignorant and amoral know precious little about the culture of poverty and the people who are its members.

Yet it is not only poor people who are unhappy. Affluent families feel threatened by violence which seems random and senseless. They also worry about some children who fail to live up to their potential and others who fail to find jobs commensurate with their talent and education. They have invested huge amounts of time and money in their children's futures, and they see that the investments are at risk, perhaps at peril. And their own lives, if not at risk, often seem disjointed and confused.

What about children on the edge of adulthood? Some, indeed, are secure, confident and happy. In high schools and colleges scattered across the land, an increasing number of young people are volunteering for and being rejuvenated by various forms of community service. These students are bright, energetic, conscientious and optimistic. They believe they can make a difference, and they believe also that their personal and community goals are within their grasp.

There are a great many others, however, who do not share the optimism of their peers. Martin Seligman, a psychologist at the University of Pennsylvania, argues that changes sweeping over American society in the second half of the 20th century have brought affluent teenagers closer to serious depression than was true for their parents and grandparents who grew up in less affluent times. Indeed, Seligman believes that today's youth are ten times more likely to suffer serious depression before they reach 30 than were their parents and grandparents. He believes we are, in fact, experiencing an epidemic which is spreading faster than AIDS. Many professionals who counsel students on college campuses agree with Seligman.

What are the causes? Seligman believes the reasons involve a combination of factors which have overemphasized the self-reliant and free individual and, at the same time, weakened our belief in and reliance upon the Commons. The celebration of individualism has been brought about by a productive system that has "opened an enormous market for customization, for individual choice," and by rapidly spreading affluence which has provided increasingly large numbers of people with an incredible variety of choices. The result is what Seligman calls a "California self"; a "maximal" self which "has almost everything but a tan." This self is preoccupied with acquiring things and experiences which produce feelings of pleasure and well-being.

Seligman traces the loss of faith in the Commons to the wave of assassinations which began with the death of John F. Kennedy in November of 1963. Kennedy's death unleashed a reign of terror which destroyed our vision of the future. Seligman believes that "a generation altered its commitment, out of fear and out of despair, from careers of public service to careers in which we could, at least, make ourselves happy as individuals." The Vietnam War reinforced the lesson, and Watergate virtually set it in concrete. As individuals despaired of finding meaningful roles in public service, they turned increasingly inward in their search for happiness. Furthermore, Seligman thinks that the "erosion of belief in the nation coincided with a breakdown of the family," and also "took place against a backdrop of a culture with little belief in God." "Where," Seligman asks, "can one now turn for identity, for satisfaction, and for hope? To a very small and frail unit, indeed: the self."

Seligman's analysis tends to confirm studies made in the 1980s by Daniel Yankelovich and by Robert Bellah and his colleagues. Yankelovich argued that affluent persons frequently found themselves in a "triple bind." First, such people valued their personal freedom so highly and had so many choices that they perceived each new choice and commitment "as a threat to their freedom and a challenge to other possibilities they might exercise." The first bind, then, arose from the unsettling fact that "the question of what to commit to and sacrifice for" remained "forever open." The second bind stemmed from the sluggish performance of the economy. While their self-fulfillment expectations continued to soar, their incomes were plagued by inflation and a tight job market. The third bind grew out of the way these affluent people interpreted their world. They spoke, Yankelovich asserted, a language derived from theories of self-psychology. "They are forever preoccupied with their inner psychological needs. They operate on the premise that emotional cravings are sacred objects and that it is a crime against nature to harbor an unfulfilled emotional need" (Yankelovich 56). Such people might well derive greater satisfaction by addressing the needs of society and other people, but the language and interpretive framework on which they have come to depend keeps them from contributing to what Seligman might term the needs of the Commons.

Bellah and his colleagues also found that middle-class Americans had come to depend on the language of therapy which was, indeed, based on theories of self-psychology. These individuals found it difficult to make commitments, and when they did make a commitment, as in the case of marriage, the language on which they had come to depend made it hard for them to justify the commitment on any grounds except those based on personal needs and desires. In bringing up their children, affluent parents without strong religious convictions tended to be clearer about goods they wanted for their children than about a good they could require *of* their children. The result, in the children's eyes, was that parental love was "narrowed to a reward for doing well." Consequently, "Moral standards give way to the aesthetic tastes and technical skills of the achievement-oriented upper middle class." Goodness "becomes a matter of being good at things; being right, a matter of having the right answers" (Bellah et al. 60).

In *Habits of the Heart* the authors note that radical individualism leads to radical emptiness; the completely free self turns out to be completely empty. In fact, however, the authors point out that our lives are *not* completely empty. We are bound to other people by memories of the past. "In order not to forget that past, a community is involved in retelling its story, its constructive narrative, and in so doing, it offers examples of the men and women who have embodied and exemplified the meaning of the community." Our participation in "communities of memory" takes us outside of ourselves and also turns "us toward the future as communities of hope." These communities of memory "carry a context of meaning that can allow us to connect our aspirations for ourselves and those closest to us with the aspirations of a larger whole and see our efforts as being, in part, contributions to a common good" (153).

Erik Erikson has argued that failure to contribute to the common good leads finally to a kind of radical despair which is characterized by the fear of death. Conversely, people who come to value and accept what they have done in and for the community develop a feeling of ego integrity which partakes of the style of ego integrity developed by their culture or civilization. Such people understand that there is a kind of reciprocity between their own integrity and that of their culture. "Ego integrity, therefore, implies an emotional integration which permits participation by followership as well as acceptance of the responsibility of leadership," said Erikson in *Childhood and Society*. Erikson concludes by arguing that ego integrity depends, in the final analysis, upon trust which crosses generational lines.

Webster's Dictionary is kind enough to help us complete this outline [of the stages of growth] in a circular fashion. Trust (the first of our ego values) is here defined as "the assured reliance on another's integrity," the last of our values. I suspect that Webster had business in mind rather than babies, credit rather than faith. But the formulation stands. And it seems possible to further paraphrase the relation of adult integrity and infantile trust by saying that healthy children will not fear life if their elders have integrity enough not to fear death. (269)

Bellah and his colleagues believe that communities of memory do exist and that our participation in them, however slight, can soften the thrust of radical individualism. Erikson goes a step further and argues that those who do not manage an identification with the patrimony of their civilization, that is to say, are unable to feel that their lives have made a difference to their communities, will end by experiencing a feeling of deep despair. That despair, in turn, will destroy the trust of the younger generation, and, if prolonged, will destroy the fabric of our society.

It is time to deal more fully with the second and third questions raised at the beginning of this essay. Why are so many people so unhappy? Why are counseling centers on campuses across the country flooded with troubled students? Why are so many voters so angry, so frustrated? Why is political debate marked by so much mud-slinging and so much heat and so little light? What does this unhappiness suggest about our future?

There are several possible explanations. The first has to do with a lack of trust. We do not trust those we elect to govern. We do not trust lawyers to give disinterested advice. We do not trust doctors enough to follow a genuine course of preventive medicine. We do not trust the institutions we have created to fulfill their appointed tasks. Lack of trust has its roots in both public and personal experience. On the public side, the world seems out of control. Peace is illusive, suffering is pervasive, and justice does not always prevail. We are part of a global community, but the global community is torn by age-old conflicts, by modern disease, and by far-reaching provincialisms. Highly sophisticated technological systems control or shape many features of modern life, but they do little to resolve conflicts or to give purpose and meaning to our corporate life.

On the personal side, as Yankelovich and Bellah and his colleagues predicted, many people are at a loss to determine what choices will ultimately be satisfying and fulfilling. In 1969 Kenneth Keniston suggested that a significant number of middle-class youth had discovered that their affluent parents were not getting the satisfaction they had expected to get from their wealth. They were, in short, bored, and they could not hide their boredom from their children. The children, in turn, questioned whether the "rat race" was worthwhile, and some found solace in the world of drugs.

On another front, colleges and universities have sold the high price of the education they offered on the grounds that this education would equip students to use their talents fully and effectively. Fully and effectively meant that students would get high-paying jobs and that they would have the discipline and expertise to have a significant impact upon their communities. The economy's growth, however, turned out to be sluggish, and the desired jobs did not always materialize. At the same time many found it difficult to join with neighbors who shared the same geographic boundaries but had little sense of or desire for community.

The end result is a shrinkage of vision. To many, the larger community seems unmanageable and the community close at hand seems, in the words of Bellah, et al., more an enclave than a community (74-75). These people find the field of politics unattractive, both because the practitioners frequently lack vision and because their peers lend so little support to those who do run for office. They reach out by volunteering for a specific task, one which is often local and readily manageable. They will build a house for Habitat or comfort the sick and the dying, but they refrain from attempting to articulate a vision of what the good community might be like and also from attempting to reshape institutions like schools, churches, and those that deliver health care.

Such problems are exacerbated by a series of widening gaps that mark contemporary American society. The first, and most important, is the widening gap between rich and poor. This gap, if not vigorously addressed, will continue to grow. Those who want to reduce the role of government are, whether consciously or not, voting to make the rich richer and the poor poorer. Since the poor constitute a minority, they lack political clout. They also frequently lack opportunities to change their status. The problem, measured simply in terms of human neglect, is horrendous; it is further intensified by the simple fact that an economy based on high mass consumption doesn't work very well when people are underpaid and unemployed. We would all be better off if those at the bottom of the scale garnered a greater share of the wealth.

The growing gap between rich and poor is mirrored by a growing gap between the educated and the uneducated. A great many Americans, including those with college degrees, are receiving inferior educations. Part of the problem derives from a lack of funds and part from a lack of vision. The public schools in America are suffering. Teachers have too many students in their classes, and they are asked to teach too many periods. They are also underpaid. Ironically, wealthy parents, who often argue that you can't improve public education by throwing money at the schools, spend very large sums of money to send their children to private schools. Public schools *can* be better, but it will take much greater tax revenues to accomplish that result. It will also take a concerted effort by those who are well educated to see to it that schools measure up to higher standards.

A student who is lucky enough to acquire a superior secondary education (one which contains a balance of training in languages, rhetoric, sciences and the arts) will get into the better colleges. That student will have opportunities that seldom come to those with inferior educations. Those opportunities depend, however, on more than knowledge of a discipline. They depend on self-knowledge, on civility, and on qualities of discipline and imagination. An education, if thoughtfully designed and rigorously pursued, can nurture these qualities, but unless present trends are reversed, smaller and smaller numbers of people will actually get an education which is worth what it costs; that is, one which disciplines and liberates the mind and enriches the imagination.

Similarly, there are growing gaps in the quality of health care which people receive. The affluent can afford insurance programs which subsidize not only major medical expenses but everyday medical care as well. Unfortunately, many are left out. One result is that Americans spend too little on preventive medicine and too much on catastrophic care.

There is also a growing gap between those who behave toward others in a civil fashion and those who do not. That contributes to the politics of anger. It also contributes to a spirit of divisiveness which brings out the worst in Americans.

These gaps will not diminish by a policy of laissez faire. They must be addressed by public policy and supported by tax dollars. At issue is the survival of American civilization. If we persist in lowering the taxes of those who have the means to help solve our most pressing problems, we will destroy the national community and with it our civilization. As matters stand, loyalty to community is eroding, and the erosion will accelerate unless Americans take positive steps to reverse the trend.

When bridges corrode, rust becomes visible. Even that visibility does not always guarantee that we will move to repair them before they cave in. When schools deteriorate, the results are harder to see, and we are reluctant to fix what we do not think is broken. We must demonstrate, however, that we care about each other, and that we understand that our lives are bound together, not only by our history but by thousands of things and events which are constantly rendering us more and more interdependent and, by the same token, making us less and less able to stand alone. If we do not address the erosion of our communities, if we persist in our efforts to stand alone and in our efforts to find happiness in a mythical world where problems are solved solely by private initiatives and taxes are forever low, the 21st century will put an end to civilization as we know it.

Works Cited

Bellah, Robert, et al. *Habits of the Heart.* Berkeley: U of California P, 1985.

Erikson, Erik H. *Childhood and Society.* 2nd ed. New York: Norton, 1963.

Keniston, Kenneth. "You Have to Grow Up in Scarsdale to Know How Bad Things Really Are." *New York Times Magazine* 27 Apr. 1969: 27+.

Seligman, Martin. "Research in Clinical Psychology: Why Is There So Much Depression Today?" *The S. Stanley Hall Lecture Series.* Vol. 9. Ed. Ira S. Cohen. American Psychological Association, 1989.

Yankelovich, Daniel. *New Rules: Searching for Self-Fulfillment in a World Turned Upside Down.* New York: Bantam, 1981.

II

Leisure and Recreation

*O*ne of the dreams that have obsessed people from the beginning
has been that of non-work time and recreation. Being driven from Eden
was humankind's first binding sentence; ever since, we have tried to
return. Never mind that every labor-saving device ever invented has
really only opened up reality to more work and less leisure, technology
has again promised us our return to Paradise. But technology aside,
people are demanding and getting more leisure and its sister dream,
recreation.

With more leisure and recreation time come many problems and
threats. Just as the idle mind has always been considered the devil's
workshop, idle hands and undirected leisure time bring problems of what
to do, how to occupy that time. Occupying it, subsequently, creates
problems, the exploitation of other people, degradation of the
environment, exhaustion of natural resources. If the original people were
driven from Eden for defying the laws of God and nature, the
transgressions only continue. People pollution is our second greatest
problem today; the greatest may well be the movement of people through
time and space.

Such movement is the engine that drives economies. Some
countries, like Britain, could hardly subsist without tourism. American
sunshine states derive more than half their income from tourists. The Big
Apple would actually be smaller in size without its millions of tourists.
The flip side of the positive results these visitors bring, however, is
destruction and degradation of the physical environment and violent
changes to traditional cultures. Environmentalists claim that tourists
lower the altitude of the Alps four inches every year. Human wastes are
being left frozen for thousands of years in Antarctica. But perhaps the
greatest impact is to be felt in such third-world tourist attractions as
Mount Everest. Since Mount Everest was climbed by Edmund Hillary

and Tenzing Norkay in 1953 it has become increasingly attractive to both mountain climbers and permanent residents. With an airfield and thousands of outsiders flying in yearly, Tibet's total way of life—culture, language, economy, religion—is being radically altered.

Never before have so many people been able to travel and recreate so easily as now, especially citizens of developed nations who have the most money. English is the common language throughout such countries. English is the international language in every airport throughout the world. It is the language of business and culture in over 70 countries. American culture is the underground culture throughout the world, particularly in rebellious developing third-world countries.

Concurrent with the expanding development of tourism goes a heavy strain on physical and cultural aspects of all environments. In every sense the real question is whether those environments can survive the debilitating strains. The informed opinion is, probably not. But such threat of environmental apocalypse has not slowed down the desire and need to promote and engage in more and more tourism.

The Play World of the New Millennium

James Combs

Every age varies in its attitude toward the future. The now much-maligned 1960s, for instance, was a time of great upheaval but also of great optimism. The popular oracles of the day—Marshall McLuhan, Charles Reich, Alvin Toffler, Herbert Marcuse, Norman O. Brown, Theodore Roszak—all expressed great, and even utopian, hopes for the future. McLuhan, for instance, wrote of communications linking the world into a "global village" of shared experience that would overcome strife and division. Brown envisioned a world of sexual freedom that would free us from our inhibitions and repressive acts, and thus raise our capacity for love and lower our capacity for violence. Marcuse saw a new world being created by the young political radicals, and Reich and Roszak saw hope in the youth culture that would create a new and more humanely "green" world. Even those who saw grave dangers in the war establishment, the growth of population, the rape of the environment, and racial and gender division seemed to share a conviction that all such problems could and would be solved. For those who look back on the mythic 1960s with nostalgic yearning, part of that remarkable era's charm now is that it was the last moment that many Americans entertained much hope for the future.

There is an odd sense in which those most affected by the hopes for change expressed by the popular thinkers and activists of the 1960s were the last to believe in the myth of progress. The various conservative, Christian, and capitalist movements since are more reactionary and defensive than truly progressive; they tend to believe in the irredeemability of most people, the necessity of enforcing class and caste systems to control undesirable mobility and activism, and the defense of enclaves of wealth and power—the State, corporations, wealthy neighborhoods, theological domains—with both political and police force. Liberals of the '60s, for example, believed that integrated schools, rising living standards and opportunity, and expanded social tolerance could end poverty, racism, and social exclusion.

But the contemporary right (exemplified perhaps by Charles Murray's *The Bell Curve*) scoffs at such progressive thinking as naive and dangerous. If, as Murray claims, African-Americans are somehow inherently "inferior" in intellect (as measured by that psychometric chestnut, the I.Q. test), then it follows, according to the canons of conservative logic, that the progressive hopes of the '60s were worse than wasted, and that all efforts at social amelioration of the shameful condition of the "underclass" are misguided at best and certainly a waste of public money.

Thus, hope for progress in race relations or class mobility is abandoned in favor of the establishment of a "custodial state" that controls the errant behavior of the irredeemable miscreants at the bottom of society. The metaphorical public institution becomes not the school but rather the prison, and the message from elite circles of power is not to encourage hope but to instill fear. Contemporary ruling elites posit the necessity of an hierarchical society characterized by class and caste that sounds statically neofeudal and nonprogressive. And more important, this dominant view supports popular wisdom and political powers who prefer to believe that the poor and dispossessed do not deserve help. Since the 1960s, the most important political idea in American politics, and dominant rhetorical theme, has been the folly of hopefulness and the wisdom of fearsomeness.

This popular theme of hopelessness and fearsomeness has all kinds of political uses. Hoped-for reforms, such as universal health care, are undermined and defeated by powerful interests, further convincing people, especially the have-nots, that the social benevolence of institutions such as the State, insurance, and medicine is not forthcoming, and that any hopeful expectations of such public compassion will be quickly dashed. Such a practice makes for a political culture of alienation, with low voter turnout and participation and high levels of cynicism and lack of hope. But as long as political alienates are quiescent, then powers and interests are safe from reform and accountability.

The political and social nastiness of the 1990s, we may think, stems from the very success of this rhetorical stance. To sustain the definition of the situation as hopeless requires constant attack on proponents of hope, and indeed cynical denigration of the idea of hope itself. Important rhetoricians, ranging from talk radio celebrities to the Speaker of the House, bespeak the rhetoric that denies public responsibility for the health, welfare, or education of the many, especially the deprived, and supports the practice of private irresponsibility for the well-being and security of employees (e.g., job security, unionization, environmental and safety standards, retirement or health benefits). Thus the fears of the haves are allayed by propagating hopelessness among the have-nots.

The perpetuation of generalized malaise and resentments directed at symbolic social targets (e.g., welfare mothers, liberals, the press) helps to preserve the status quo, but leaves serious problems unsolved. Indeed, the very rhetorical strategy is to make fun of reformers and rational proposals. The comic rhetoric of Agnew, Reagan, Quayle, Gingrich, and so on lets people identify with their rulers against their common enemies by portraying their foes (the Clintons, for instance) as fools. If people cannot take presidents or policy proposals seriously, then support for a leader or a reform becomes difficult to garner. Apparently we no longer can take anything important seriously, which of course diminishes its importance. The idea of benevolent government is laughed to death as a kind of sick joke, and such proposals as extending health care to all treated with snickering contempt. Similarly, reformers who extend concern for people in need are deemed reckless sentimentalists. The elite structure of *fin de siècle* America seems to regard "the people" with condescension and contempt, a mass to be manipulated and deprived rather than a public to be served and cultivated.

The political situation of the 1990s might be described by a rational and outside observer as self-destructive and frivolous, an odd kind of politics of jocular malevolence that courts social fragmentation and allows economic dislocation. As public effort and expenditure are directed less for the "therapeutic" functions of the modern State (e.g., public school, health, welfare) designed to improve the well-being of the citizenry and more at the "punitive" functions (e.g., prisons and orphanages, police powers, public discipline), the potential for truly dreadful upheaval with uncertain consequences becomes all the more likely. But what is truly odd about these reactive innovations is that apparently no one expects them to work; lacking a deep belief in social progress, the proponents of "downsizing" government and curtailing or eliminating many traditional State activities seem to advocate deconstructive change without really believing in it.

The core assertions of ruling elites in the "nasty '90s" typically stem from pessimism about humankind and social harmony and even cynicism about human motives and public solutions. The political language used is a rhetoric of delusional fantasy that is likely not *really* believed in, only mouthed to appeal to the deep longing Americans have to escape from the harsh and stubborn realities of the time and to deny the grim prospects the future may hold. Lacking belief that one is "conserving" anything of value, then political talk is (with talk radio and right-wing punditry) just talk, or talk that serves a magical rather than a political function, conjuring up demons and making blessings and curses. Much such talk is Canutean, ordering the tidal waves of history to cease but without any expectation they will do so. If the 1960s demonstrated that liberalism in practice liberates no one, then the political legacy of the 1990s may well be to prove that conservatism in power conserves nothing.

Much of the flamboyant rhetoric and many of the names of the grandiose schemes of the 1990s, then, sound suspiciously like whistling in the dark, betraying a rather scared and juvenile effort to escape from history. Such bravado we might term "the pathology of normalcy," the attempt to believe in some mythic past, social order, and American character as if such normalcy, if it ever existed, was still valid and adequate to face the future. But for many Americans, the future simply isn't what it used to be. It is now simply hard to believe, and for that matter for propagandists to sell, the promise that the future will be better.

It has become increasingly difficult for social elites to perpetuate confidence in the future, again likely because they have trouble believing in it themselves. For the American future as imagined by many forecasters could well be bleak. Thoroughly respectable conservatives such as Edward Luttwak and Kevin Phillips envisioned nothing less than apocalyptic change for the worse unless draconian measures were taken. Luttwak thought us headed for "argentinization," with elites in palaces on the hills and the rest of us struggling in decaying towns and slums. Twenty-first century America, he predicted, will be characterized by huge permanent debt, structurally high unemployment and underemployment, stagnant or falling living standards, and severe and intractable social problems. Worse, social elites who control political, economic, and cultural institutions are less willing to "invest" in the country. Political elites are reluctant to spend on urban renewal, job training, and schools; economic elites move from the creation of widespread wealth through employment in areas such as manufacturing to the creation of "paper" wealth concentrated in elites through the cyberspace of financial markets; and cultural elites attack public support for institutions of "high culture" (the National Endowment for the Humanities, the Corporation for Public Broadcasting), and indeed the study of popular culture, as well as multicultural and global- perspective programs in schools. From lofty elite perches, investment in the quality of life of the "lower orders" and "dangerous classes" must appear to be a poor one indeed.

If elites now have little confidence in the masses, the masses also have little confidence in elites. A glance at polls show the disappearance over time in the belief in the benevolence and competence of politicians, business leaders, and eminent divines. Phillips notes how Washington is now perceived as "the parasitic capital of a declining empire," populated by "the rich and privileged," all of whom are part of "a broader transition toward social and economic stratification, toward walled-in communities and hardening class structure." Washington ranks with Wall Street and Hollywood as symbol of the remote power and privilege of elites, wherein "the nation's richest city (the Washington area) has itself become a vested interest—a vocational entitlement—of the American political class" (Phillips 37). The irony of this post-democratic era is that while the ruling classes (who believe themselves to be part of the "meritocracy" that have the skill, and thus the right, to rule) appear to have nothing but contempt for the people; the people have nothing but contempt for their rulers. Liberal analyst Christopher Lasch writes of "the revolt of the elites," making for "a two-class society" rule by classes who "have ceased to think of themselves as Americans in any important sense" and identify with "an international culture of work and leisure—of business, entertainment, information, and 'information retrieval'" (Lasch 47). And *Harper's* editor Lewis H. Lapham, like Phillips, raises the specter of past revolutions (luxuriant and decadent classes ruled 18th-century France) and devolutions (Rome declined and fell due to an inability to solve problems of political instability, elite decadence, and temporal entropy).

We have turned the pursuit of happiness into a mad self-destructive quest based in our narcissistic vision of "a romantic panorama of man at play in the meadows of paradise" (Lapham 300). As the people in the upper 20 percent of society increasingly control more wealth and power, and the middle and lower classes decline in income and status, mobility and security, the potential for social conflict becomes high.

The immediate American future, then, is one likely to be characterized by political fragmentation and perhaps even chaos, economic inequality and dislocation, and cultural struggles over constraints and expressions. Phillips (and writer Gore Vidal) even raise the Romanesque specter of devolution, the United States breaking up into regions (e.g., Ecotopia in the Northwest) with some measure of autonomy, much as the Soviet Union and eastern Europe have devolved into ethnic nationalisms and regional groupings, and as Canada soon may experience with the secession of Quebec and Indian regions. More likely are drastic measures by political elites to deal with increasingly unsolvable problems such as debt and unemployment, the breakup of cities in enclaves of the rich and ghettoes of the poor, the expansion of police powers to control unruly populations, and the attempt to stem migration and suppress social movements.

We may anticipate various forms of tribalism and new identities among, for instance, bored and alienated Generation X whites and dispossessed African-Americans. It is likely that significant parts of American inner cities will be controlled by gangs, who will in effect be the tribal government of those neglected and segregated areas. Murray's vision of a "custodial state" will include the vast expansion of prisons, homeless shelters as holding areas, and the expansion of capital offenses (and, perhaps, the return of public degradation rituals, including televised punishments such as executions and floggings). In a sense, this transformation would mark the end of civil society as we have known in the United States, institutionalizing a kind of postcivilized and neobarbaric social order strangely reminiscent of the early Dark Ages.

The potential for political fragmentation and the desperate attempt by elites to impose order through increasingly draconian measures would be exacerbated by economic disinvestment and innovation. The flight of capital because of fears the United States would break apart or become hopelessly unstable politically would further intensify the problem of structural debt and deprivation of the expanding number of have-nots dropping out of the shrinking middle class. For one of the more remarkable economic phenomena we are witnessing is the declining need for labor, with much more work done by computers, robotics, and other organizational refinements.

Futurist Jeremy Rifkin, in his book *The End of Work*, notes that the unfinished agenda of capitalist organization is the minimization of the use of human labor. Thus such current practices as "downsizing," reliance on temporaries, and expansion of overtime presage the eclipse of jobs, careers, benefits, and advancement as an economic expectation. The same process is at work in public institutions, with the decline of trust in public solutions and the elite decision to minimize state participation in education, health, and other therapeutic functions. It may be the case that the State will indeed "wither away," to be replaced by the myth of corporate benevolence. The corporate alliance that controls health care will "sponsor" access to the system based on wealth and status, and sustain itself through the myth of benevolent health organizations (e.g., hospital chains) and medical roles (e.g., doctors).

Many of the social conflicts that will emerge in "postmodern" America will be fought out, and find expression in, the realm of culture. If it is the case that the political world is coming apart, in a strange way the cultural world is, to use McLuhan's term, "imploding." The world is increasingly "wired" together, but as Thoreau remarked about Maine and Texas being connected by telegraph, do we have anything to say to each other? Contemporary elites apparently feel that both school curricula and popular culture are saying things dangerous to inherited values that support extant hierarchies of power. We may expect recurrent battles over the form and content of education, often revolving around the cynical question of whose propaganda is going to prevail. And we will no doubt see attacks on popular artifacts by political rhetoricians, in the tradition and manner of Dan Quayle's famous attack on *Murphy Brown*.

But in a larger sense, the struggle will likely be over the kinds of popular experience that are thought to be appropriate. This will range from people with censorship agendas to symbolic condemnations of popular objects (e.g., *MTV*, Madonna, tabloid news) to libertarian defenders of free speech, no matter how vulgar, to admirers of popular fare (e.g., critic Camille Paglia's admiration for Madonna). But in a world of overwhelming varieties of popular communications, ruling elites will be sorely tempted to control and restrict the more egregious and critical messages. How much success they will have remains an open question, but in an "emergency" situation, the invocation of "national security" might abrogate significant portions of free expression.

As we approach the millenium, the questions of arrangements of power, wealth, and expression will become more intense and apocalyptic. Just as the world went a bit crazy in the years leading up to 1000 A.D., we should anticipate that a similar "sense of an ending" will invite popular creations that speak to the hopes and fears raised by a millennial turn. We have already alluded to the images of decline and fall and imperial devolution conjured up by punditic oracles. Indeed, since the 1970s it has become common to find popular portrayals of a dismal and chaotic future.

Elsewhere I have loosely classified recent "clusters" of movies with dystopian themes about the future: Caesarian, Gibbonian, Mad Maxian, Orwellian, and Huxleyian. Those popular movies, and other forms of expression, that celebrate martial virtues and the reassertion of violent, usually male, power are artifacts of a desire for decisive and certain solutions that reassert and relegitimate tough authority, ranging from the protection of the family (*Fatal Attraction*) or social organizations (*Heartbreak Ridge*), or both (*Aliens*).

The appeal of Caesarism includes the military-police theme of "praetorian daring," applauding the exploits of brave and determined heroes skilled in violence (e.g., *Diehard, Top Gun*). The Gibbonian theme treats imperial arrogance and decadence in the midst of social decay (*Down and Out in Beverly Hills*), the organizational quest for power in the midst of poverty and despair (*Robocop*), and resentment and alienation on the hopeless bottom of society (*Do the Right Thing*). The Mad Maxian vision is postcivilizational, imagining an impending Dark Age characterized by a reversion to barbarism, ruled by the brute force of tribal bands, and burdened by scarcities (*Road Warrior, Blade Runner, Waterworld*) in either a desert wasteland or urban Gothic setting. The Orwellian fantasy foresees rule by a malevolent elite that governs through the use of vast personal control apparati and the technology of pain and mind control (*Brazil*). The Huxleyian scenario posits an elite that believes itself to be benevolent ruling through the manipulation of behavior based in a technology of pleasure (*A Clockwork Orange, THX 1138, Logan's Run, Sleeper*). All these dystopian themes suggest that we have lost confidence in the future, and can only imagine coming worlds in which we either lose control and things descend into chaos, or malevolent powers gain control over us without our consent or restraint.

We cannot even discount the possibility in the near future of what Jewett and Lawrence call "pop fascism." They cite various fantasy heroes of monomythic politics, from *Star Wars* to Rambo to Ollie North, wherein the violent redeemer exercises zealous will and becomes triumphant over evil, acting on behalf of the virtuous folk who have been betrayed by corrupt or cowardly politicians. Such a redeemer figure would no doubt have the praetorian bearing of a North, the folksy spirit of a Perot, and likely the appearance of a mature movie star, a Reagan or a Charlton Heston. But in any case he would preside over an American variant of "reform fascism," with the personal power of a Caesar, attempting to revitalize a decaying republican order (like the Weimar Republic) by abrogating its democratic elements, exercising vast police powers and using the media for propaganda, incorporating barbaric male impulses into a militant warlike atmosphere, and attempting to make ordinary people feel part of a renewed community with divine mandate. The imminence and felt necessity of an American pop fascism could be anticipated by the expanded celebration of such heroes and heroics in popular culture, wherein a popular fantasy of moralistic vigilantism translates into a political movement. The popular culture allowed under the rule of pop fascism would obviously be designed to serve the new order, under the guidance of a propaganda minister who would be something of a combination of Joseph Goebbels and Walt Disney.

Whatever future history has in store for us as a nation, we may be sure that popular culture will serve as valid evidence as to the political fantasies we entertain, both in terms of what we fear may be happening and what we hope does happen. To understand that future we must comprehend that culture. Indeed, in the presence of so many bleak and dreadful scenarios as to what the future may hold, we may be forgiven if we prefer to entertain hope for hope. In some measure, the desire for future hope no doubt helps explain the enduring popularity of *Star Trek*. The various manifestations of *Star Trek* display various and familiar popular formulas, and have a distinct technological bias, but its root appeal, one may suspect, is that it portrays a future with hope. To be sure, there are political conflicts that turn violent, and a variety of strange cultures to understand, but nevertheless the idea of progress is restored in the advance of political organization, science, and exploration, and in a kind of egalitarian professional society as represented by the crew of the starship *Enterprise*. They offer hope that rationality and good intentions can once again make us the master of our universe, and help us to believe that the present is not hopeless and that the future can be a garden rather than a desert.

From Work to Play

There is, however, another hypothesis about the future that should be considered. This is nothing less cosmic than what we might call a "civilizational premise," that the modern world in the West has been based upon the cluster of myths of progress, work, and happiness, but that now in the emerging post-modern world, the premise of civilization is changing to the pursuit of happiness and the achievement of fulfillment through play.

In the Weberian (and for that matter, Marxist) worldview, the activity of work had mythic sanction and efficacy: work produced the result of individual and social progress through the creation of prosperity with the eventual result of happiness. Both the idle rich and idle poor were condemned as useless and deviant; writers like Veblen made fun of "the leisure class" devoted to "conspicuous consumption" and "pecuniary decency," and conservative writers damned the poor on welfare as morally unworthy. The middle class, and the middlebrow press that catered to their fantasies, imagined both rich and poor to be engaged in unfruitful and wasteful play, having fun at their expense. The rich were believed to live like the new celebrities, as portrayed in the lurid press. The poor were thought to be cunning "operators" (like Reagan's apocryphal "welfare queen") who lived a free and easy life at public expense, breeding more illegitimate children to expand their enjoyment of a soft life. In both cases, middle-class contempt for both rich and poor likely included a latent element of envy: Both the rich and the poor "get away with" playing while I work? Despite all the ideological rhetoric about the joy of work, most people knew better; work was onerous, and play—those periods of carefree leisure, fun, and recreation—more pleasurable.

Despite the central and honored place given work in modern society, the general thrust of recent history has been to reduce the amount of time and energy devoted to work and to increase the domain of play. The advent of Hollywood was perhaps the signal event for the advance of the play ethic in the 20th century. But certainly by midcentury, the proliferation of a "multimedia society" made the availability of cheap play universally available and desirable. During the postwar prosperity of the 1950s and 1960s, the social ideal of work was transformed in ways that shifted the locus of life—what was worth doing—from the realm of work to the realm of play. Leisure time and discretionary income combined to create a leisure industry.

The burgeoning entertainment industry made the choices available for recreation, vacation, travel, and the like readily available. The "youth culture" exalted Dionysian play as a primary activity, and attempted to delay adolescence and enjoy these new leisures. Indeed, the thrust of the consumer economy has been to move us from an economy of needs to an economy of wants, giving impetus to the appetites and desires, and the need for novelty, stimulation, and "the good life." Popular culture became a vast instrument for the consumption of experiences as we increasingly demanded and sought the pleasures and diversions of play. And politics became increasingly occupied with the task of maintaining prosperity and thus the means to enjoy the good life, at least among the possessing classes.

But such changes simply increased the ascendancy of the play ethic. Rather than business as a norm, fun became the norm. Whereas a previous generation of entrepreneurial hopefuls might have admired a captain of industry or master of finance who worked hard to build and run an empire without cease until death, now they admire a success who made spectacular good and took the dream of "early retirement" (e.g., Peter Lynch). Whereas once popular celebrities could be ruined by bad behavior, now such shenanigans are rewarded as admirable if childish fun, something we all wish we had the money and freedom to engage in.

Our fantasy is that celebrities live a life of constant and egregious pleasure-seeking, and wish that we could enter the play-world they inhabit. Indeed, politicians have long known of the power of the political spectacle, providing ritual play for the masses through a variety of means—parades, court ceremonies, holidays, executions, news conferences, and so on. Too, many people expect politicians to live the good life, whether they approve of it or not (e.g., entertained by lobbyists, enjoying the perquisites of office, having a secret and hypocritical life of corruption and debauchery). It was noted long ago that elites were moving from being idols of production to idols of consumption; with the rise of figures such as Reagan and Gingrich, we may be seeing the legitimation of political idols of consumption, living a public life of luxury and acquisition reminiscent of the Roman equestrian classes in the declining imperial period. Celebrated elites in general would serve an important play-function as models of legitimate exhibitionism, acting as guides to the new luxuriant and narcissistic culture.

America in the early 21st century, then, may carry the logic of the consumerist good life to an astonishingly new kind of society, ironically undermining the work ethic that had created and sustained the old. Business as a norm ("time is money") will be replaced by play as a norm ("time off for fun"). If the premise of civilization becomes play, then the goals of the expanded leisure class (encompassing at least the upper-middle class) will shift from achievement to enjoyment, from the pursuit of rational work goals to the joy of pleasurable play goals.

The possessing classes will be admired and emulated down the social scale, indeed giving impetus to the pursuit of play rather than work among those who can less afford it. The Veblenesque display of superior status will include conspicuous appearances at major events (inaugurals, Super Bowls, awards ceremonies) from which the ordinary will be excluded. Nevertheless, those of inferior status and wealth will nevertheless grasp the spirit of the new society, and devote themselves to enough work to finance play, or abandon work altogether. It may be the case that the "slackers" of Generation X, who will someday be the dominant age group in American society, will become the creative force that gives shape to a play-society. In such an eventuality, we would see the end of civil society as we have known it, and the formation of a ludenic society with Dionysian rather than Apollonian principles and practices. The mark of success will be one's access to play, especially enviable and elegant play, and one's ability to organize life around fun activities. *Homo faber*—humankind the worker—will become an object of social contempt among the playing classes, and social stigma will attach to those condemned to the onerous jobs that remain necessary. *Homo ludens*—humankind the player—will be judged by the extent to which one commits to play-roles and the sportive and jocular spirit of a ludenic society.

The possible world of the future we described in the first part of this essay and our speculations about a ludenic society are not necessarily mutually exclusive projections of the American future. There will be much intellectual conflict between those who cling to the norms of the work ethic and business civilization, while ironically those very forces create the new norm of the good life defined as play through such forms of communication as advertising, making us all part of the revolution of desire. And we should expect much social conflict between those who have the means of play and those who do not.

If we have large segments of the mass population submerged in a world of work without hope of advancement, prosperity, and ample time to play, with rich elites living in the inaccessible pleasure-domes of the play-world, then the potential exists for serious upheaval that interferes with elite play. Social and political stability in the American future, then, might well depend upon the extent to which democracy evolves into a kind of "ludenocracy" or "playocracy," wherein the means of mass play—spectacles, lotteries, executions, tabloid news, drugs and alcohol, media play, and so on—are readily accessible. It might be necessary to subsidize the large segments of the populace who are poor or unemployed with "play stamps" much like food stamps in order to satisfy their socially sanctioned urge to play and to divert them from political activities such as voting or rebellion.

Popular culture would obviously be essential to the "playings" of a ludenic society. For in a ludenic society, life is conceived to have a very different purpose than before. The medieval ideal of life as a pilgrimage posited the human purpose as piety; the modern ideal of life as a secular career posited the purpose of achievement; the postmodern ideal of life as a carnival will posit the individual ideal as having fun. The locus of life becomes the playday rather than the workday.

In such a society, "where you live" is in the delights of the carnival, not in the pieties of the prayer closet nor the rationalities of the office. (We might speculate that this involves the ascendancy of a new social ideal and role model: whereas the classical world exalted the ideal of political activity, the medieval world the ideal of religious piety, and the modern world the ideal of economic achievement, the coming postmodern play world will honor the ideal of cultural play, wherein cultural experience becomes the locus of action for humankind.) The goal of life is to belong to the leisure classes, and to experience the play-forms of the social midway. The dominant form of social discourse would be comedy; rather than the pietistic effort to overcome human tragedy, or the melodramatic effort to manage pragmatic results, energy would be directed at comic relief.

A play society derives its vitality from its levity and jocularity, and denigrates earnestness and seriousness; traditional heroism is deemed foolish, and comic heroism a matter of playing the fool. Even formerly "serious" realms of action such as politics become impossible to take seriously, and indeed success accrues to those who are comic heroes willing to play the fool and maintain an air of levity. Ronald Reagan was a key figure in this transition, but so too was talk radio and popular journalism, with their attitude of cynical jocosity; by the millenium, all political discourse would take the form of a jest, and democracy would evolve into a kind of fun-house distortion of the ideal, a grotesque comedy of carnival entertainers with crackpot ideas and a gift for farce (Combs and Nimmo).

The play world of the future might come about as the result of the collapse of the modern institutional system (e.g., the inability of the State to cope, the bankruptcy of world finance), or as a reaction to the over-rationalized and -organized world of controls and disciplines the system imposes (e.g., surveillance, testing, "productivity"). The play-world could occur in the ruins of a postcivilizational period, with Dionysian revels among the decayed monuments of Washington and Wall Street. Or it could come about as rebellion against spreading world controls, and the attendant destruction of the environment. Play as a value could rise as a response to the Romanesque death of the old world, or to the increased controls of a successful death culture that wants to stamp out all forms of individual vitality, spontaneity, and joy. In the former instance, play would be crucial in the creation of a new society; in the latter, play would be forbidden unless it had official sanction. In any case, we do not really know what a society founded on play would look like, or how stable it might be.

The proliferation of popular culture has made play into an increasingly primary expectation, to the extent that shared popular experience is the communications link between people in the "global village" (actually more likely a "global city"). We may fear the darker aspects of a Dionysian society, with excessive displays of narcissism, extremes of sexual permissiveness, and even violence (read Euripides' *Bacchae* while listening to Stravinsky's *Rite of Spring*!). But with the current sense that things are playing themselves out at the *fin de siècle*, and that the millenium augurs new human possibilities, we may expect popular play with the idea of something new and unprecedented. It may be that those younger generations who are familiar with popular culture can use that knowledge to create a world that is different, and hopefully better, than the present. Their comprehensive knowledge of the expanding world of play might inform them of the value of play as a social principle, and help them shape a future that sustains life over death, perpetuating the human species—what Aristotle called "the laughing animal"—into the world of *Homo ludens*. Like any future, the world of the 21st century can be either a desert or a garden; we may hope that the play-force of popular culture helps transform it beyond the wretched present into a garden of earthly delights that celebrates a truly playful culture of the populace. But one thing is clear. The drive of popular culture will be so powerful that all societies will be carried along. To survive we will have to understand it. Such a burden placed on popular culture studies in the 21st century is heavy but necessary.

Works Cited

Combs, James. "Pox-Eclipse Now: The Dystopian Imagination in Contemporary Popular Movies." *Crisis Cinema: The Apocalyptic Idea in Postmodern Narrative Film.* Ed. Christopher Sharrett. Washington, D.C.: Maisonneuve Press, 1993. 17-35.

Combs, James, and Dan Nimmo. *The Comedy of Democracy.* Praeger, forthcoming, 1996.

Jewett, Robert, and John Shelton Lawrence. *The American Monomyth.* 2nd. ed. Lanham, MD: UP of America, 1977. 248-78.

Lapham, Lewis H. *Money and Class in America.* New York: Ballantine, 1988.

Lasch, Christopher. "The Revolt of the Elites." *Harper's* Nov. 1994: 46-47.

Luttwak, Edward. *The Endangered American Dream.* New York: Simon & Schuster, 1994.

Phillips, Kevin. *Arrogant Capital.* Boston: Little, Brown, 1994.

Rifkin, Jeremy. *The End of Work.* Putnam, 1995.

A Lion's Share of Tourism in the 21st Century

Ray B. Browne

The driving demographics which will guide up to 10 billion people on the earth by the beginning of the 21st century compel us to re-examine our position on the use of nonwork, leisure, tourism time. Long ago nonwork time was not necessarily considered positively as desirable, as according to the old proverb idleness was looked upon as the devil's workshop. Now we are compelled to look upon non-work time as the tourist person's area of development and exploitation.

As we move into the next century, the areas of tourists and tourist-workers are already crowded. We cannot possibly expect to put three times as many airplanes, cars and buses in the air and on the roads to accommodate all the new people who will want to go on vacation. We cannot expect to enlarge airports to three times their present capacity. Yet as everybody demands and gets more time off from work, society must prepare for a useful, at least enjoyable and non-destructive employment of the time, else we might have a societal devil's workshop. The public will have greater expectations from the tourist business: cheaper rates, greater accessibility, finer facilities and with all greater preservation of the environment and nature. The demands are incompatible.

We cannot expect nature to accommodate 40 billion hands and feet using the natural resources, which haven't expanded, and preserve pristine nature and wildlife. Yet everybody believes that he/she has the constitutional right to enjoy the natural elements of tourism. For example, when it is suggested that the Grand Canyon and the Colorado River cannot accommodate everybody who wants to shoot the rapids, the people who oppose overexploitation are called elitists who are denying the enjoyment of the Canyon to everyone. When it is suggested that the ecology of certain parks is too fragile to support unregulated tourism, many people feel that it is unfair to restrict their unfettered enjoyment. Still people are pouring into Yosemite until they are stacked higher than El Capitan, and have to be restricted. Africa has more safari tourists than wild animals being viewed. There definitely are more whale watchers than there are whales.

Yet most tourists believe, to one degree or another, that wildlife has a constitutional, God-given, right to life, liberty and the pursuit of happiness, just as human beings do, and that natural environments must be preserved. Just as humankind likes to think about the sanctity and safety of our own homes, we believe in the sanctity of animal homes. We even call them—when we have preserved them—sanctuaries. So people in the tourist business must somehow work with the people and with wildlife and with the mixed emotions about the issues of animal and environmental rights.

One way to do it is through representative tourism. That is, a representative number of people enjoy a tour as our surrogates, and all of us experience and enjoy through them. This is, of course, a suggestion, though it is not new, which brings out many strong negative responses. Many people think it is discriminatory and just another perk for the rich and powerful. But the sheer weight of the problem demands some such regulation. If we believe that our political life must be served by our electing one among us to represent, to voice, to exercise our political liberty, then we quite properly might ask why not send a small percentage of us out to enjoy those aspects of nature which are too fragile to accommodate us all. If facilities cannot tolerate us all, why not a representative group?

There are of course many objections. Unlike political life, vacation enjoyment is not something one does by proxy; everybody wants it for himself/herself. Yet we know from TV, movies, even pornography, that the next best thing to actual experience is seeing someone else participating. Further, many of us apparently want only an opportunity for an on-site photograph. When we visit a site all we are interested in is having a picture made. Years ago we provided such opportunities at home or at the studio. Now we can provide very sophisticated opportunities for inclusion in videos and very realistic settings. With the ever-growing number of documentaries, such as on cable TV and PBS, a reasonable substitute can be provided for our actual presence on a tourist site. Contrary to the initial objections of many, such reasonable substitutes need not further isolate us from participation in life's activities. They could in fact become agents for greater participation and inclusion.

Objections will arise from the trade, of course, Reduced numbers of tourists, some people will say, will cause the tourist industry to collapse, airlines to fold; and the total economy, which in most places is closely tied in with tourism, will collapse.

But regardless of the tourist business, which might suffer some initial setbacks, the whole of society will not collapse with a reduced rate of total tourism. Tourism business, though it may constitute from one-third to one-half of a particular community's business, may be the wrong kind of income. Tourism does not create wealth. It merely shuffles it around. With people released from the tourist business, business could create something valuable, something tangible. The adjustment, although somewhat traumatic, could benefit us all. If that suggestion is too draconian, I have another.

In addition to the exponential growth of total populations, society is changing in another way, this time with a positive possibility for the tourist trade. The current drives toward ethnicity and nationalism have unleashed forces which seem at least to threaten conventional society itself. Regardless of the ultimate result on society at large, this ethnic rationalism presents an opportunity to enlarge and enhance tourism. Many Americans are now rediscovering their roots and finding enrichment in this discovery. They may want to visit the "old country" but may not be financially able to return and tour the countries from which their ancestors came, no matter how strong the nostalgic tug at the heart.

Yet these latter-day would-be pilgrims may fulfill their fondest desires. Throughout the United States, and other countries, there are ethnic and nationalistic enclaves which are tightening their cultural ties and development through museums, festivals, dances, foods, and other manifestations of the "old life," which recreate rather effectively the life the tourists want to experience. So these local representations present a golden opportunity to provide a return to "roots" without the expense of going overseas for it.

If these aspects of ethnic life, and other marketable ways to enjoy leisure time, seem too thin to satisfy the desires of many tourists to spend a week or two away from home, then the various sites can be marketed collectively. In northwest Ohio, for example, the 3 million people who visit Cedar Point yearly could be coaxed into spending the rest of their vacation period visiting other sites in northern Ohio such as Seaworld, Edison's birthplace, President Hayes's home, Sauder Village, Fort Meigs, and nearby, Henry Ford Museum and Greektown in Detroit. If these are not sufficient inducement to lure the tourist, this area, at the crossroads of two of the most heavily traveled arterials in the country, might wisely think of developing some new ones.

My third suggestion is somewhat more broadly based on a longer range, with infinitely more ramifications for the trade and society at large.

With tourism there is an inevitable abuse, use and destruction of resources. Some British believe that the price of tourism, which alters and destroys traditional British culture, is too high. The French both love and hate the tourists, who dilute the French culture. As the number of people on earth increases, the number of fingers and toes that touch and break things will be hard to tolerate. We put up signs for people not to lean on the glass, touch the flowers, rub the medallion, chip the monument. But it is hard to keep people from tactile participation. There is an almost inbred feeling among tourists that they pay out their good money and therefore have a right to handle and destroy, oblivious to the rights of their successors.

We fight this urge in many ways but with mixed success. We are also not entirely successful in creating the proper respect for the need to conserve the environment and the culture in which things exist. We could be far more successful if we worked in greater detail and depth in preparing the tourists for the environment of the destination. Some simple and obvious ways could be very beneficial. An excellent way would be for the airliners going to foreign countries to present videos of the cultures of destination-countries, telling the customs, way of life, the flora and fauna. These videos would of course be free; people not interested could turn their attention elsewhere, but it would be my guess that only the most callow would not be at least partially interested. We now pass out printed brochures, sometimes, which at best are superficial and somehow insufficient. There might also be preparation at the point of entry of the tourists. Again, videos could be shown, printed brochures could be designed to be more effective, and tourist guides could very profitably preface their tours, where tourists go on such trips, with more background material. Some tour guides do relatively fine jobs, but most of us know that the majority of them merely repeat by rote.

But perhaps the most effective and the most needed change in the tourist business in the future will be an extension of education, and will begin in the classroom. It may be too much to ask the incoming tourist to spend a day or two in a classroom before being released into a country's society. But it clearly would be a worthwhile idea if the embassy or Intourist office had a one-day, or even one-hour, seminar for those people coming into the country. It might have been done in the home country before the tourists left. But wherever, it would be helpful. The instructors could be paid by a small surcharge of the tourist facilities, or indirectly. The result would be happier and less destructive tourists, with less negatively affected destinations and increased tourism.

But in many ways the success of the tourist business of the future can be greatly assisted by those professionals who come into daily contact with the tourists, the guides, cultural attachés and In-tourist officials. It is they who will direct, explain, mollify and modify the tourists' behavior. For those professionals somewhat more particular education would be helpful—education in the humanities, that is. The humanities are those elements in our culture which characterize us as *Homo sapiens*, which enrich our daily lives and make us cohere as groups and nations. In our present-day life the humanities are the popular culture, the everyday culture around us, in our country and by extension in all the countries of the world. There is an American popular culture and there is an overriding world popular culture. If one understands his/her own popular culture it will be much easier to understand that of other countries and other peoples, and to explain it to tourists so that they appreciate the differences and the similarities.

Some years ago I was lecturing for the U.S. Information Service in Moscow. One of the people at the American Embassy was a Bowling Green State University Ph.D. in American Culture who had been a student in my Popular Culture classes. She told me that she had served for several years in the office of the cultural attaché in several Near Eastern countries and was now in Moscow. She insisted that the training she had received in Popular Culture Studies had served her best in her duties. These studies had trained her to best relate to the people among whom she lived and worked, and allowed her to explain the United States most effectively to the non-Americans among whom she worked, who were eager to learn what "America is really like."

Her observation has been borne out dozens of times by the students who have come to BGSU from other countries, from such places as Japan, Australia, China, Germany, the Near East, and elsewhere. Generally these foreign students come to BGSU to get training in American Studies so that they can teach United States culture back home. They soon discover, however, that what they really want and really need for back home is the training in Popular Culture Studies. Their students don't really want American Studies in the traditional sense, but Popular Culture Studies, the real, everyday culture of the United States. At the moment I know a Ph.D. from China who got his degree at Michigan State University, took a course or two in Popular Culture Studies and discovered when he got back to China that he really needed more of the latter field so that he could satisfy the needs of his students and school. So he is now back at BGSU for a year to develop his skills. From both directions, then, the preparation for people working with foreign cultures and those tourists who are going to meet those cultures is Popular Culture Studies. These studies are particularly useful to those people who will touch the travels of any and all—travel agents, those working in hotels and embassies, as translators, in all forms of business. It would be unrealistic to ask that all people who are in or going into the tourist trade, especially that associated with overseas travel, become Ph.D.s in Popular Culture, even if such a degree were currently possible. But it would be useful for such people to take courses in Popular Culture Studies, perhaps to major or minor in such studies, and the more taken the better prepared the tour person should be.

What would such courses consist of? Essentially they would consist of the theory and rationale for people's behavior, the differences and similarities in the behavior of people of different countries, what makes them different and what similar. Such explanations could be especially effective in our present-day and future society when the "global village" that media specialist Marshall McLuhan predicted turns out to consist not of small groups of friendly natives but ethnic enclaves armed to the teeth and shooting to kill.

The Popular Culture courses point out that all peoples like and need games and spectacles. The games and spectacles of one nation are not superior to or inferior to those of another. They are merely seemingly different and actually more alike than different. The courses point out how habits of dress, eating habits and entertainments are more similar than different. And the courses can point out how the "cultural imperialism" of the United States can be explained, rationalized, and "justified" to non-Americans as well as to Americans. Proper backgrounds in Popular Culture Studies oil the ways of life for us all.

Of these possible changes in tourism of the future, perhaps the last mentioned is the most important, for it actually encompasses the other two. Through the travel agents it explains the possible greatest gratification to be found in travel and touring—and the best way for tourism to remain in business without ultimately destroying the world in which it operates. With such an arrangement the lion could have his/her share of the world and we, the most voracious consumers of all times, could have ours. Such accommodation would be beneficial all around.

"And then I saw the monkey . . .":
Teaching Travel Culture

Carol Traynor Williams

Humankind has always traveled—"walked," said the late travel philosopher Bruce Chatwin. We have looked for food ("Raids are our agriculture," Chatwin quoted a Bedouin proverb) or a mate not incestuous, or fled the stranger (in Middle Latin, *wargus*, the stranger or "expulsus," is also the wolf). To be human is to travel, to travel is to be primally human. In the new millenium, more of us will have more access to finding "somewhere else." But, what does this newly (more) equal opportunity mean? Who will go, who will be bumped? Will most of us go on getting squashed in the crowd? It is time that our travel brochure took on this new kind of human odyssey and helped prepare us for the traumas ahead.

In this 20th century of chicken-and-egg mass war, mass communication, and democratization, more of us traveled more, and worked less. In the postmodern world of surfeit, consuming becomes our "work," and travel one of the rarities we can consume without feeling guilty. "Travel," says John Krich, "is one item American affluence buys that . . . we're convinced is unmitigatedly good for us" (12). To heck with all we chop and tramp down. The most endangered mountain range, geologists now say, is the much-trodden Alps, where there also are avalanches in new places, from trees cut for ski runs. A European tour director cited this; and another one said that while even a few years ago, tours gave Florence (for example) three days, today they give three hours, a "glimpse."

For as popular travel grew, so also did the hospitality industry and its specialization, "Travel and Tourism." And as the business spiraled, so did its need to train new workers. In a traditional chronology, at first training was apprenticeships—learning by doing; then, when Hospitality became respectable, came the university, where, in the last decade of the century, it is still fledgling but growing, as its parent, Business, did, finding its "theory," applying Accounting, Management, Marketing, Law, etc., to the hospitality industry, turning apprenticeships into "internships." Like practical Business students, Hospitality students tend to be irked by the Liberal Arts requirement. Learn the geology of the Alps? Study the Medicis? They do not get the connection. Here is how one university used travel culture studies to ready its Hospitality Management students for the "one world" of the 21st century.

The Real Egyptians

My dreamlife—not too unusual—is travel and writing about it. So, when a Hospitality Management degree (the only university one in the Chicago area) grew from Roosevelt University's interdisciplinary Bachelor of General Studies (BGS) program, I had an idea for its general education seminars. These students, we had learned fast, glaze at "Liberal Arts." What better way than travel culture—rarely in the Liberal Arts curriculum—to introduce Hospitality students to the wide world they should know but probably don't. Remember, this is the generation always in the news for not knowing what country North Dakota is in. As first-year students, they get an anthology's shot of "multiculturism," and that usually is it for a "Ramble Through Lebanon" (P.J. O'Rourke).

I remembered that my BGS humanities seminar was rapt a few years ago when I illustrated *The Shape of Content*, the painter Ben Shahn's book, with art postcards from Europe, and (especially) my own photographs and narrative ("This was my table every morning in the Piazza San Marco, and my cup of cappuccino . . ."). Above all, travel teachers should love travel and should tell their stories because, besides travel, we all also love stories. Travel teachers should play music, show movies (like *Enchanted April*), cook! The best reason for using travel to teach the humanities is that all the humanities can be taught: history and philosophy, as well as the arts—as can the social sciences. Politics, economics, and, of course, cultural anthropology come alive under this indirect but highly concrete, indeed sensual lens, called popular culture.

Or called more specifically, travel culture. "Travel culture" covers the trip and/or the faraway place—and also everything that goes with travel, all the media, artifacts, and milieu of the Orient Express or the "small world" of Disney; the literature and art (books, travel magazines, movies, music, etc.), and also "home" photography and travel diaries. The travel culture is not for those who want to "do" a place. It is for *being* there, if only imaginatively. In *They Went*, an anthology of travel writers on travel writing (edited by William Zinsser), Vivian Gornick wrote:

In Cairo I read a book by Lady Duff Gordon called *Letters from Egypt.* . . . It was the difference between General Westmoreland reporting on Vietnam and Frances FitzGerald writing *Fire in the Lake.* I read Lady Gordon's letters and I believed her. Her Egyptians were real; they reminded me of Egyptians I was meeting every day in Cairo. (177)

Travel culturists want to discover Egyptians for ourselves. We do not want them veiled by "interpretation." We like letters, journals, and other primary documents. (Or past, and thus innocent, records, like Ernie Pyle's 1935 description of the "Boston Post Road" as a "nightmare of roaring trucks and careening cars" [149–50], to which we can say, *Ha*, you should see the Merritt Parkway today.) We love the sign, the emblem of the real thing, the "detail" that God, or truth, is in. I became a Russian-phile when I read Truman Capote's *The Muses Are Heard*, in a "'workman's'" bar off Leningrad's Nevsky Prospekt in December 1955, where the Russians "pecked at me like magpies," particularly a toothless veteran missing an eye, so that, over and over, he could do this "trick . . . meant to be a parody of Christ on the Cross": "Taking a swallow of beer he would stretch his arms and droop his head. In a moment a trickle of beer came crying out the gaping redness of his hollow eye socket" (127–28).

The veteran traveler's imagination takes off even from guide books or maps (especially maps). But all travel buffs prize the spur of the traveler's tale. Travel narrative can be realistic social documentary or it can reach for our daydreams. Mort Rosenblum does the latter in *The Secret Life of the Seine* (1994). The former *International Herald Tribune* editor-in-chief lives on a houseboat at Paris quai. ("Suddenly, sweet notes of music wafted down to the deck. Up in the trees, masked by leaves, I saw a bandsman in blue and red with shiny brass buttons tuning a French horn" [10].) In *Roissy Express: A Journey Through the Paris Suburbs*, also 1994, François Maspero is a political documentarist; with Anaik Frantz's photographs, Maspero limns not only the African emigrants today's tourists see if they take the Reseau Express Regionale B-line train from Roissy-Charles de Gaulle airport, but also Drancy, from which the Nazis sent 70,000 French Jews to camps.

Like Robert D. Kaplan's 1993 *Balkan Ghosts*, travel literature is almost always historical, and sometimes centrally so, as in the popular type, "retracing the steps" (across Antarctica, on Asia's Silk Road, through the Adirondacks in a 19th-century-style canoe [Christine Jerome, *Adirondack Passage* 1994]). Travel narrative can be fiction, or women's studies, or a cookbook (like the Chase siblings' *Saltwater Seasonings*: Coastal Maine photographs, stories, and, oh yes, recipes). It can be traditional description or travelogue, or a mystery, such as the Miss Marple movies which make people run for trains to English hedgerow country. There is travel narrative for every teacher's and student's interest. Basically, though, there are two types of travel tale: stories of places and stories of getting there. The former focus on the place more than the traveler-teller, and might be called culture literature: e.g., Chatwin's *The Songlines*, on Australia's Aboriginals, or Rebecca West's *Black Lamb and Grey Falcon*, on Yugoslavia. Journey-tales highlight the Odysseus as much as the locale; for example, the travel adventure books like Redmond O'Hanlon's *Into the Heart of Borneo*, so popular these decadent postmodern days.

In this 20th century of democracy rampant, the world's romance with travel has grown hugely. Ironically, the energizer was war. Technology, especially of transportation and communication, also drove travel, but these technologies grew from wars. The Civil War uprooted and urbanized rural and small town America. World War I opened Europe to American "expatriates"; and the Second World War got 14 million U.S. men and women "off of the farm." The Vietnam War lies behind the current boom in Asia. As post-World War II affluence spread, first in the United States and then worldwide, the streams merged in a mighty river of travelers. As we traveled, willy-nilly we became more sophisticated. Only look at the changing face of America's fast food, from the hamburger to tacos, "French Dips," and sushi bars.

And after we came home, we became suckers for books about the Seine, movies laid in Italy, or BBC-TV series such as *Upstairs, Downstairs*. Reporting from Seattle, on May 13, 1994, *Good Morning America* introduced house-boating: "Living on a riverboat just like in the movie *Sleepless in Seattle*." At first, after World War II, anything with "Venice" in the title sold; but travelers use up where they go and need ever-stronger adventures. Why the trips up the Orinoco? To test ourselves, yes; to feel in danger so we can *know* we can make it in Outer Mongolia without the language. "[C]ulture shock," says travel writer John Krich, "isn't just a matter of being unable to find [the traveler's] favorite flavor of yogurt. It becomes a tool for stripping the personality back down to the instinctual. . . ." (57).

Meanwhile, technology and democracy wiped out the luxury liner and brought in the (ever-bigger) "cruise ship"—thanks to *The Love Boat*. Before this popular TV series (1977–86), only the wealthy cruised, travel agents say. Similarly, before *Northern Exposure* in the 1990s, only two large lines cruised Alaska (the Princess and Holland America). Now, most of them "position" Alaskan trips. (*Northern Exposure* is really filmed in Washington—also booming). The influence of popular culture on the travel industry—and now, vice-versa—cannot be overstated. The story of air travel is the same: first there were the liner-like dirigibles (pre-*Hindenberg*), and the "Pan-Am Clipper," New York-Lisbon, last hope to flee Hitler's Europe, smoky den of triple agents looking like John Garfield and Maureen O'Hara in *The Fallen Sparrow* (1943). Pan-American's flying hotel grew to become today's airbuses—and in the 1990s, in economy class, more like buses in the back country of Honduras.

Today, as always, class is mirrored in the traveler: in the 1990s, the very rich can buy privacy with their kind on a Smithsonian cruise (as can the intellectuals, who earn their way aboard as "lecturers" on flora, penguins, cathedrals, etc.) The bourgeoisie goes by tour bus—and some very good ones for the weak of limb, but not necessarily brain or taste. Another class adventures. It is economically hybrid and not small in number: the postwar generations are (in some ways) better educated, hence healthier, and as television spreads, more global minded. Not all who bike, hike, or ride third class are hippies or even young. Even after the 1960s, some of the hopefulness and personalism of that period sticks. Some of us *prefer* pensiones.

But not all. Even in the 1990s, not everyone travels. And that cycles us back to the Hospitality students in Chicago. Many are young, looking for first careers; in 1994, about 30—a sixth—are from another region: Asia, the Middle East, Europe, or Latin America. A student may be a Mexican father trying to make a better life; another a child of wealthy, and frustrated, Asian (or U.S.) parents—frustrated because the field is seen, and the child will be seen, as second rate. Hospitality students often lack self-confidence. The daughter of a Hong Kong magnate, for example, needed all the help Jan Morris could give in *Hong Kong* to see wonder even in her hometown. Ironically, those in training to become "cultural ambassadors" in the hotels, meeting and conference centers, and travel firms of this ever-more-interwoven world are all too often sadly insular.

What travel narrative can do with such students is open them up culturally. The daughter from Hong Kong added to Morris's essay and listened to the Native American talk complexly of life on the "picturesque" reservation, and the new gambling casinos. And both heard the white-haired 72-year-old student tell of a trip to Auschwitz, where he had lost family. Through travel culture more than geography can be taught, likely because the message comes at a slant, and stealthily.

Travel Story

Even if a travel account does not, like the works of Sir John Mandeville and Marco Polo, trade largely in wonders, it will still resemble the literary form of the *romance* by containing more than a mere *novel's* share of anomalies and scandals and surprises and incredibilities. (Fussell 16)

The message comes in literature, but it also comes in movies like *Summertime* (in Venice) or *The Lovers*, in which the Orient has never been more erotic and exotic. The "meaning" of a place may be Audrey Hepburn in Rome, or Paris; *A Room With a View* ("Merchant and Ivory are making a fortune out of locations," a critic says); or *A Passage to India* or *The Jewel in the Crown* (*The Raj Quartet* novels by Paul Scott). "I couldn't wait to stay in a bed and breakfast in Belgravia," says a traveler and fan of *Upstairs, Downstairs* (1973–77) and its "parent," *The Forsyte Saga* (PBS, 1969–70). "Texas" was created by popular culture, from *Giant* to *Dallas*. Fans of *84 Charing Cross*, a cult movie, walk Charing Cross Road in London looking—alas in vain—for the bookshop in which Anthony Hopkins read Anne Bancroft's letters from far-off America. Visitors to Minneapolis do the same for "Mary Richard's" house (*The Mary Tyler Moore Show*, 1970–77). But the most active (not counting history buffs) are tracers of Sherlock Holmes's trails, or Agatha Christie's.

Mysteries and detective stories may be the best travel literature next to the official stuff. Like so much in the mystery genre, this may owe to Christie, who traveled with her archaeologist husband and romanticized the Orient Express and the Nile (*Death on the Nile*, 1937), not to speak of the English countryside. Perhaps this by-product (place) comes from the lack of characterization in the classic mystery, in which only the detective is much characterized. Everyone else is an accomplice or antagonist, or is getting murdered. This is an overgeneralization; but mystery "supports" often are eccentrics, cameoed, like Ross Macdonald's Californians, Sara Paretsky's Chicago-types, or Christie's secondaries (each unique, fans say).

Randy Allen White, one of the best contemporary mystery writers, creates a number of complex and varied characters in his three books on Sanibel Island, off the south Florida Gulf coast—along with plots both original *and* logical, and with a sense of place so strong a Sanibelian can hear the waves' sough and the palms in the breeze. Locales, usually regions, are almost as common to detective stories as detectives; and (as I try to show students), the tie is mutually enriching: as between Tony Hillerman and the American Southwest, which, in the last few years, has been *Conde Nast Traveler* readers' favorite U.S. place.

The mutual boost between travel literature and its locale is also shown where, surprisingly, it does not hold; most notably, the Caribbean and Latin America. The Caribbean overflows with tourists and traveller-adventurers, and so with fans for books, movies, etc., set there. Yet these are few, and underread. Toni Morrison's *Tar Baby* (1981) and Martha Gellhorn's *Liana* (1944) stand out with vivid, lush description; but they are "serious" stories about racial mixing, as are the works of contemporary native Caribbean writers such as Michelle Cliff and Paule Marshall. The Caribbean, it seems, is truly too close to America to be fantasy.

The works of Gabriel Garcia Marquez, Carlos Fuentes, Manuel Puig, Mario Vargas Lhosa, Isabel Allende, and a number of others from South or Central American countries, are realistic fantasy, or fantastic realism, often mixed with politics, on the top of the list of important serious contemporary fiction, and the opposite of the image U.S. President Franklin D. Roosevelt and the Rockefeller family created in the 1940s: Latinos rhumba-ing like Carmen Miranda, "The Lady in the Tutti-Fruitti Hat." Travel agent Susan Weiss says that in the travel business today Latin America is the "great untapped resource. . . . What it needs is a good Mayan mystery series." Latin American's problems are that it is far away and its ports too far apart and not major cities—unlike the Caribbean, near the U.S., with islands close together, and "made" by the cruise ship.

If Puig's *Kiss of the Spider Woman* is too serious, it is in the company of Tolstoy, Joyce, and Faulkner. Serious novelists focus on characters. Even in most popular novels, even *Gone with the Wind*, "the land" is not as memorable as the O'Haras, et al., and their story. Australia is not what is remembered from *The Thorn Birds*. Historians also focus more on story than locale (except military historians, whose work draws travel buffs). On the other hand, travel books of a time are one of the best ways to learn what it really looked like then and how it was to live there. For example, Lady Mary Wortley Montagu, "the first woman to travel abroad for curiosity's sake" (Mary Morris, editor, in *Maiden Voyages*), wrote of the "Turkish ladies," whose veils and *ferigees* (cloaks) gave them "entire liberty of following their inclinations without danger of discovery." Lady Montagu envies them (*Maiden Voyages* 5–6).

Besides making history interesting, travel books and films are unmatched in giving the most memorable messages—indirect ones—on the politics and ecology of a region, and in communicating its customs and culture. For example, in the aptly surreal *Zoo Station* (1987), Ian Walker writes of the socializing of east and west Berliners: "[T]he easterners were thinking . . . *Isn't this very drab compared to what they're used to*? The westerners in turn went out of their way to compliment their hosts on the positive aspects of their way of life . . ." (189), not, it seems, what Lenin saw happening when socialism met capitalism!

Who *are* these men and women who travel and write? Often they are as powerful a pull into their stories as their locales. Patrick Leigh Fermor, for example, may have been in the "political torpor" he apologized for when he walked through 1930s Transylvania and Carpathia (*A Time of Gifts* and *Between the Woods and the Water*), but he went on to behind-the-lines heroism in World War II. Bruce Chatwin, who died at 48 in 1989, was the travel-adventure writer's travel-adventurer, as much the metaphysician as the storyteller. In 1993 Helen Winternitz and Tim Phelps went *East Along the Equator*, particularly into Zaire, the colonial Belgian Congo, rotting under the U.S.-backed Joseph Mobuto's dictatorship; they went on to write *Capitol Games* (1992), the history of the Anita Hill-Clarence Thomas hearing (October 1991), which Phelps made happen when he broke the story in *Newsday* (as did Nina Totenberg of National Public Radio).

The women travelers are nearly unbelievable in the collection *Maiden Voyages*. Lady Mary Anne Barker (from *Station Life in New Zealand* [n.d.]), straightforwardly reports walking from 7 A.M. until after dark, through bush, up and down almost vertical cliffs, over huge fallen trees. . . . Alexandra David-Neel (*My Journey to Lhasa*, 1927), not only led her Tibetan guide through pathless glacial mountains one night; to keep them from freezing, she lit the wet flint and steel by warming them against her body, a skill she had learned from the Tibetans (*thumo reshiang*: "the strange art of raising the internal body heat" [*Maiden Voyages* 149]). Women's studies and travel are a pair!

Men's travel writing is often droll. I laugh aloud alone at Bill Bryson's traveling in Europe. Some of the early women reporters can be funny; e.g., Frances Trollope on the "Domestic Manners of the [19th century] Americans" (in *Maiden Voyages*). But, generally, women writers, being empathetic, are serious, and in the later feminist years of this century, and in their growing numbers, they have brought to the genre as a whole their characteristic search for identity.

The quest, and empathy, mark one of the best newer books, Brad Newsham's *All the Right Places: Traveling Light Through China, Japan, and Russia* (1989): "Burned onto the steps [in a Hiroshima museum] was the shadow of a man. . . . What, I wondered, was his last act? To smoke a cigarette? . . . Admire a passing woman?" (87). This contemporary American traveler, buffeted by new sensitivities, stands behind a Japanese boy in the museum, looking at a replica of a woman carrying her melting breasts in front of her. The boy turns, and Newsham looms over him. "His mouth flew open, his knees buckled, and he grabbed those around him for support" (87). Little Japanese girls ask, "'Wife-u? . . . Bay-be?'" not knowing that Newsham travels because his wife has asked for a divorce. This tension of opposing, complex people, culture, moods, would work well in fiction. Knowing it is true makes it more powerful.

When Paul Theroux wrote of his one-night coupling at the end of the Trans-Siberian Express, in *The Great Railway Bazaar* (1975), he founded postmodern travel literature, in which the traveler is deeply implicated in—even the protagonist of—the travel. (Truman Capote's *The Muses Are Heard* was a progenitor.) Later, walking the coast of England (*The Kingdom by the Sea*) and *Riding the Iron Rooster* through China, Theroux needed an editor—he is a *very* postmodern, morose, and whiny traveler. But as good as the best, and emblematic of the seduction of travel and travel literature, is the title essay in his 1985 collection *Sunrise With Seamonsters*. This title is that of a Turner painting of sunlight and sea veiled behind light-suffused mist, and the essay is about direful adventures (monsters) in a beautiful and familiar place, the waters off Cape Cod, where he has grown up. He writes the end of a particularly hubristic row in his dinghy.

The wind had beaten all the Sunfish and the windsurfers to the beach at North Truro, but there were children dodging waves and little dogs trotting along the sand, and people preparing barbecues. I pulled the boat up the beach and looked out to sea. Nothing was visible. That unpredictable place where an hour ago I was afraid I might drown now looked like no more than a frothy mockery of the sky, with nothing else on it. (355)

Here is the truth of the dark night every rower and traveler knows: how close the haven (little dogs trotting on the sand), how close the snuff-out. This is the story underlying all the good travel tales, hooking us to this form of story.

Tim Cahill is an adventurer, ecologist, and writer; I carry with me an image from his essay about the Marquesas islands. Written for *Islands* magazine in 1985, it is in Cahill's 1989 collection, *A Wolverine Is Eating My Leg*, and with differences, in the 1993 collection, *Pecked to Death by Ducks*. Cahill lived on the same black beach the French painter Paul Gauguin had lived on ("[A]bout eleven-thirty, when it gets too hot to work [in one of the two bungalows on the beach], I walk down to the Gauguin beach for a swim" [*Wolverine* 166]). He hiked the mountainous islands, finding the giant stone gods, the *tiki*, and the wild horses the

French had brought to the Marquesas. "[L]ike the goats and pigs and breadfruit, the horses multiplied beyond count in the provident land. . . . Horses run free in the steep, sloping jungles. . . ." And then this image: "They can be seen drinking from rivers, a waterfall in the background, orchid petals or plumerias on their backs where they brushed the vegetation" (*Ducks* 46).

It is an image from Gauguin's paintings. (Not quite, for Cahill has just told of the women of Puamau watching *The Towering Inferno* on the television the Polynesian government gave to keep the Marquesans from moving to livelier, overcrowded Tahiti. A static painting can draw us into its depths, but it cannot move us along, gathering up stories, some contradictory, bringing them together.) The waterfall, the horses' backs, the orchids. It was a unique conjoining—Tim Cahill's moment, but written by him and read by me, and so the "foreign" is part of me. In a sense, I created it—its beauty, its meaning—in my reader's privacy. "It feels as real as my real memories," a student said when we explored how we learn from travel writers' images. Perhaps it is even more real because as in every connection through art, the "reading" is uniquely private: the film, music, painting, story, and me.

I use this kind of narrative to draw the less experienced student into the real world of travel and meeting—a world funny and ironic, lyrical, rhythmic, metaphysical; an arena of terror, discovery, recognition, as old as Marco Polo, as new as the child shouting, "Go, go." But all this is about us. We are at the center of this heart-stopping view travel gives of death as life's fellow traveler. And that—the center—is not where we should be. Here is one of many similar passages in good travel writing. It is from David Yeadon, one of the best adventurers, and writers, in *The Back of Beyond* (1991), on canoeing through the Costa Rican jungle:

A white heron eased itself langorously into the wet air . . . a Morphos butterfly with an eight-inch wingspan enjoyed a free ride on our boat for a while before fluttering off in flashes of bright blue.

Screams came from deep in the rain forest. "Howler monkey," said George. I nodded. I'd heard them before. Now I'd like to *see* them—just one would do. . . . Between brief bouts of jungle noise, utter silence. . . . In the stillness I was struck by the total aliveness of the forest. . . .

In that tiny boat I felt like an openmouthed intruder, hardly understanding anything of what I saw, irrelevant to the place, almost envious of the jungle as an unquestioning participant in the enormous rhythms of life, responsive to a far deeper purpose. The little tribulations of our conscious lives and the apparent inability of us human beings to find a comon harmony with all the myriad life systems around us seem to leave us spinning on the surface like flotsam, so tangled in our petty patterns that we fail to comprehend the larger whole of which we are a part. And while we're trying to understand what we dimly sense unconsciously, we slowly destroy ourselves and the earth too. . . .

And then I saw the monkey.

Stendahl says that a "landscape . . . itself" is not "interesting"; that "there must be a moral and historic interest." And Paul Fussell, in his introduction to *The Norton Book of Travel*, says that beyond all the vivid particulars travel writing gives us, must be a "larger meaning . . . metaphysical, political, psychological, artistic, or religious—but always, somehow, ethical" (16). That is why the properly humbling message that we are not gods in this universe is the most vital lesson travel art gives a student today. Ah, but the message goes down easier, is so much more memorable, because of that black beach, that unique codger in the tavern, that one howler monkey we saw, at last.

This is what, and how, we try to teach in travel culture. For a varied student body, we pick a range of texts (e.g., the *Maiden Voyage* collection, *Balkan Ghosts*, *Nelson Algren's Chicago: City on the Make* [or another local work]), excerpts (as from Cahill on the Marquesas), books chosen from a bibliography, movies (e.g., *Five Easy Pieces*, for the "role" played by the island off Washington State), trips to the Art Institute of Chicago (and especially its collection of impressionists, with texts on their French region). For students lacking experience in the humanities, we give reading guidelines, such as: Analyze descriptive passages—which are the better ones and why? Select some examples of metaphorical language. Note the kinds of information given: political, sociological, cultural, economic, demographic, architectural, meteorological. How is nature observed, and what is the relationship of the traveler to nature and the elements? In people met on the journey, what characteristics are focused on? How do these people and the traveler interact? What are the distinguishing marks and patterns of the writer's handling of towns, cities, villages or other communities? (These are, more or less, my colleague Bob Graham's questions.)

Better would be to get students when they are children—as C-Fun does. Children for Uniting Nations is a nonprofit group of volunteer parents, children, and teachers in Arlington, Massachusetts, who work for multicultural education. When Greg Thompson and John Shea graduated from Harvard Business School, they linked up with C-FUN and made B-Fun: B for "bicyclists" because they were bicycling around the world. They sent back letters and audio cassettes, plus coins, stamps, news stories, menus, candy wrappers, and other particulars of each country they traveled in. Volunteers from the Madison Park High School in Arlington sent copies to some 500 schools—over 20,000 young people. (In their "wrap-up," Shea and Thompson listed Nepal as their "favorite" country, and spoke of the "amazing spices" in Thai soups and noodles.) With a lot of B-FUNs, students would not need our seminars— and there would likely be a lot more Hospitality students.

Yet one needs to be older to understand the point of Michael Parfit's *Chasing the Glory*. Pilots of small planes, when they soar into the sun, may see a bright light circling their shadow on a cloud. This halo is called a *glory*. Parfit outlines the loveliness of the America he flew all over, dropping in, soaring; and all the different, unique people he met. But in the prologue he says that in Szechwan, China, and in Germany in the west, if the sun was behind the mountain, and mist below, pilgrims on the top of the mountain would see a "bright circle" around their shadow, feel divine, and fly off the cliff. This brilliance and shadow is the glory that so beautifully is, and really is not, and the soaring airplane that always must come down, and the travel that—big as the U.S.A. is— has to end. Doesn't it?

It is best if we know the terrain and the natives where our airplane lands. It is time to leave a vocabulary of "foreigners" (and "natives"), and learn to pronounce the "strange sounding names" of those "far away places" of the popular song from the days when Carmen Miranda and pineapples were exotic. It is time to keep the fresh view the new gives us, and to emphasize the continuum of peoples and lands, the "us," not the "them." Teaching this continuum can be the province and accomplishment of the fledgling academic travel culture curriculum being tested and proved in American schools at this century's turn and in so doing smooth many a bumpy conflict in world's societies which will otherwise destroy many a traveler and that traveler's society.

Works Cited

Bryson, Bill. *Neither Here Nor There: Travels in Europe.* New York: Morrow, 1992.

Cahill, Tim. *Jaguars Ripped My Flesh.* New York: Bantam, 1987.

——. *Pecked to Death by Ducks.* New York: Vintage, 1993.

——. *A Wolverine Is Eating My Leg.* New York: Vintage, 1989.

Capote, Truman. *The Muses Are Heard.* Random, 1956.

Chatwin, Bruce. *The Songlines.* New York: Penguin, 1988.

Fermor, Patrick Leigh. *A Time of Gifts: On Foot to Constantinople, from the Hook of Holland to the Middle Danube.* 1977. New York: Penguin, 1979.

——. *Between the Woods and the Water: On Foot to Constantinople from the Hook of Holland: The Middle Danube to the Iron Gates*. New York: Viking, 1986 (Penguin paper, 1987).

Fussell, Paul. Introduction. *The Norton Book of Travel*. Ed. Paul Fussell. New York: Norton, 1987. 16.

Globus Gateway Tour Director. "The Grand Age of Democratic Travel." *Travel*. John Hemenway host, PBS, 7 May 1994 in Chicago.

Gornick, Vivian. "An American Woman in Egypt." *They Went: The Art and Craft of Travel Writing*. Ed. William Zinsser. Boston: Houghton Mifflin, 1991. 101–20.

Jerome, Christine. *Adirondack Passage: The Cruise of the Canoe Sairy Gamp*. New York: HarperCollins, 1994.

Krich, John. "Travel Books." *New York Times* 11 June 1989: 12, 57.

Morris, Jan. *Hong Kong*. New York: Random, 1988.

Morris, Mary, ed., in collaboration with Larry O'Connor. *Maiden Voyages: Writings of Women Travelers*. New York: Vintage, 1993.

Newsham: *All the Right Places: Traveling Light through China, Japan, and Russia*. New York: Villard, 1989 (Vintage, 1990).

Parfit, Michael. *Chasing the Glory: Travels Across America*. New York: Collier Macmillan, 1988.

Pyle, Ernie, ed. *Ernie's America: The Best of Ernie Pyle's 1930s Travel Dispatches*. Introduction by David Nichols. Foreword by Charles Kuralt. New York: Random, 1989.

Theroux, Paul. *The Great Railway Bazaar*. Boston: Houghton Mifflin, 1975.

——. *The Kingdom by the Sea: A Journey Around Great Britain*. Boston: Houghton Mifflin, 1983.

——. *The Old Patagonian Express: By Train through the Americas*. Boston: Houghton Mifflin, 1979.

——. *Riding the Iron Rooster: By Train through China*. New York: Ivy, 1989.

——. *Sunrise with Seamonsters: Travels and Discoveries 1964–1984*. Boston: Houghton Mifflin, 1985.

Yeadon, David. *The Back of Beyond: Travels to the Wild Places of the Earth*. New York: HarperCollins, 1991.

——. *Lost Worlds*. New York: HarperCollins, 1993.

Yesterday's Gone:
Sports in the 21st Century

Gerry O'Connor

Not an easy call. Especially after Annus Diabolis, olde '94. Tonya Harding, the Great Baseball Strike, the Hockey Lockout, and O.J. Simpson. Hardly the stuff of dreams.

Less sensational but almost as depressing were replacement picket-persons, the fact that the heavyweight boxing champion and the President of the United States are roughly the same age, trash talking, the Big-Mac-Hold-the-Pickle-with-Fries-Bowl, "Hey, it was only a practice I missed," all sports agents, Darryl Strawberry.

Sure, there are a few lights at the end of the play-of-the-week tunnel: Jerry Rice, Wayne Gretzky, Akeem Olajuwon, Pernell Whittaker, Cal Ripken—consummate professionals who excel at the highest level of their sports with integrity and dignity. Unhappily, these individuals are endangered species. The stereotypical modern professional athlete is a totally self-absorbed, arrogant, showboating celebrity.

More about the Neon-Deon syndrome later. First, a look at some of the features of sports today that will intensify over the next 20 years or so.

In *From Ritual to Record*, Allen Guttmann identifies a distinguishing characteristic of modern sports as specialization: the increasing reliance by professional teams, most notably football and baseball, on individual expertise in *ad hoc* situations. This observation by the well-known sports historian will not exactly shock the guys at the All-American Sports Bar. In fact, they would probably tell Guttmann that the specialists are already themselves specialized. Many NFL teams, for example, have two place-kickers, the 45-yards-and-under-marksmen like Matt Bahr, and their long-range back-ups like Pat O'Neill.

Pro football is easily the most specialized of all team sports now, and all indications point to its becoming so specialized in the next 10 years that virtually no fans—and few players—will understand its complexity. Nickel-and-dime defenses will inflate to $5 and $10; teams will routinely be penalized for having "17 players on the field"; and Steve Tasker will join the *Monday Night Football* announcing crew to analyze kickoffs.

103

Similarly, baseball—assuming it survives—will have reduced to absurdity the once noble calling of the starting pitcher. *Total Baseball* and *The Baseball Encyclopedia* will agree that the last complete game ever pitched in the majors was by Tom Glavine of the expansion Havana Stogies on July 4, 2000. Notably, Glavine ended the game by striking out pinch-hitter Cal Ripken, playing in his 2,844th consecutive game, albeit with the expansion Tijuana Diablos.

Another characteristic of modern sports that has reached self-parodying absurdity by the mid-'90s is stats, "quantification" to the wannabe scholars like Guttmann. Once the fabled arcanum of legendary masters, trivia is now as commonplace as the beer commercial. This fast-lane of the Information Highway is way too swift for the average fan, but it does have enormous appeal for high-tech coaches, network analysts, and gamblers. Extrapolated into the 2000s, classic coaching confrontations—Where have you gone, Vince Lombardi?—will have degenerated into dueling computers. Bill Gates will have replaced Jerry Glanville on Fox and your $10 parlay bettor will get his bet-the-house picks from his own PC.

In fact, the whole world of betting will have changed dramatically by the early part of the next century. The hypocrisy of the mid-'90s will have been replaced by the New Greed. In 1995, the date of this writing, it is still illegal to bet on sports unless you're in Vegas. Yet almost every newspaper in the country publishes daily a ton of information that has only one purpose: to help someone make an illegal bet. Lines, spreads, odds, overs and unders—these are all printed in the morning paper with the school lunches and bird sightings. Bobby Knight once compared this journalistic practice to publishing the phone numbers of prostitutes. Sorry Bobby, but Lost Wages, Nevada, is the future.

Outside of Vegas, the two biggest bookies today are the church and the state. From Bingo and Beano to Lotto and Megabucks, the church and state survive because of gambling. Which is, of course, why they have conspired hypocritically for years to make honest bookmaking illegal. Every bookie who has ever been fined or jailed is owed some Bigtime Heavenly Vig.[1]

The wake-up call to the state came in the early '90s with the spectacular success of Foxwoods, a native-American owned casino in Ledyard, Connecticut. As this humble scribe can verify firsthand, Foxwoods makes more money than the Sultan of Brunei. The State of Connecticut is, after the house, the next big winner. Millions in taxes, thousands of well-paid employees, collateral tourist bennies for the whole region. The roulette wheel lands on black every time in Foxwoods.

By the year 2000, however, Foxwoods will have competition from its neighboring states, all of whom have counted the license plates in that sprawling Connecticut parking lot. From a gleam in the crazed eye of Bugsy Siegel, casino gambling will have become as accessible and widespread as fast food. And as surely as a flush beats a straight, sports betting will become an integral part of the casino scene everywhere in America.

But since not everyone who wants to bet the Cowboys and the under[2] is able to get to a casino—Normie and Cliff do not leave the bar—the casino will have to come to them. No problem. Interactive TV. Virtual Reality. Universal Credit Card. Cash? Who needs it?

As dramatically as the computer will change how games are played and where fans will watch, drink, and bet—Hey, some things will never change—the science of genetics will change who plays those games. Everyone knows you can't dodge a bad gene, but most of us forget that you can't dodge a good one either. Look around professional sports today in the mid '90s and you will see the first genetic wave of the future. Grant Hill, Ken Griffey, Barry Bonds, Moises Alou, Eric Metcalfe, Brett Hull, et al. By the early 2000s the dystopian mythology that Robert Coover creates in the ninth "inning" of his novel *Universal Baseball Association* will have come to pass. All professional athletes will be swimming in the same cosmic gene pool.

That something genetically sinister has been happening underground for a long time is today believed by more than a few conspiracy-theory fanatics. They point to, for example, the apparent existence of a choking Thomas gene. This was first suspected in 1960 when overwhelming favorite John Thomas failed to clear a height in the Olympic high jump four inches under his own world record. Years later, Debi Thomas fell on her Olympic fanny chasing Katarina Witt. Finally, in two successive Super Bowls, Thurman Thomas lost his helmet and then the football. So say the conspiracy theorists.

Finally, and climactically, the biggest single feature of sports in the early 21st century will be the athlete as celebrity. Hardly sprung full grown on ESPN, this notion goes back to the Roaring Twenties of Babe Ruth, Red Grange, and Jack Dempsey. The Sultan of Swat, the Galloping Ghost, and the Manassa Mauler, as those wildly alliterative nicknames proclaim, were the stuff of which the writers made heroes and the people made myths. Joe Louis in the '30s and Joe DiMaggio through the '40s, both touched the soul of the people. And then Jackie Robinson appeared and gave the black people a hero who was not only better and more intelligent than the white player in the all-white game of baseball but one who was proud to be black.

The athlete as hero continued to evolve through Mantle and Mays, Unitas and Namath, to the first representative from a participant sport— Arnold Palmer. Conservative and white, Palmer played golf with presidents but had a middle-class army celebrate his electrifying style of play. At the same time that Palmer was democratizing golf, Muhammed Ali was personifying the rebellious spirit of the '60s. No wonder that in its 40th anniversary issue in September 1994, *Sports Illustrated* wrote about Ali that "no one remotely like him has ever been seen on the sporting scene."

From Ali to Michael Jordan is a quantum dunk. For in naming Jordan second only to Ali as sports giant, *Sports Illustrated* points out that Jordan was "America's superstar teddy bear, the approachable one, the demigod of the masses . . . whose appeal was uncomplicated and thoroughly wonderful." Those thoroughly wonderful years came to pass. Michael Jordan's heir apparent with the Chicago Bulls, Scottie Pippen, is best known for refusing to go back into a game when told to by his coach. Pippen's refusal is both a microcosm of what has happened to professional sports, especially basketball, and an omen of what is to come.

From Babe Ruth to Michael Jordan, the athlete hero was not just a great player with a charismatic personality. He was eponymous; he personified the spirit of the times. The athlete hero was spiritually in touch with the people. He was somehow accessible.

All that has already changed. In the Great Baseball Strike of 94–95 three baseball players (David Cone, Tom Glavine, and Cecil Fielder) went to the White House for a summit negotiation and basically blew off the President. Don Nelson, coach of the Dream Team II and the Golden State Warriors, is "fired" by two rookie players, Chris Webber and Latrell Sprewell. Wade Boggs proclaims, in the *Boston Globe*, "We are entertainers. And the sky's the limit, brother, when you can make the money."

That the professional athlete has become a contemptible jerk is surprising only in how quickly it happened. The free-ride mentality has after all been around for some time now. No current professional football or basketball player ever had to pay college tuition—or for that matter for anything else in life. But when rookie Glenn Robinson holds out for $100 million, then you know that it's a whole new ballgame. As, again, *Sports Illustrated* documented in its cover story of January 30, 1995, the NBA is being sabotaged by "pouting prima donnas" who refuse to practice, attend team meetings, or tie their shoelaces. Isaiah Rider of the Minnesota Timberwolves called a press conference to ridicule his coach, while Derrick Coleman of the New Jersey Nets handed his coach a blank check for the fines his $7.5 million a year salary can easily accommodate. These millionaire NBA jerks have no respect for coaches, owners, fans, or the game itself.

How bad will it get? Clearly, as long as the megabucks are there, it will get worse. Outstanding college football and basketball players will jump into the draft after their freshman year. Team spirit, school pride and loyalty—all the mantras of the past—will become as obsolete as the dropkick and in-shoot.

Once in professional sports the superstar of the future will immediately market himself, become a product, logo, image, symbol. In his heyday Michael Jordan earned $30 million a year with only $3 million of it from playing basketball. Already Shaquille O'Neal has far surpassed those numbers. Win-one-for-the-Gipper has become Buy-two-from-Nike.

And it never ends. The celebrity athlete can look forward to a lifetime of endorsements, like Arnold Palmer. If he is really lucky, he can open his own museum, as Ted Williams did. Not quite so lucky, he can open his own restaurant, like Mickey Mantle, or queue people for hours to pay for his autograph, like Joe DiMaggio.

Did I say "it never ends"? Yup, 'cause just when you think it's safe to call Shoeless Joe Jackson a sleaze, along comes William Kinsella with his Field of Dreams.

Shortly before his tragic death in 1978 Lyman Bostock refused to accept his salary because he was playing lousy.

Lyman Bostock, where are you?

Notes

1. Vig is the percentage that the House, or a bookie, keeps from every losing bet. Usually, you have to put up $11 to bet $10. Thus, if bettors in Vegas backed both San Francisco and San Diego in the Super Bowl for exactly $10 million each, then Vegas made $1 million profit.

2. The under refers to the over-under line: the number of points that Vegas establishes as expected-to-be-scored in any given game. Last year's San Francisco Super Bowl blowout was an over.

Works Cited

Boston Globe 7 Sept. 1994: 66.

Guttmann, Allen. *From Ritual to Record: The Nature of Modern Sports.* New York: Columbia UP, 1978.

Sports Illustrated 10 Sept. 1994: 42.

III

Sense of Community

Human beings are social animals, from the need to group together for protection as well as the desire to be near one's kind. As the number of human beings throughout the world has increased, and with the growing diversity in kinds and interests, there has been a strong centripetal force threatening to tear the communities into shreds. Nevertheless the force to hold them together has persisted. Now with the renewed rise of emotional forces such as clans, tribes, ethnopiety, nationalism, blind hatred and fear, the forces working on the sense of community have become ever stronger. Now they threaten existence. While the forces of instant communication and visibility—the power to "be there" anywhere, any time—are pulling peoples together, other equally strong forces are pushing people apart. So the threats and results are immense and vital.

Cultural Fragmentation in the 21st Century

Arthur G. Neal

Our time period is one in which the proliferation of knowledge and the elaboration of cultural forms has somewhat of an explosive character about it. Under the rubric of specialization, the social system is expanding outwardly in all different directions at the same time. The cultural explosion is far from having run its course. The result is a time period in which a great deal of experimentation, upheaval, and stress are occurring within the social realm. Within this context, the study of popular culture is necessary for an understanding of the many phases and aspects of contemporary social living. It is through the elaboration of popular culture that efforts are directed toward a fine-tuning of the prospects and limitations of the world in which we live.

The proliferation of popular culture grows out of the contradictions that are inherent in social life. Regardless of how well a society is organized, it does not endure for very long. The old order becomes fragmented by the volcanic disruptions that significantly alter the conditions under which men and women live. Individuals are thrown back on their own resources when they are no longer able to assume that social life as it was known up to this point will continue into the future; when they can no longer assume that their general understanding of events is adequate as a guideline to action; when they can no longer assume that their own understandings of the world are likewise shared and applied by other people.

The conditions of cultural fragmentation provide the raw materials for a great deal of cultural elaboration as humans attempt to make sense out of the conditions of their existence. There are three types of cultural fragmentation of primary concern. The first is the form of fragmentation generated by national traumas. A fracture occurs between contemporary conditions and the social heritage from the past. Uncertainty develops over what the future holds, and new opportunities are provided for innovation in the social realm. Research on individual and collective responses to national traumas offers the potential for a great deal of conceptual and theoretical development in the field of popular culture. The cultural fragmentation resulting from national traumas provide the raw materials for clarifying both the underpinnings of everyday life and the process by which new meanings and creative understandings of the human condition are elaborated.

The second type of fragmentation is reflected in a blending of the triumphs and the tragedies of the human experience. During the 20th century, human hopes and aspirations collided with serious frustrations of human efforts. Innovations in the realm of technology contributed to an increased standard of living for the general population, but at the same time increased the risk for a serious environmental catastrophe at some time in the future. In modern forms of popular culture, both potentials for a better world and images of an apocalypse are clearly evident.

The third type of cultural fragmentation grows out of the polarization of life-worlds in modern society. The major forms of pluralization in our time and place are reflected in deep divisions over issues related to gender, race and ethnicity, and social class. The social activism of those who are severely disadvantaged by existing social arrangements requires a rewriting of the social heritage. The quest for social justice will continue as a major source of conflict. Martin Luther King's question, "Where do we go from here" remains one of the primary questions that will need to be addressed in the 21st century.

National Traumas and Collective Memories

The concept of trauma is typically applied to extraordinary experiences in the personal lives of individuals. Trauma involves an element of shock, such as the shock of being stung by a bee, touching a live electrical wire, undergoing surgery, or being in a serious automobile accident. The concept of trauma, however, may be applied to the collective experiences of an entire group of people. Here conditions of trauma grow out of an injury, a wound, or an assault on social life as it is known and understood. An extraordinary event becomes a national trauma under circumstances in which the social system is disrupted to such a degree that it commands the attention of all major subgroups of the population. People pay attention because the consequences appear so great that they cannot be ignored.

Men and women may desire stability, order, and predictability in their personal lives. However, the realities of the 20th century included several volcanic disruptions of everyday life. The tranquility of the social order was disrupted by the severe economic hardships of the Great Depression, by the Japanese attack on Pearl Harbor, by the Cuban Missile Crisis, by the assassination of President Kennedy, by the Vietnam War, by the assassination of Martin Luther King, by the forced resignation of President Nixon, and by the explosion of the space shuttle Challenger. Just as the rape victim becomes a permanently changed person as a result of being violated, a nation becomes permanently changed as a result of an encounter with a collective trauma.

As with other centuries, the 20th century was the best of times and the worst of times. It was a century in which we split the atom, landed a man on the moon, and eradicated smallpox worldwide. It was also a century in which more people met with violent death than in any previous century in history (Elliot). In the first half of this century, social life was shattered by two major world wars. There were more than 40 million civilian and military casualties in World War II alone; an additional 6 million people were annihilated in the holocaust of Nazi Germany, and a comparable number of killings resulting from purges in the Soviet Union. Single bombing raids during World War II resulted in as many as 100,000 civilian fatalities. Dropping the atom bomb on the Japanese cities of Hiroshima and Nagasaki dramatized the potentials of warfare and increased human awareness of the dangers inherent in the modern world.

Under conditions of national trauma, the borders and boundaries between order and chaos, between the sacred and the profane, between good and evil, between life and death, become fragile. People both individually and collectively see themselves as moving into uncharted territory. The central hopes and aspirations of personal lives are temporarily put on hold and replaced by the darkest of fears and anxieties. Symbolically, ordinary time has stopped: The sun does not shine, the birds do not sing, and the flowers do not bloom.

Perhaps no other event in human history matches the trauma of the holocaust of Nazi Germany. The authority of the national state was utilized for the systematic annihilation of a subgroup of the population. While genocide has occurred at other times and places, nothing matches the severity and the banality of the German death camps. Basic human rights were violated in the official policy directed toward annihilating the Jewish population of Europe as a means of ethnic "purification." The horrors and atrocities inflicted upon human beings by other human beings in Nazi Germany became ingrained in historical memories as one of the major traumas of all times.

How could a country that produced some of the greatest works the world has ever known in music, literature, and philosophy also produce an Adolf Hitler or the holocaust? Why did the masses in Germany follow the mandates of the Nazi Party when it was not in their own best interests to do so? These are among the many questions that were pondered at the end of World War II. They are among the historical questions that will still be pondered in the 21st century. The violations of basic human rights with the growing emphasis on "ethnic cleansing" in many parts of the world are particularly disturbing to those who seriously ponder the historical lessons from the recent past.

We usually think of memory as reflected in the retrieval of information that is stored in the brains of individuals. However, in the final analysis, memory is a collective phenomenon (Halbwachs). It is through the use of language and other symbols that we construct the possibilities and the limits of the world around us. Images of ourselves and of our external environment are shaped by memories that are passed on from legions of men and women we have never known and never shall meet. To provide some assurance that the past will be remembered properly, acts of commemoration are directed toward the creation of national shrines, monuments, memorials, and holidays.

Following the opening of the U.S. Holocaust Memorial Museum, an extraordinary number of people came. Museum officials found it necessary to request that people stay away or postpone their visit to a later date. The people came because of the importance of drawing upon the traumas of the past for reflections on the human condition. In these reflections, it becomes clear that the range of possible worlds that human beings are capable of creating is very vast indeed.

Reflections on Nazi Germany, however, should not serve to gloss over the atrocities of our own past. Our own history includes the systematic annihilation of Native Americans by settlers bent on confiscating their tribal lands; the brutality directed toward captives transported from Africa for the American institution of slavery; and the vigilante activity of the Ku Klux Klan. The list could go on, but the point is that such traumas occurred in the past, can still occur today, and will continue to occur in the future. The specters of environmental contamination, the depletion of energy resources, and nuclear annihilation are among the possibilities we imagine in our more solitary moments. If any of these do occur, the explanations must necessarily lie with the joint enterprises resulting from the ideologies, decisions, and actions of a very large number of people.

Novels, movies, documentaries, and other forms of popular culture during the early part of the next century will draw upon the traumas of the 20th century. Those historical events that had a high degree of closure to them will be relegated to the back areas of collective memories. But it will be difficult to put aside those events that evoked intense levels of sadness, fear, and anger. The stories will continue to be told and retold about why we were so disastrously unprepared at Pearl Harbor, how close we came to nuclear war during the Cuban Missile

Crisis, and what circumstances surrounded the assassination of President Kennedy. Developing an adequate understanding of these events is an unfinished task for the near future.

Humans take an active part in determining what their collective memories will be. Events are fashioned through a filtering of experiences. Some experiences are dismissed, while others are elaborated and given high levels of significance. Selective inattention and forgetting are ways of minimizing the risk of cluttering up memories with information that is perceived to be trivial. In contrast, we tend to remember what we sense as being important for us to remember (Casey). Individually and collectively, we seek to repeat those activities that were rewarding in the past and to avoid those activities that were associated with pain and suffering.

Social awareness is of a different order for those who only hear about an event and those who experienced it directly. For this reason, the differential responses of individuals to national events are shaped to a very large degree along age and generation lines. The fear of nuclear war cannot have the same meaning to the youth of today that it had for the generation that lived through the Cuban Missile Crisis. The emotional arousal of Kennedy's assassination cannot be fully comprehended by those who were not alive at the time.

As new generations confront the problems of their time and place, the inventory of data from the past is re-evaluated. Some experiences from the past become embellished and elaborated in the quest for contemporary relevance. Other experiences tend to be relegated to the background of consciousness because they are no longer perceived as useful.

Generation Effects

New members are added to a social system and older members die off. Through the replacement of members, societies take on dynamic qualities through the opportunities provided for new beginnings and fresh starts (Mannheim). Each generation is influenced disproportionately by what was happening historically during their formative years. These are the years in which major life decisions are made at the individual level about formal education, selecting a career, entering the labor force, getting married, and becoming a parent. The large number of decisions in early adulthood place individuals in a position of hyper receptivity to the events that are occurring during their time and place. Personal encounters with national traumas during the formative years tend to have a disproportionate effect on any given generation unit (Schuman and Scott).

For example, those entering into early adulthood during the Great Depression had direct experiences with economic hardships. Through knowing what scarcities were like, they became disproportionately oriented toward savings, investments, and the accumulation of assets (Elder). In contrast, the generation entering into early adulthood during the 1950s and 1960s had direct experiences with economic abundance and tended to take access to the good life pretty much for granted (Simon and Gagnon). They tended to see the older generations as overly materialistic and money-oriented. They were more concerned with following impulse tendencies, seeking self-actualization, and making free use of consumer credit. Spend now and pay later became an accepted point of view for this privileged generation. The hedonistic values of here and now tended to take priority over long-range financial planning.

Collective memories frequently are drawn upon to support a political position or to document the urgency of avoiding a particular line of action. For example, the debates in the U.S. Senate over the Gulf War reflected generational effects. Older members of the Senate drew upon their experiences with World War II, saw a similarity between Saddam Hussein and Adolf Hitler, and argued against any form of appeasement or compromise. Nothing short of a direct forceful military response to Iraq's invasion of Kuwait was seen as adequate. In contrast, Vietnam veterans in the Senate were concerned about the long-range implications of our involvement, predicted heavy American casualties, and maintained that we lacked guidelines on how to get out (Schuman and Rieger). Thus, memories of both World War II and the Vietnam War were implicated in the debates over contemporary policy options. Some subsequently saw the use of American military might against Iraq as a demonstration of how we should have fought the war in Vietnam.

Many veterans of World War II remember their war experiences as the most meaningful and exciting experiences of their lives, while others remember primarily the tragedies that were involved. Many children who lived through the Cuban Missile Crisis still vividly remember their fears of nuclear war. The deep divisions within the nation over the Vietnam War are reflected in the emotional responses of visitors to the national memorial for the veterans who lost their lives in that war. With the celebration of Martin Luther King's birthday, memories of the tragedies of his death reappear as Americans reflect on issues of social justice. Thus, collective memories have enduring effects.

The more recent generations are notorious in their disregard for the long reach of their historical past. Henry Ford's comment that "history is bunk" is a sentiment shared by many young adults. There is a sense of comfort in putting bad times behind us and thinking positively about the present and the future. Following a lecture on social problems, one of my students spoke for her generation when she said, "All this talk about the American institution of slavery and other atrocities in American history just makes me feel sad. I was not alive then and did not have anything to do with such practices. Besides, we don't do that kind of thing any more. I would prefer not to hear about it."

Such attitudes are also evident in the responses of the younger generation to the continuing national preoccupation with who killed JFK. As one of my younger students put it, "Who cares? The man is dead, and nothing can be done about that." For students old enough to remember, the response was more nearly one of saying "we still care." The intensity of the emotional response at the time of Kennedy's assassination was great enough that the experience became permanently implanted in the memories of many Americans. The simple explanation that a lone gunman killed the President remained insufficient as an explanation in view of the complexity of the emotional responses of an entire generation.

The significance of the divisions along generation lines has been intensified as a result of people living longer, and many dramatic changes have occurred. For example, during the course of the 20th century more than 25 years were added to the life expectancy of Americans, and with the decline in birth rate, the population is growing older. The median age of the population has increased, and an increasing percentage of the population is retired from the labor force. These dramatic changes have sharpened the contrasts in generational experiences and intensified the separations within the social realm.

Generations are foremost among the divisions within the social system and thus a primary source for the pluralization of life-worlds. In many respects, the generations go their separate ways, hold different worldviews, and differ in immediate concerns and preoccupations. Schisms develop over differential lifestyles, communication problems develop, and difficulties surface over the inability of individuals to take each other's point of view.

Generational effects became evident in responses to the counterculture and the student revolts of the 1960s. The conflicts centered not only around the disrespect for authority, but also around the development of lifestyles that were shocking to the older generations (Feuer). The patriotic concerns of the World War II generation collided with such forms of public protest as the burning of an American flag or refusing to register for the draft. Attitudes toward sexual permissiveness collided with conventional notions about sexual morality. Styles of dress, forms of music, and the taking of psychedelic drugs were shocking forms of behavior to the older generation.

While national traumas have relevance for all subgroups of the population, their enduring effects are more intense for those who were directly involved as participants. A great deal of attention has been given to the post traumatic stress syndrome of Vietnam veterans. However, there are enduring effect of the combat experience for the veterans of all wars (Herman). The combat veterans of World War I returned with the psychological trauma of relentless exposure to the horrors of trench warfare. Many of the survivors of the Japanese attack on Pearl Harbor continue to suffer from inescapable memories and symptoms of depression. Many of the veterans of World War II still relive their combat experiences in their memories and suffer from sleep disturbances, survivor guilt, and recurrent moods of sadness. The needs both of the social system and of individuals are addressed through such forms of commemoration as the creation of national shrines, monuments, memorials, and national holidays.

Commemoration

The act of commemoration is a formal means of giving recognition to the importance of past events and designating them as worthy of collective remembrance (Schwartz). Symbolic representations of the past are designed to give special recognition to great men and women, to heroic undertakings, and to personal sacrifices for the benefit of the nation. The act of commemoration is essentially a means of tuning up cultural values and promoting images of society as moral community.

Most of the war monuments and memorials in the American repertoire of commemoration have typically glossed over the tragedies and the horrors of war (Mosse). The urge to find some higher meaning in the war experience has led to justifications for the sacrifice and the loss. The horror of war is generally displaced by an emphasis upon its glory. Encounters with death and destruction are camouflaged by an emphasis upon the sacred task of defending the nation. The speeches at sacred shrines on Memorial Day, the Fourth of July, and Veterans Day are all designed in a variety of ways to tune up patriotic values through the glorification of war. Emphasis is placed upon the men and women who "voluntarily" sacrificed their lives for their country (Warner). The underlying message seems to be that Americans in general correspondingly should be willing to make personal sacrifices for the collective good.

In contrast to previous wars, the Vietnam War provided very little in the way of glorious victories to commemorate. Yet, the trauma of the war required some form of symbolic representation (Wagner-Pacifici and Schwartz). A special kind of memorial was required. The granite wall sloping into the ground with a listing of the names of the military dead elicits an awareness of the grimness of war. Collective sadness surfaces in a reflective way for the millions of Americans who make a pilgrimage to the wall each year.

In contrast to the required travel in visiting monuments and shrines, the commemoration of historical events by people dispersed throughout the country is promoted through the creation of national holidays. Not only does the holiday permit commemoration throughout the nation, it also provides a structure for selectively remembering the traumas and the glories of the past. Dwelling routinely on tragic events would reflect a morbid form of anxiety and would be regarded as pathological. Yet, those events that had an extraordinary emotional impact on the society cannot be easily dismissed or completely ignored. For this reason, special anniversaries reflect on the events in question. The reflections especially become necessary for those events that remain unsettled or incomplete.

The designation of Martin Luther King's birthday as a national holiday was a way of giving recognition to the importance of social justice in the life of the nation. The King legacy taps into the moral consciousness of the nation and serves as an emblem of a willingness to make personal sacrifices for a broader cause. On the anniversary of his birth, the news media taps into collective memories by selectively reproducing his speeches, by showing photographs of civil rights demonstrations and marches, and reflecting on contemporary issues of social justice. In this respect, the holiday is also a holy day as Americans ponder the dominant values of their society and the contradictions inherent in modern social living.

While the epic struggles of the Civil Rights Movement put an end to the more blatant forms of discrimination in the public sphere, symbolic racism still persists in the thoughts and actions of individual men and women. Residues of the ideological justifications supporting the institution of slavery in the early history of the nation are still with us today. The discriminatory practices based on race stand in sharp contrast with the constitutional guarantee of equal rights for all citizens. The many faces of the contradiction are still with us today. In reflection on the issue of race, a great deal of concern is directed toward the persistence of discriminatory practices in American life. Additional remedial action is needed in confronting one of the more serious problems of our times. The contested struggle over racial and ethnic contradictions is far from having run its course and will persist in the future.

In contrast to remembering Martin Luther King on the date of his birth, John F. Kennedy is remembered on the date of his death. Remembering Kennedy does not stem so much from commemorating his accomplishments as from reflecting on his unfulfilled potential. Perceptions of his youthfulness and his idealism promote speculation on how the world would have been different had he lived. Rather than suggesting historical events as an unfolding of impersonal forces, the creation of the Kennedy legacy focused on how a great man can make a difference. Freed from the reality of practical politics, the imagery of Kennedy has a dream-like quality about it. Some believe Kennedy would have circumvented the quagmire of the Vietnam War, would have negotiated a settlement of the arms race with the Soviet Union, would have normalized relationships with Cuba, and would have advanced the cause of civil rights. Remembering Kennedy thus taps into personal hopes for a better world.

There are circumstances when it is necessary to analyze and dwell on historical events in order to get rid of them. Americans who accepted the conclusion of the Warren Commission that Lee Harvey Oswald acted alone in killing the president have been able to complete the mourning process, to store the event in the back reaches of their generational memories, and to put the event behind them. Americans who reject the report of the Warren Commission, however, still suffer from some degree of trauma. The six seconds in Dallas are played and replayed in their memories. The excavation of new evidence and the creation of new explanations only serve to perpetuate feelings of disturbance and uneasiness. The concerns are likely to dissipate only through the passing of the generation that was so deeply moved by the emotional trauma of his death.

While some national traumas are selectively remembered, others are relegated to the background of collective consciousness. The forced resignation of President Nixon is a case in point. Whether the assassination of a president or the criminal conduct of a president is of greater or lesser significance is not the issue. Instead, collective memories are more likely to be activated by the lack of closure than by the historical significance of the event. Through the forced resignation of the president, closure to the Watergate Affair was achieved. His public disgrace and removal from office were generally seen as a proper form of justice (Schudson). Misconduct in public office was seen by many Americans as typical of the way the political system works, and Nixon was seen primarily a man who had been caught.

Popular Culture and Mass Entertainment

In popular culture and mass entertainment, collective memories are reflected in the many ways in which stories are told to new generations about their historical past. In movies, television programs, and fictional writing, storytelling takes an embellished form. Whatever events occurred in the past are now immobilized, and those who tell stories about them are free to shape them as they wish. The constraints surrounding the events as they unfolded no longer apply. Plausibility to the reading and viewing audience is of more concern than historical accuracy.

Previous events are reconstructed through touching them up, selectively filling the missing gaps, humanizing them, and embellishing them with extraordinary forms of drama. In this respect, mass entertainment is a form of dream time in which specific imagery becomes highly focused, and events are experienced as only fragmentary. The raw materials that may be drawn upon in dream time are infinitely variable and suitable for producing new and novel combinations.

In the realm of mass entertainment the past becomes a form of selective memory, since the factual details of what actually happened in history are often neither known nor knowable. We may never know in a definitive sense why we were caught so disastrously unprepared at Pearl Harbor, what actual circumstances surrounded the assassination of President Kennedy, or how close we came to nuclear war during the Cuban Missile Crisis. Through the use of imagination and through drawing upon the predisposition of reading or viewing audiences, collective memories are elaborated and embellished. Historical events are treated both as symbolic events and as pseudo events that are used for reflections on the problems and challenges of contemporary living (Boorstin). Under these circumstances history becomes a form of remembering in which the mixture of fact with fiction is of less concern than the stimulus value of the production.

In dramatizing historical events, the mass media becomes a type of collective mirror that reflects the individual's self-image and the image of society. From the mirroring of multiple aspects of social life, we may conclude that we live in a dangerous world, that people sin and suffer from it, that heroic undertakings have successful outcomes for some and disaster for others, and that our personal problems are small ones as compared to the problems of people at other times and places. A sense of comfort may develop through recognizing that contemporary troubles are small ones in comparison to the difficulties people faced in the past. In this respect, collective memories provide individuals with frameworks for locating their present lifestyles along a continuum somewhere between "the best possible" and "the worst possible" of all social worlds (Cantril).

The selectivity in telling the stories of the past is not so much a deliberate attempt to deceive as it is to give past events a contemporary relevance. A connection is being made between extraordinary events of the past and present life circumstances.

Historians are frequently appalled by the inaccuracies and distortions in the portrayal of past events in popular culture and mass entertainment. After all, historians are professionals who have been given the responsibility of constructing "accurate" records of the past for keeping the nation properly informed about itself. The historian is necessarily concerned with the accuracy of the story that is told in a way in which others are not. They are the keepers of "authentic" and "official" versions of the past. Their professional code of ethics requires objectivity and accuracy, and their work is subjected to professional scrutiny and evaluated by peers.

Trusteeship over the official versions of what happened in history properly falls within the jurisdiction of professional historians. But even here, it is evident that we do not live in a world of "solid facts." The rewriting of history stems less from new forms of evidence than from attempts to develop new perspectives and new understandings of past events. The lessons from history are never direct and self-evident. Their meanings must be constructed anew by each generation as they confront the changing circumstances of their time and place. While the actual occurrences of historical events may be frozen in the past, the new meanings they are given become a part of the dynamics of any given society. The rewriting of history may not be based so much on uncovering new documents or new evidence so much as placing past events within the living framework of contemporary concerns.

Discussion

In conclusion, we may ask, "Who are the keepers of collective memories?" The correct answer is, "We all are." The intersection of personal biography with historical events is crucial to the many aspects of knowing who we are and what we are to become. The questions "How did we get to where we are now," "Where are we now," and "Where are we headed as we move into the future" are basic to personal and collective identities. The task of the individual is to find his or her place within the broader scheme of human affairs. In this process, some see themselves as being located at the center of what is happening in their time and place. Others see themselves as being located on the periphery of the consequential events of their society. Some seek to become active participants in shaping the social and political climate of their society. Others prefer to remain politically apathetic and to pursue their own self-interests.

Linkages between the past and the future take several forms in the cognitive frameworks of individuals. Some tend to glorify an earlier time through constructing a golden age as they selectively perceive it. Frequently, this is expressed in nostalgia about some previous decade of the recent past. The problems that prevailed during the time period that is idealized tend to be downplayed. However, dwelling on the past is more than a form of collective daydreaming. It builds upon the hope that present conditions can be improved by drawing on models from the past.

In contrast to those who glorify the past, those of utopian thought are oriented toward creating a future that will be an improvement over any set of arrangements that existed previously. The emphasis is not upon building on the past but upon a critical analysis of present problems and seeking innovative solutions to them. Rather than seeing the future as a continuous flow of events from the past, the future is seen as discontinuous and an improvement over the present. The basic task is seen as inventing new forms of social organization that are more suitable for meeting basic human needs.

While a meaningful distinction can be made between romantic and utopian styles of thought, the two frequently are equivalent in the functions served for adherents. Each involves estrangement from the contemporary present; each contains notions about how mistakes are made in the collective realm; each seeks to intervene and alter the process of social change. While the products of utopian thought are generally regarded as unique and qualitatively different from the past, they may appropriately be regarded as drawing upon tradition and seeking improvements. While the romantic style of thought seeks to recreate the past, they are necessarily confronted with the fundamental historical changes that have modified the conditions under which men and women live.

The philosopher Santayana once said that "those who do not learn from history are condemned to repeat it." However, the problem of properly learning from history is a difficult task. Any given event is necessarily surrounded by multiple realities and nuances in the course of its development. As John Dean noted during the Watergate hearings, "The mind is not a tape recorder." We select and elaborate on events in order to make them coherent to ourselves and to others. Such selectivity is frequently pragmatic as past events are drawn upon for self-serving purposes.

The need for rewriting history becomes evident to subgroups of the population who see themselves as being disadvantaged by the ways in which the stories have been told. Following the Civil Rights movement, there was a clamor for rewriting history to make a formal acknowledgment of the heroic struggles under conditions of slavery and of the many contributions African-Americans have made to American life. With the emergence of the Womens Liberation movement, there was a perceived need to recognize the many contributions women have made to the history of the nation and to the many ways women have been disadvantaged by patterns of discrimination. New versions of the past are now being presented by Native Americans who seek to set the historical record straight. Thus, telling and retelling the stories of the past is a necessary activity. The selective vantage points of subgroups of the population will continue to demand recognition as we move into the 21st century.

In the final analysis, collective memories may be understood as forms of mythmaking. Their significance lies less in their accuracy than in the meanings they have for adherents. From an objective standpoint, there is a wide gap between "the pictures in our heads" and "the world outside." There will always remain an external world that exists independently of our perceptions of it (Lippmann). We construct the world into systems of meaning that can be drawn upon when the need arises. Myths and illusions are useful in sustaining personal identities and commitments as well as in supporting a political position of advocacy or documenting the urgency of avoiding a particular line of action. But as forms of myth, collective memories become endowed with sacred meanings as they are drawn upon to embellish perceptions of society as moral community.

References

Boorstin, Daniel J. *The Image: A Guide to Pseudo-Events in America.* New York: Vintage, 1961.

Cantril, Hadley. *The Pattern of Human Concerns.* New Brunswick, NJ: Rutgers UP, 1965.

Casey, Edward S. *Remembering: A Phenomenological Study.* Bloomington: Indiana UP, 1987.

Elder, Glen H., Jr. *Children of the Great Depression: Social Change in Life Experience.* Chicago: U of Chicago P, 1974.

Elliott, Gil. *The 20th Century Book of the Dead.* New York: Ballentine, 1972.

Feuer, Lewis S. *The Conflict of Generations: The Character and Significance of Student Movements.* New York: Basic, 1969.

Halbwachs, Maurice. *On Collective Memory.* Ed. Lewis A. Coser. Chicago: U of Chicago P, 1992.

Herman, Judith Lewis. *Trauma and Recovery.* New York: Basic, 1992.

Lippmann, Walter. *Public Opinion.* New York: Macmillan, 1961.

Mannheim, Karl. "The Problem of Generations." *Essays on the Sociology of Knowledge.* 1928. London: Routledge and Kegan Paul, 1952. 276-322.

Mosse, George L. *Fallen Soldiers: Reshaping the Memory of the World Wars.* New York: Oxford UP, 1990.

Schudson, Michael. *Watergate in American Memory: How We Remember, Forget, and Reconstruct the Past.* New York: Basic, 1992.

Schuman, Howard, and Cheryl Rieger. "Historical Analogies, Generational Effects, and Attitudes Toward War." *American Sociological Review* 57 (1992): 315-26.

Schuman, Howard, and Jacqueline Scott. "Generations and Collective Memories." *American Sociological Review* 54 (1989): 359-81.

Schwartz, Barry. "The Social Context of Commemoration: A Study of Collective Memory." *Social Forces* 61 (1982): 374-402.

Simon, William, and John H. Gagnon. "The Anomie of Affluence." *American Journal of Sociology* 82 (1976): 356-78.

Wagner-Pacifici, Robin, and Barry Schwartz. "The Vietnam Veterans Memorial: Commemorating a Difficult Past." *American Journal of Sociology* 97 (1991): 376-420.

Warner, W. Lloyd. *American Life: Dream and Reality.* Chicago: U of Chicago P, 1973.

Community, Boundaries, Social Trauma, and Impact in the 21st Century

H. Theodore Groat

This essay addresses two related issues that have been examined by a variety of scholars in the social sciences and humanities. The first concerns the so-called "eclipse of community" and the hypothesized emergence of "mass society." Here my interest in community is focused on its recent rediscovery as a sociocultural phenomenon. The second related issue I address also concerns the resilience of community, and specifically my own prognostication for continued, intense conflict as communities based on ethnic and cultural differences are increasingly traumatized by events in the postmodern world. Trauma, literally, is something experienced at the individual level as a wound or emotional shock. Here I use the concept of *social* trauma metaphorically to refer to a shock experienced by a collectivity or group encompassed by community boundaries. The trauma may be differentially experienced at the individual level but is collectively shared as well by community memberships oppositionally situated on the basis of symbols, meanings, and identities. I argue that social trauma results especially from the intrusions of an increasingly pluralistic and deinstitutionalized world into the social-psychological dynamics of cultural identity and meaning-giving ideational constructs. The invidious and hierarchical bifurcations of societies and nations into "them" and "us" is an important part of this process.

The Loss and Rediscovery of Community

The sociologist Nisbet (*Sociological*) refers to community as one of sociology's basic "unit ideas." Drawing upon the classic sociological work of Comte ("moral" community), Le Play ("empirical" community), Tonnies and Weber (community as "typology"), and Durkheim (community as "solidarities"), Nisbet's idea of community includes all forms of relationships characterized by emotional depth, moral commitment, sense of intimacy, social cohesion and historical continuity. Community is, above all, a social environment where thought and feeling, tradition and commitment, membership and volition, are fused. The volitional relationship (i.e., the potential for agency) between members of communities and their proximate environments is particularly noteworthy. Thus community may be expressed by any of a great variety of social placements: locality, religion, nation, race, ethnicity, class, crusade, or commune. Think of family as the archetype of community.

For Nisbet (*Quest*), the high degree of emotional depth, intimacy, and social cohesion implied by community is possible only within a context of authority—an authority firmly rooted in the statuses and roles of the *structure* of community itself (e.g., parental statuses and roles in the family, clergy in religion, teachers in education, etc.). Without such authority, Nisbet believes, community is at high risk of being fragmented, weakened, or even lost; and the loss of community will be accompanied by temporary social chaos and a possible monopolization of power in the hands of the state. Freedom, from this perspective, can flourish only within a context of competing authorities (with their competing demands for allegiance). Thus Nisbet's conceptualization of community places him squarely within the classic sociological tradition.

Empirically, the contributions of the famous Chicago School of sociology outlined in fascinating detail the disorganizing influences on community life of urbanization and industrialization. Wirth, for example, focused on the disorganizing effects of increasing population size, density, and heterogeneity. Elsewhere the Lynds found the same social forces at work in their famous *Middletown* studies, and a generation later Vidich and Bensman characterized the small town as being sociologically gutted by the larger mass society. Stein summarized much of this classic research by concluding that community in modern societies was being "eclipsed" by the macro-forces of urbanization, industrialization and bureaucratization. About the same time, others were writing for a much broader audience about the faceless "organization man" (Whyte), the "lonely crowd" (Riesman), the dehumanized "white-collar" worker (Mills, *White Collar*), and the hegemonic influence of the "power elite" (Mills, *Power*). Indeed, themes of alienation, individuation, and loss of community have permeated much of the most popular and most influential postwar sociological literature through the 1980s to the present. The immensely popular *Habits of the Heart* (Bellah et al.), with its obvious agenda of carrying these themes to a wider audience, is the best recent example of this tradition.

The other side of the coin, of course, is that during this same postwar period both quantitative and qualitative studies began to document the persistence of local community orientations. Community was being "discovered" in street corner societies (Whyte; Liebow), working-class neighborhoods (Gans), personal networks in both cities and towns (Fischer), white-trash enclaves (Harvey), support groups (Wuthnow) and above all, perhaps, within tribal, ethnic and national enclaves (Kramer; Conner). Clearly, if by community we mean a symbolically constructed system of values, norms, and moral codes providing a sense of identity and meaning within bounded memberships (Cohen), community has not yet been eclipsed.

There are at least three good reasons, however, for believing that the "decline-of-community" literature and the "rediscovery" literature are not as incompatible as they might seem. First, the concept of community has a long history of loose definition, which means that one person's "community" is not necessarily another's (Hillary). Second, community can be conceptualized as a continuous as well as a categorical variable, which means that the debate can be framed in terms of the *degree* of community, or "community-ness," rather than as an either/or proposition. Finally, as Hunter shows, there are three distinguishable theoretical dimensions to community: (1) a spatial unit functioning to meet sustenance needs; (2) a system of patterned social interaction; and (3) a cultural and symbolic order of collective identity.

We can readily find all three of these dimensions in the earlier classical statements concerning loss of community. The increases in organizational scale noted by Tonnies, for example, are viewed as reducing the extent to which local residents can sustain their basic needs *at that level*. In turn, organizational changes lead to new patterns of social interaction—a shift from the primary interactions of place and kinship to the more rational and individualistic relationships within market economies. Ultimately community, having lost its sustaining qualities at both the functional and primary interaction levels, presumably loses its capacity for nurturing collective identity. Consequently, there is a decline in the "sense of community." The problem with this argument is that, as reflected in Durkheim's concern with both the mechanical and the organic forms of solidarity, there is a duality to social life. An increase in organic solidarity for economic sustenance, for example, does not necessarily mean the demise of mechanical solidarity for community identity.

The loss-of-community school overemphasized the seemingly determinant qualities of changing social organization while simultaneously largely ignoring the social interactions that generate identities and meanings within an ideational, meaning-giving, cultural context. My argument, therefore, is that there was an over focus on the macro-level forces at the expense of the micro-level interactions and the cultural context of symbolic meanings. Structuralists, after all, believed that modernization, technology, and changing social organization were leading us down the path of greater homogeneity toward the inevitable global village. Many believed, for example, that Japanese society dared not borrow and build upon Western technology without risking the very essence of what it means to be "Japanese." Similarly, the idea of cultural imperialism suggests that through mass media, mass information, mass production, mass marketing, and mass consumerism, the less developed societies will become increasingly duplicates of the core countries of the West. And others believed, in their sociological naivete, that the wide-ranging concerns shared through participation in a new global economic order would trend toward the erasure, and then the homogenization and tranquilization, of a multitude of tribe-like and bounded interests and identities. Ultimately all this would result in a monolithic urban culture that would spell the decline of multiple community identities. What Cohen labels this "myth of inevitable conformity" (36) is driven by an underlying theory of social change which seems to lose sight of the duality of social life, and by the assumption that people "are somehow passive in relation to culture: they receive it, transmit it, express it, but do not create it." By drawing upon the micro-level dynamics of symbolic interactionism, however, one can agree with Cohen (37) that both structural and cultural forms imported across community boundaries are typically infused by the importing community with its own indigenous meanings and made to serve the importing community's own symbolic purposes.

Thus much of the focus of community studies has been on the structures and forms of social life as they are affected by the macro-level organizational forces of urbanization, industrialization, bureau-cratization, communications technology, and the like. My argument, in contrast, is that there is an important "other side" to community—the side that implicates symbols, meanings, interpretations, and cultural boundaries. This is community as constructed at the micro-level through the interactions implicit in everyday life. And for this reason I have taken culture, rather than structure, as my point of departure. Community without indigenous cultural identifications and clearly defined boundaries would be a social morphology devoid of human meanings and, indeed, truly vulnerable to being eclipsed or lost. A brief examination of "intentional" communities, and their typically short life spans, should help to clarify this point.

American society has a long history of deliberate attempts to create responsive environments through the literal construction of intentional communities. The notion of communes as responsive environments is, of course, an idealization of group life that goes back to the sociological tradition of community as a major unit-idea. Human nature is viewed by communitarians primarily—or at least most importantly—as social rather than individual or biological. Human "problems," therefore, are defined as overwhelmingly social even though their manifestations are frequently identified at the individual level. Communes have always been experiments in finding the right combinations of, for example, behavior, dress, sex, diet, drugs, property rights, and family life to maximize both a sense of kinship—again emphasizing the special importance of the family metaphor and the perfectibility of human life— by creating environments that are believed truly responsive to human needs.

Beyond this emphasis on kinship and human perfectibility, however, intentional communities have strived to achieve a social order that is held in sharp contrast to the perceptions of chaos and disorder in the larger society. If the larger society is viewed as uncertain, unpredictable, and nonresponsive to human needs, the commune, in contrast, is where the environment can be made certain and where control, agency, order, purpose, and meaning can be socially constructed.

In her analysis of the commune experience, Rosabeth Kanter concluded that the central problem for communes is one of social organization. By this she meant that different kinds of social arrangements (environments) have differential affects for the fostering of commitment. Commitment requires a degree of identification with the community to the extent, in fact, that our internal beings require thought and behavior that support the social order. In other words, we are committed when the values and norms of our communities have become synonymous with our felt needs as individuals, i.e., when we follow community norms and standards of conduct because that same behavior is what we need to feel good about ourselves.

Kanter outlined the commitment mechanisms within social organizations around instrumental, affective, and moral categories. Thus "sacrifice" and "investment," for example, are instrumental mechanisms in the sense that the more we must sacrifice to belong, and the more of a stake we have in belonging, the greater the degree of commitment we will experience. Similarly, emotional commitment is built upon renunciation of the "outside" world and the sense of communion that emerges from homogamous backgrounds, sharing, and collective participation in ritual. Finally, moral commitment, the evaluation of values and norms as good/bad, right/wrong, follows the dual experiences of mortification (e.g., sanctions and mutual criticism) and transcendence toward membership in some greater design (e.g., with nature, God, a cause, or a charismatic leader). The experience of transcendence is to feel that one's own life experience is a part of some greater, all-embracing environment of meaning.

But what eventually happens to most communes? They fail. Typically the larger, more organically structured environment intrudes in nonresponsive ways. The practical needs of making a living, for example, lead to more open boundaries and greater value flexibility. And the rudeness of environmental intrusions such as new technologies in communication or transportation foster boundary penetrations that tend to restructure the communities. As Warren states: "vertical ties" between the inside and the outside become relatively more forceful than the "horizontal ties" linking the institutional components on the inside to each other. In the classic vocabulary of sociology, expressive, emotional *Gemeinschaft* gives way to a more efficient, practical *Gesellschaft*, and community is eclipsed. Thus in terms of organizational or systems analysis, where community might be emphasized as an intervening level of social structure, lower-order social systems such as towns, universities, neighborhoods, and families are indeed reshaped by the ecological dominance inherent in such macro-level forces as industrialization and global economic interdependence.

While this does happen, it is only a part of what happens. The rest of the story is that communities have not only a structural and organizational dimension but a cultural and relational dimension as well. Community today is rearing its head in the frequent overlaps between and within localism, ethnicity, race, religion, class, language, and nationalism. And the symbolic meanings of cultural homogamy provide greater resistance than their structural counterparts to being fragmented or eclipsed. Strong commitment can thrive, even in the face of massive structural change, where there is a strong moral ecology of community. The problem for intentional communities, therefore, is not only the organizational one emphasized by Kanter. Without an indigenous cultural tradition, a moral order based on mechanical solidarity and collective history, community is truly vulnerable. From this perspective it seems unsurprising that deliberate attempts by diverse and heterogeneous people, lacking historical continuity and collective memory, are seldom successful in constructing from scratch a sustainable community.

To summarize, there are two sides to community: (1) the organizational, structural, or spatial, which traditionally has been focused on the notion of territoriality; and (2) the cultural, relational, and symbolic, which is more concerned with a sense of solidarity resulting from emotional and traditional (nonrational) attachments. While these two sides of community historically have shared considerable overlap, they are analytically distinct. My interest in community in this essay focuses on the second side: community as a meaningful, self-aware collectivity united by a culture of shared meanings. This conceptualization of community implies personal identity as the other side of the coin, analogous to Mead's "generalized other." The generalized other is the community context within which the individual is provided with a unity of self. From this perspective, inherent in a particular way of life or web of communications is the idea of a social person. Thus community, identity, and selfhood remain highly salient and resilient features of the modern world.

The Importance of Cultural Boundaries

Alan Wolfe, writing about the tensions between democratic ideals and sociological realities, states, "Without particular groups with sharply defined boundaries, life in modern society would be unbearable" (311). My argument is along similar lines: without the cultural content and fabric of community, social life everywhere would be unbearably vulnerable to the macro-forces of structural change. The cultural side of community, therefore, as much as the structural, is functionally indispensable for human beings.

Human beings are "meaning makers" for whom the sense of self is developed within particular ideational systems that broaden, deepen, and generally enrich human experience. The cultural parameters of the socialization process so imprint on human self-definitions as to effectively make feelings of personal efficacy and empowerment inseparable from the dominant meaning-giving values and goals prescribed by the cultures within which our lives our lived. Culture is not just "out there"; rather, its symbolic manifestations constitute the centrality of our sense of being human, of having agency to make choices and to affect outcomes. The cultural side of community, therefore, refers to "its patterns of meanings, its enduring expressive aspects, its symbols that represent and guide the thinking, feeling, and behavior of its members" (Griswold 11).

As social beings we are products of intense, emotionally gratifying patterns of social interaction that enable us to construct definitions of ourselves, of who we are, and what symbolizes our essence (i.e., what it means). This is why the concept of community suggests identity as the other side of the coin. Further, as social beings we also understandably feel threatened by stimuli that would potentially deny us the securities of the defined boundaries that constantly reinforce and, indeed, make possible, our sense of who we are. Semiotically, our awareness of who we are depends on the awareness of who we are not. In the sense of its complex contribution of feeling, sentiment, and emotion to our self-identities, culture is both insidious and compelling. Human beings seek the psychological comfort and legitimating reinforcement of community as shared cultural symbols that evoke strong emotions. Without the shared cultural symbols there would be little predictability, and without predictability there would be little sense of personal efficacy. The need for community, therefore, is a universal human need. Without community membership we cannot know who we are. Moreover, community implies both members and nonmembers; so there is seldom if ever a feeling of community membership without a concomitant sense of the *non*membership of others somewhere "out there," i.e., there can be no inside without an outside.

The idea of community is a *relational* idea. Given communities are inherently defined by oppositional postures relative to other communities (Cohen 58). Thus community implies a sense of discrimination, of a distinction between communities. Boundaries—legal, physical, social, linguistic, religious, ethnic—would not be necessary if members of communities did not want and need to distinguish themselves from others. So the boundaries have meanings precisely because they symbolize differences in the very essence of both kinship and selfhood. The most important boundaries, therefore, are in the individual consciousness, where they function to enclose likeness and mark off difference (Cohen 12). Symbols are both subjective and enabling. They do not merely contain meaning. They enable us to create and express meaning. Members of the same community, therefore, are able to more or less make similar sense of things. And this "sense of things" is a continuous, interactive process of creating, recreating, and internalizing culture.

Earlier I suggested that the loss-of-community literature emphasized the structural over the cultural. Part of the reason for this is that the older, classical anthropological concepts of culture were easily reified and made to seem relatively autonomous and deterministic. The development of the culture concept has recently been traced by the anthropologist Hammel from the Greeks and Romans (e.g., as an identifier of membership) through the great anthropologists Tyler (e.g., as autonomous, shared content), Kroeber and Benedict (e.g., as pattern or system), and Malinowski and Radcliffe-Brown (e.g., social expectations and conformity). The sociologist Durkheim was among the first to conceptualize culture as a symbolic system, but his consensus model of culture presupposed a given structural pattern. Some fairly recent conceptualizations of culture, however, provide an analytic advantage over more traditional forms. Geertz was the first to reject the possibility of any objectivity in culture. Rather, culture is to be read and interpreted as text. Culture is not something objectively "out there" in any autonomous sense. It is constituted. From this perspective, culture is a result of negotiated symbolic understandings. Culture not only shapes our behavior; our behavior redefines and shapes our culture. In his informative essay Hammel combines these historical developments of the culture concept as follows:

The theory of behavior underlying the . . . ideas [about culture] presented here posits a cultural fund or repertoire of behavior (culture as content) specific to actors in particular circumstances of time, place, and social position (culture as identifier). Actors are deemed to exhibit some strain toward consistency in their behaviors in an effort to reduce cognitive dissonance (culture as pattern) and are aware of the symbolic effect of their behavior on co-actors (culture as expression). Their selection of behaviors from the cultural repertoire is designed to achieve a balance between competing critics and to optimize the net social morality of their position (culture as a negotiated set of understandings). (474–75)

If, with Geertz, we think of culture as a "web of significance . . . an historically transmitted pattern of meanings embodied in symbols, a system of inherited conceptions expressed in symbolic forms by means of which men communicate, perpetuate, and develop their knowledge about and attitudes toward life," we can begin to fully appreciate the human capacity to perceive meaning in and attach meaning to social behavior. Community symbols are largely mental constructs—ideas, really—that provide us with the materials for the construction of meaning. Further, community is found wherever "people believe they have more in common with each other than with members of some other community" (Cohen 74). While at first this may sound oppressively deterministic, the conceptualizations of culture by Geertz and others not only allow for but require that individual agency be viewed as reconcilable with commonality. Differences in meaning, as Cohen notes, are transformed into the appearance of similarity through the customs and rituals of everyday behavior. Thus while community leaves ample room for individual differences in interpretations of symbolic forms, the important point is that within the range of these interpretations there is nonetheless a commonality of sentiment that contributes to perceptions of the social environment as relatively predictable and orderly.

The Need for Responsive Social Environments

There is good reason to believe that human beings feel the need for orderly, responsive, and predictable social environments, and have a low tolerance for substantial cultural diversity. The behaviors of nonhuman animals are, of course, predictable because of genetic programming or prompting. That is, most of what animals do is genetically given. But this is not the case with humans, for whom patterns of meanings and behaviors must be learned in the social processes of interaction and socialization that transmit culture. For humans to find their bearings, so to speak, symbolic sources of illumination must be drawn upon as compensation for genetic incompleteness. Without direction from cultural patterns, what Geertz calls "organized systems of significant symbols," human behavior would be virtually unpredictable, "a mere chaos of pointless acts and exploding emotions" (45–46). Along similar lines, Peter Berger (*Sacred Canopy* 51) suggests that the ultimate human terror is not evil, but chaos. The avoidance of chaos, therefore, is a primary human concern. Culture not only wards off chaos but structures and directs behavior toward certain goals, or meaning-giving ideational systems, through the use of symbols.

Earlier I noted the importance of the volitional relationship between members of communities and their proximate environments. This is where the need for human agency fits in, a feeling of having important control over one's social and physical environment. With the exception, perhaps, of some intellectuals, entrepreneurs, young adults, and transient populations (e.g., students and tourists), important and serious diversity within social environments typically is considered undesirable. Long before the current concern with random shootings, carjackings, and other violent behaviors in our urban areas, those who could afford to move away from the inner cities were well on their way.

When asked for their residential ideals, Americans have stated over and over again their preferences for small towns, albeit not far from urban areas. The suburban movement of the past half century has been a compromise between this preference for social predictability and the demands of proximity to the workplace. So it is in the suburbs, realistically, that urban populations can most successfully realize a sense of efficacy over their environments. This is largely because of the cultural homogeneity of suburban populations with respect to what Wilson (32) refers to as notions of "right and seemly conduct" and of what constitutes "improper behavior in public places." People segregate themselves from others not only for physical security, but for emotional, ideational, and moral security as well. That is, responsive environments speak to nonrational as well as to rational needs.

Predictability and order obviously depend on some minimal agreement in the interpretations of symbolic forms among people sharing a particular environment. If people living together do not share the same symbolic codes and moral solidarity, at some minimal level, sanctions against those who depart significantly from community norms will not work (Anderson). Suburban and small-town communities, as lifestyle enclaves, are frequently caricatured in both popular and scholarly work as oppressive in their conformity. But it is precisely this striving for conformity, predictability, and order that motivates older people toward walled, gated, and child-free retirement communities, middle-class people toward suburbs with carefully landscaped grounds and well-kept houses, and the wealthy toward their rural or urban seclusions with guarded entrances and airs of exclusivity.

By and large, people seek out symbolic homogeneity in their surroundings; and because people who are different in some outwardly obvious respect—age, ethnicity, religion, or wealth, for example—are thought probably to be different in normative and behavioral respects as well, they are under suspicion. Most of us live our daily lives prejudiced against the unknown consequences of heterogeneity. That is, we prejudge people who are different from ourselves as being unpredictable. Their constructed realities may not be the same as our constructed realities, leaving little to share in terms of symbolic meanings. Prejudice, from this perspective, is a consequence of the need for a shared consciousness of moral order, which in turn is indispensable for community. Because community, whether family, ethnic neighborhood, suburb, sect, or retirement enclave, functions to enforce a set of subjective understandings, there can be no community without a minimal conformity, and no conformity without a minimum of prejudice against those who might not conform. In this way, most of us are able to experience our communities as responsive environments. Our otherwise random and chaotic social worlds become both predictable and meaningful precisely because of the cultural lens through which they are viewed.

Unfortunately in American society the poor, the very old, the very young, and racial minorities, for example, have relatively fewer resources for the construction of responsive environments. That is, their limited agency for finding secure employment, high quality schools, and adequate housing, as well as in controlling deviant behaviors, is sparse relative to the resources of the more affluent. In short, the economically disadvantaged are forced to live their lives within relatively chaotic environments that are increasingly characterized by drugs and violence (Anderson 77). Indeed, there is a sense in which subcultural and ethnic minorities are inevitably "repressed" by a society's dominant culture, because the minority subculture must always contend with and adapt to the values, norms, and expectations of what Dahrendorf calls the "rules of the game," controlled by the dominant culture. Hence orderly and predictable environments for the collective memberships of minority communities often require some degree of separation and boundary maintenance, as on college campuses, where a syncretic process combines elements of both minority and majority cultures into new communities of shared understandings. At the individual level, within racial/ethnic populations, a high degree of assimilation or an extensive armamentarium of highly developed bicultural capital (Bourdieu 13) are other ways minorities can adapt to the dominant cultural forms. Even here, however, the outward manifestations of behavioral assimilation and bicultural adeptness often simply "mask" the sense of difference. By and large, as Kramer notes, "Like all people, members of a minority group feel comfortable only among those with whom they can identify and this usually means each other. They can't relax with outsiders because they can't anticipate what outsiders are likely to do" (67).

The Invidious Nature of Communities

Cynthia Fuchs Epstein writes: "Belief in difference invariably results in inequality, in invidious distinctions" (232), and continues with the idea that while cultural distinctions "need not logically lead to invidious comparisons, . . . nearly all inevitably do" (234). When we begin to focus on community as symbols, emotions, and ideologies, in contrast to structure, we confront the notion that people believe in community and therefore that community must be real in its consequences. This line of reasoning emphasizes community as a symbolic construct of ideas (values, norms, codes, etc.) within which people as social beings find meaning. Because what we think of as modernism has resulted in important structural changes in community, often with a greater emphasis on economic rationality and individualism (e.g., Bellah et al.), there is a tendency to think of modernity as somehow sweeping away the contemporary social importance of community and making it seem something parochial, quaint, nostalgic, and old-fashioned. However, since community has a compelling emotional, nonrational, and ideational as well as a structural basis, there is nothing inherently contradictory between modernism and community.

There is popular agreement that the Old Order Amish, for example, constitute communities precisely because they remain "old-fashioned" in their rejection of modern conveniences and lifestyles. This view, however, misses an important point: that the Amish have socially constructed their Amish identities and sense of community by making the deliberate, conscious choice not to live as their non-Amish neighbors (Olshan). Robert Redfield notes that folk becomes civilization precisely "through the appearance and ideas of reform, of alteration . . . by deliberate intention and design" (113). Modernity, far from resulting in the loss of community, means, "*What previously was experienced as fate now becomes an arena of choices*" (Berger 21, emphasis in original). From this perspective, we might better understand the Amish as a modern community that has chosen to separate itself from others through symbols, boundaries, and a special universe of discourse precisely in order to construct and maintain identity and meaningfulness as Amish people. They sense themselves as having important control and agency within the constraints of their own bounded social environment. Within the context of this control there is a moral ecology, a sphere of solidarity with relative autonomy and a socially constructed consciousness of the "good life." The Amish share a network of subjective understandings about who they are and what they are about, complete with symbolic codes (e.g., dress, language, religion, gender roles, etc.) for classifying their life experiences and for defining those on the inside from those on the outside.

Returning to the invidious qualities of relational community, we have already noted that belief in difference usually results in hierarchies of inequality. The reason for this is that, since community is impossible without its relational character, the opposition of one community to others (or at least to other social entities) necessarily implies a boundary. That is, there is always a sense of discrimination. Note that it is the *belief* in difference, rather than any objectively real difference, that is the basis for this kind of boundary work. The most important and consequential boundaries, therefore, are in the minds of the beholders. And this is why the essence of community is a collective *consciousness*. That is, it is through the emergence of conscious differences vis-à-vis others that we experience community (Kramer 43).

Boundaries enclose likeness, mark off difference, and are maintained by symbols. Consider vocabulary. Certain words may be thought of as "hurrah" words: freedom, democracy, God; while other words are "boo" words: communism, flag-burner, atheist (Cohen 14). Each of these words is a symbol that allows those who use them to supply and express part of the meaning. Because we all bring to the interpretation of symbols our own idiosyncratic biographies, large numbers of people may share the same symbols in a general sense without necessarily sharing the meanings in a precise sense. The generally shared meanings are learned in the same context of community membership as that in which we learn to be social and to acquire a particular culture. Community cultures, therefore, may be conceptualized as networks of symbolic codes.

Symbolic codes not only define who is included and who is excluded, but also who is worthy and who is not, who is "civilized," "amoral," "deserving," "impure," and the like. Symbols define the centrality of moral order, or community, by legitimating the ethnocentric distinctions we make between insiders and outsiders. Not that some people intrinsically are more or less "worthy" than others. Rather, members of communities position themselves vis-à-vis outsiders on cognitive maps with a continuum or grid of symbolic reference points ("goodness/badness," "pure/impure" points, as it were). These maps are learned effortlessly during infancy and childhood as part of the socialization process; and they function as beacons that direct our cognitions toward selective symbolic features of our social worlds. The fabric of these maps is woven from each community's social constructions of its history, mythology, and other ideational or meaning-giving systems of thought. Through this process of social learning, community members come to believe in the values by which they live, the goals they seek, and the satisfactions they receive.

The core of the ethnocentric map for the majority of Americans is the Western European cultural tradition. Americans, like others, tend to evaluate their social worlds semiotically as sets of homologies: likeness and unlikeness, similarity and difference (Alexander 291–92). A "binary discourse" of communication, reasoning, and differential evaluation is virtually always present, and used by members of communities to distinguish themselves from outsiders. This discourse is situational and occurs within the context of a kind of hierarchy of boundaries, from the more inclusive to the more exclusive: Westerners vis-à-vis non-Westerners; New Englanders vis-à-vis Southerners; Boston brahmans vis-à-vis west-end Italians. Minow's work on inclusion and exclusion convincingly argues on the one hand that "boundaries and categories of some form are inevitable" while, on the other hand, there can be no such thing as a "neutral" boundary (374). Neutral boundaries are impossible because boundary distinctions tend also to be power distinctions that can be used by the more powerful to define both boundaries and the rules for boundary crossing in terms of their own vested interests. Social exclusion may not always be excusable, but since groups by nature are exclusive they function by keeping nonmembers out. This becomes particularly troublesome, even traumatic, when boundaries based on racial, ethnic, or other subcultural identities are arbitrarily assigned rather than freely chosen.

An important question is the extent to which any society can have meaningful diversity without hierarchy. As Wolfe points out, many of the boundaries in contemporary American society are "given," i.e., involuntarily imposed upon people who are perceived as being different in some important respect. For example, clearly there is a difference between the restrictive and oppressive boundaries encircling the racially and ethnically segregated victims of urban American poverty and those that enrich rather than diminish the quality of life for Americans who voluntarily choose to live, say, in Jewish or Italian enclaves. Boundaries that are voluntarily achieved rather than involuntarily ascribed seem obviously more compatible with democratic and egalitarian principles (Wolfe 316), although sorting out the historic sequence and the hierarchical nuances of ascription vis-à-vis achievement is often problematic. There is often a thin line between socially constructed boundaries that we might applaud as freely chosen, and boundaries that are imposed on people against their will. For example, to the extent that the majority of white Americans define themselves on the basis of where their ancestors came from, they necessarily define another visible category of Americans—blacks—as having come from somewhere else (Wolfe 317). One group's freely chosen boundary thus becomes the basis for a boundary imposed upon others.

Contemporary Trauma in a Shrinking World

Cultural analysts argue that cultural change is uneven in its pace, intensity, causes, and consequences (Griswold 63). During lengthy periods of relative calm ideational systems and the status quo generally go unchallenged. Social identities during these times are securely anchored in the context of community symbols and meanings. At other times cultural innovation, change, and creativity are intense and unsettling. New ways of thinking sometimes lead to the defiance of convention, and normative orders are sometimes overturned. In American society as well as much of the world, the 1960s and early 1970s represented this kind of cultural change.

Why the 1960s and 1970s? In the United States there was a combination of compelling factors: demographic (the baby boom bulge), political (a controversial war), economic (continued inequality within general prosperity), civil rights (the agenda of African-Americans), and ideological (the women's movement), to list a few. The consequence was an extended period of extraordinary cultural change that included both ideational and behavioral dimensions: acid rock and LSD, Black Panthers and Women's Liberation, pop art and long hair, antiwar protests and self-actualization, the Pill and IUD, female labor-force participation and increased divorce, sexual freedom and cohabitation.

Europe during this time also was shaken by a youth culture centered on leftist politics, while much of Africa and other parts of the world were bursting with cultural innovation precipitated by the withdrawal of colonialism. Such unstable times create "disturbances in the moral order" (Wuthnow 154), and what Williams sees as the loosening grip of ideological hegemony. Communities of meaning are challenged by the intrusion of ideas that are different and guidelines that seem threatening. The resulting disorientation often brings the experience of anomie until new meaning-giving systems can be constructed to reorient people toward their new social circumstances.

On a worldwide scale it seems reasonable to believe that we are presently in the early stages of extraordinarily new social circumstances brought about by technological developments in communications. I have already stressed the importance of cultural boundaries to community cohesion and to a collective sense of meaning and purpose. While this by no means suggests complete homogeneity of thought, it does mean that large numbers of shared meanings are recognized by the majority of community members. During times of cultural revolution, then, what happens to community?

Human beings throughout most of their history have lived in oral cultures that depended upon face-to-face communication. Communities under these circumstances were necessarily limited to small, relatively homogeneous social orders. And, except for divisions of labor by age and sex, everyone thought and behaved pretty much the same way. Beyond this oral culture, Wendy Griswold traces the development of three major media revolutions and the consequent transformations of culture and society. The first two revolutions were the development of the phonetic alphabet and print. Alphabets in which characters represent sounds are much simpler to learn than those based on complete words or ideas; and manuscript literacy on a much wider scale becomes possible. It was movable type, however, in combination with the phonetic alphabet, which democratized literacy and knowledge and laid the groundwork for the European cultural explosions we think of as the Renaissance, Reformation, and Enlightenment.

According to Griswold, "Because literacy became much more universal as a consequence of printing, we can say that print itself made modernity possible" (142). The transition from modernity into the postmodern era was marked by the third great communications revolution: the electronic media. Radio and television broadcasting, as well as the two-way transmission capabilities of telephone, fax, computer networks, and electronic mail, form the core of this technology. Together, they have unleashed a virtually limitless potential for immediate and intimate communication between people anywhere in the world. Further, all kinds of cultural access, which used to be limited by time and space as well as by literacy and education, have been greatly democratized.

For purposes of my argument, however, the electronic media's most compelling characteristic is its unique capacity to penetrate cultural boundaries. Older notions of cultural centers and peripheral areas are changing. Television, for instance, can be watched and understood by huge audiences with minimal education or other skills. The messages of electronic media are impossible to stop, even in police states, so there is a continuous flow of ideas that may contain new or contradictory cultural messages. The question, then, is whether mass exposure to cultural differences is moving us toward an increasingly tolerant global village, or toward an increasing number of fractious countermovements seeking to defend their cultural turfs against outside threats posed by the electronic media and other postmodern sources. If culture is the bearer of identities and meanings, then is not a further fragmentation of communities—as recently witnessed in Eastern Europe—as likely as the more optimistic scenario?

One can interpret the current nationalistic and communitarian hostilities in the former Eastern bloc of Europe as expressions of the human need to fortify and highlight cultural boundaries when those boundaries are being pressured, challenged, penetrated, and "polluted." From this perspective, the collapse of multinationalist states such as Yugoslavia created political vacuums within which perceptions of threats to differences and distinctions can flourish. Davies's historical analysis of responses to sexual deviance makes the point that when groups are subjected to outside pressures they turn their attention to purifying their categories of distinctions. Cognitive reference maps, to put it in terms discussed earlier, become focused more clearly on binary groupings of people, ideas, and cultural objects into categories of "them" and "us." We could generalize Davies's perspective, therefore, as suggesting that when meaning-giving systems—including such symbolic referents as language, religious beliefs, moral standards and other cultural objects— are perceived as being somehow endangered, a common response of community members is to emphasize precisely those cultural traits which most clearly define collective identities and meanings. Thus cultural upheavals may or may not lead to new meaning-giving systems of thought; old ones may simply be given new life. The aggressive emergence of multiple national identities in the former Federal Republic of Yugoslavia, in combination with the purification rituals of "ethnic cleansing," highlight by example the invidious, hierarchical, and relational nature of community discussed earlier.

The most extreme and most horrifying example of the invidious, relational nature of the emotional (nonrational) side of community, and of the use of boundaries, is probably the ethnonational bond (Connor 386). Nationalism refers to the emotional attachment to one's people and is distinguishable from patriotism, which refers to loyalty to one's state. Hence most countries, or states, are multinational states rather than nation-states. Some countries, such as Nigeria and India, contain dozens or even hundreds of different ethnic populations, and in about one-third of all countries the largest national group is not even a numerical majority. In all but the most homogeneous countries, therefore, there is an unrelenting tension between ethnic communities striving for their own cultural sovereignty within the state and the state's need to integrate the ethnic communities into a politically cohesive unit. The struggle in these circumstances is over both hierarchy and identity, i.e., over issues of both distributive justice and the preservation of cultural identities. The interest of the state, in contrast, is necessarily the assimilation of differences into an eventual ideological as well as cultural hegemony. Further, part of the dynamic friction in most heterogeneous societies is due to the tendency for the largest, or at least most powerful, ethnonational groups to view the state as an extension of their own ethnicity. For example, consider the English person's tendency to refer to England as his/her country and to "the English" to describe all of the country's people.

Most of the world's people live in societies in which the nation and the state compete for their allegiance: Basque, Tibetan, Flemish, Corsican, Kashmiri, Quebec, and African nationalism in opposition to Spanish, Chinese, Belgian, French, Indian, Canadian, and American patriotism. When able to do so, people ordinarily choose nationalism over patriotism, as evidenced most recently by events in Eastern Europe and large areas of sub-Saharan Africa. The appeal of ethnonationalism is powerful because it is a large-scale form of community in which people are emotionally bonded by exaggerated perceptions of their similarities and separated from others by exaggerated perceptions of their differences. The boundaries between the "insiders" and the "outsiders" seem so clear.

When based on combinations of ethnicity, race, religion, or language, cultural assertiveness can be both psychologically satisfying and undemanding in its simplicity (Griswold 106). That is, members of communities can effortlessly apply the simple rules of affiliation to sort out the "familiar" from the "unfamiliar," the "we" from the "they." When the moral order is challenged or comes to seem less certain, a strategy of psychological retrenchment through cultural affiliation stands in marked contrast to such alternatives as negotiating new interaction patterns with people who are different. The emotional appeal of community through affiliation is frequently intensified by the belief, at some level of consciousness, that members of nations share a common bloodline (Connor 377). It seldom matters that scientific evidence for the purity of any national bloodline is suspect, or that all racial and ethnic affiliations are in fact cultural constructs.

The cultural constructs of ethnicity and race often seem so "natural" that intellectual and political leaders find it easy to combine cultural and political agendas by manipulating bifurcated perceptions of "them" versus "us." Consider Bismark's metaphorical exhortation "Germans, think with your blood," and Hitler's declaration that Germans "enjoy the consciousness of belonging to a community . . . conditioned by . . . a blood-relationship" (1438). Numerous leaders, including Mussolini, Churchill, Mao Tse-Tung, Ho Chi Minh, as well as the political elite in colonial America, appealed to perceptions of their people as flesh of its flesh and blood of its blood, i.e. of family and kin. Note the passage John Jay wrote for the Federalist Papers: "[I]t appears as if it was the design of Providence, that an inheritance so proper and convenient for a band of brethren, united to each other by the strongest ties, should never be split into a number of unsocial, jealous, and alien sovereignties" (Hamilton et al. 9). Ethnic nations are, it seems, often united by a feeling of consanguinity.

In terms of identity, the metaphor of consanguinity symbolizes not just the present but a felt, albeit nonrational, sense of history. One identifies with one's people throughout time. This intense identification with community need not be limited to states, of course. Freud, the great student of emotion and the unconscious, noted that he was "irresistibly" bonded to Jews and Jewishness "by many obscure and emotional forces, which were the more powerful the less they could be expressed in words, as well as by a clear consciousness of inner identity, a deep realization of sharing the same psychic structure" (273–74).

The sense of community which lies at the heart of this kind of consciousness gives us a basis for understanding a substantial amount of the world's current inhumanity, oppression, and genocidal tendencies. Amnesty International's annual reports of officially condoned oppression of national ethnic minorities is chilling: Tibetans by Han Chinese; West Bank Arabs by Jews; Kurds by Iraqi Arabs, by Persians, and by Turks; Dinkas by Sudanese Arabs; Zhosas and Zulus by

Afrikaners; and Mayans by Guatemalan mestizos. Civil wars and genocidal trends have also recently characterized relations between countless other groups, including the Serbs and Croats, Sikhs and Hindus, Punjabi and Sindhi, Khmer and Vietnamese, Assamese and Bengali, and Tutsis and Hutus.

Because ethnicity and race are cultural constructs that have resulted from historical circumstances, they are also in a sense artificial. In theory, something that has been socially constructed should be susceptible to social deconstruction. Western social thought since the 18th-century Enlightenment has considered the modern era to be distinct from all those preceding it. Reason, secularization, democratic process, education, and technology were viewed as harbingers of a modern world where such particularistic and ascribed characteristics as skin color, religion, language, family name, or community of origin would matter less and less. And while the founders of modern sociology—Marx, Durkheim, and Weber—seriously worried about the possible downside affects of capitalism, anomie, and rationalism—there was still an optimistic sense that human beings in the 20th century could in a variety of ways defend themselves against the intense individualism of modern society.

Modernization theory, then, has tended to view industrialization and urbanization, a more specialized division of labor and enhanced communication and transportation, as eroding ethnonational and other regional and subcultural identifications. For example, to take ethnic membership seriously as a primary identifier would be considered premodern and provincial, and in sharp contrast to the more cosmopolitan and sophisticated identities of people as "citizens of the world." With modernization, traditional village life would become economically, politically, and culturally integrated with the broader, more universalistic principles of a more rational world. Every increase in the social forces of modernization would result in a greater understanding of differences and an increase in tolerance for diversity. A widely shared core of modern cultural values would sweep away the narrow-minded prejudices of the past. Both heterogeneous states and smaller-scale communities such as cities, towns, universities, and neighborhoods would be obliged to learn about and even celebrate remaining cultural diversity. And all the while a new, more humanistic culture would evolve that would then incorporate the fragments of different ethnicities, races, religions, ideologies, and other meaning-giving ideations into a greater global village. The problem is, this has not happened. Even in the most advanced postindustrial societies, the transformations predicted by theories of modernity have not materialized. Whether in terms of religion, race, language, ethnicity, or history, the traditions of cultural identity have remained surprisingly compelling.

Global Villages

What *has* happened is that the immediacy and intimacy of electronic communication have exposed people worldwide to the personal lives of strangers and their strange lifestyles. Unedited human activities, as they occur, can be instantly shared by vast audiences. We can now watch and listen to starving children as they starve, Olympic athletes as they compete, astronauts as they circle the globe, and soldiers as they engage in combat. Human emotions and cultural differences have become entertainment. And there is little evidence that this entertainment quality has united more than divided the globe. Those are "somebody else's" children who are starving, whether in Biafra or Somalia, and we become numbed by the repeated images; we root for "our" athletes, not "theirs"; those are "our" astronauts, after all; and "our" weapons and troops are superior to those of Iraq or others. It is true that Americans, or even the larger Western bloc of allies, can share a common purpose and a feeling of togetherness in such efforts as the Persian Gulf War. But again it is a unity generated by relational interests, i.e., a common enemy, "them" versus "us," that on a worldwide basis seems to divide as much as to unite.

Within our own society, modernization and greater affluence increasingly make it possible for people to live in "lifestyle enclaves" with others just like themselves (Bellah et al. 71). Thus residential segregation by age, income, stage of family formation, recreational and occupational interests has probably increased rather than decreased in recent decades. The underlying principle behind this segregation, according to Michael Weiss in *The Clustering of America*, is that "most people tend to move where they can afford to live, among people who are like themselves" (xiv). Hence retired people who share an interest in golf, or young child-free professionals with interests in tennis, body building, and the singles scene, can elect to live in communities where their friends and neighbors are most likely to share their values and lifestyles. Weiss argues that the clustering principle not only brings people with similar life styles together, it also "guards" the character of their communities, resisting outsiders who might bring change and uncertainty.

While both Bellah and Weiss recognize the cultural as well as the geographic or territorial dimensions of community, their emphasis is on community as place. People cluster together to share common interests in lifestyle enclaves. But the postmodern communications revolution makes it possible for people to live within "cultural enclaves" as well. As Griswold points out, "Individuals with very different meaning systems—from cyberpunks to fundamentalist Muslims—can create and receive their own distinct cultural objects and confine their interactions to those others who share their meaning systems" (148). Again, the operating principle is sameness rather than diversity. One could argue, as Griswold does, that the process of separation between insiders and outsiders is even more intense for relational than for geographic communities. In relational communities united by electronic media, members interact on the basis of self-defined cultural interests.

Where, then, is community to be found in the postmodern world? The electronic revolution has made possible the reproduction and dissemination of cultural symbols from all times and places, making it possible for anything to be combined with anything else. Thus, in a sense, communities are denied any particular history, future, or reality. With postmodernity, images become superficial. Fragmentation and discontinuity become part of our everyday lives. Ironically, the modernism that was to bring the world greater unity and tolerance seems to be changing simultaneously along two lines. First, the pastiche of images communicated by electronic media have helped create a postmodern culture increasingly characterized by cynicism and meaninglessness, shallowness, superficiality, diversity, and a weakened sense of history (Griswold 148). At the same time, however, the intrusions of postmodern culture are being met and resisted by countermovements in the form of cultural enclaves, lifestyle clusters, and fundamentalist beliefs that guide large numbers of people in their quest for the greater securities of homogeneity, order, predictability, and meaning. Clearly the global village has not yet arrived, and even the prospects for greater economic and political unity seem diminished and overshadowed by the most intractable conflicts of the post-cold-war era: those involving cultural meanings far beyond strictly economic or political concerns.

Works Cited

Alexander, Jeffrey C. "Citizen and Enemy as Symbolic Classification." *Cultivating Differences: Symbolic Boundaries and the Making of Inequality*. Ed. Michele Lamont and Marcel Fournier. Chicago: U of Chicago P, 1992. 289–308.

Anderson, Elijah. *Streetwise: Race, Class, and Change in an Urban Community*. Chicago: U of Chicago P, 1990.

Bellah, Robert N., Richard Madsen, William M. Sullivan, Ann Swidler, and Steven M. Tipton. *Habits of the Heart: Individualism and Commitment in American Life.* New York: Harper, 1985.

Berger, Peter L. *The Sacred Canopy: Elements of a Sociological Theory of Religion.* Garden City: Doubleday, 1967.

——. *Pyramids of Sacrifice: Political Ethics and Social Change.* New York: Basic, 1974.

Berger, Peter L., Brigitte Berger, and Hansfried Kellner. *The Homeless Mind: Modernization and Consciousness.* New York: Random, 1973.

Bourdieu, Pierre. *Distinction: A Social Critique of the Judgement of Taste.* Cambridge: Harvard UP, 1984.

Cohen, Anthony P. *The Symbolic Construction of Community.* New York: Tavistock, 1985.

Connor, Walker. "Beyond Reason: The Nature of the Ethnonational Bond." *Ethnic and Racial Studies* 16 (1993): 373–89.

Dahrendorf, Ralf. *Class and Class Conflict in Industrial Society.* Palo Alto: Stanford UP, 1959.

Davies, Christie. "Sexual Taboos and Social Boundaries." *American Journal of Sociology* 87 (1982): 1031–63.

Durkheim, Emile. *The Division of Labor in Society.* New York: Free, 1964.

Epstein, Cynthia Fuchs. "Tinkerbells and Pinups: The Construction and Reconstruction of Gender Boundaries at Work." *Cultivating Differences: Symbolic Boundaries and the Making of Inequality.* Ed. Michele Lamont and Marcel Fournier. Chicago: U of Chicago P, 1992. 232–56.

Fischer, Claude S. *To Dwell Among Friends: Personal Networks in Town and City.* Chicago: U of Chicago P, 1982.

Freud, Sigmund. *The Standard Edition of the Complete Psychological Works of Sigmund Freud, Vol. XX (1925–26).* London: Hogarth, 1959.

Gans, Herbert J. *The Urban Villagers: Group and Class in the Life of Italian-Americans.* New York: Free, 1962.

Geertz, Clifford. *The Interpretation of Cultures: Selected Essays.* New York: Basic, 1973.

Griswold, Wendy. *Cultures and Societies in a Changing World.* Thousand Oaks, CA: Pine Forge, 1994.

Harvey, David L. *Potter Addition: Poverty, Family, and Kinship in a Heartland Community.* New York: Aldine De Gruyter, 1993.

Hamilton, Alexander, John Jay, and James Madison. *The Federalist: A Commentary on the Constitution of the United States.* New York: Harper, 1937.

Hammel, E.A. "A Theory of Culture for Demography." *Population and Development Review* 16 (1990): 455–85.

Hillary, George A., Jr. *Communal Organizations: A Study of Local Societies.* Chicago: U of Chicago P, 1968.

Hitler, Adolf. *The Speeches of Adolf Hitler, April 22-August 1939.* vol. 2. London: Oxford UP, 1942.

Hunter, Albert. "The Loss of Community." *American Sociological Review* 40 (1974): 537–52.

Kanter, Rosabeth. *Commitment and Community: Communes and Utopias in Sociological Perspective.* Cambridge: Harvard UP, 1972.

Kramer, Judith R. *The American Minority Community.* New York: Crowell, 1970.

Liebow, Elliot. *Tally's Corner.* Boston: Little, Brown, 1967.

Lynd, Robert S., and Helen M. Lynd. *Middletown.* New York: Harcourt, 1929.

——. *Middletown in Transition: A Study in Cultural Conflicts.* New York: Harcourt, 1937.

Mead, George H. *Mind, Self, and Society from the Standpoint of a Social Behaviorist.* Chicago: U of Chicago P, 1934.

Mills, C. Wright. *The Power Elite.* New York: Oxford UP, 1956.

——. *White Collar: The American Middle Classes.* New York: Oxford UP, 1951.

Minow, Martha. *Making All the Difference: Inclusion, Exclusion, and American Law.* Ithaca, NY: Cornell UP, 1990.

Nisbet, Robert. *The Quest for Community.* New York: Oxford UP, 1953.

——. *The Sociological Tradition.* New York: Basic, 1966.

Olshan, Marc A. "Modernity, the Folk Society, and the Old Order Amish: An Alternative Interpretation." *Rural Sociology* 46 (1981): 297–309.

Redfield, Robert. *The Primitive World and Its Transformations.* Ithaca: Cornell UP, 1953.

Riesman, David. *The Lonely Crowd.* New Haven: Yale UP, 1953.

Stein, Maurice R. *The Eclipse of Community.* Princeton: Princeton UP, 1960.

Suttles, Gerald D. *The Social Order of the Slum.* Chicago: U of Chicago P, 1968.

Swindler, Ann. "Culture in Action: Symbols and Strategies." *American Sociological Review* 51 (1986): 273-86.

Tonnies, Ferdinand. *Community and Society.* 1963. Ed. Charles P. Loomis. New York: Harper, 1987.

Vidich, Arthur, and Joseph Bensman. *Small Town in Mass Society.* Princeton: Princeton UP, 1958.

Warren, Roland. *The Community in America.* Chicago: Rand McNally, 1978.

Weber, Max. *Economy and Society.* Berkeley: U of California P, 1978.

Weiss, Michael J. *The Clustering of America.* New York: Harper, 1988.

Whyte, William Foote. *Street Corner Society: The Social Structure of an Italian Slum.* Chicago: U of Chicago P, 1955.

Whyte, William H. *The Organization Man.* New York: Simon and Schuster, 1956.

Williams, Raymond. "Base and Superstructure in Marxist Cultural Theory." *Problems in Materialism and Culture.* London: Verso, 1980. 31–49.

Wilson, James Q. "The Urban Unease: Community vs. the City." *The Public Interest* 12 (Summer 1968): 25–39.

Wirth, Louis. "Urbanism as a Way of Life." *American Journal of Sociology* 44 (1938): 8–20.

Wolfe, Alan. "Democracy versus Sociology: Boundaries and Their Political Consequences." *Cultivating Differences: Symbolic Boundaries and the Making of Inequality.* Ed. Michele Lamont and Marcel Fournier. Chicago: U of Chicago P, 1992. 309–25.

Wuthnow, Robert. *Meaning and Moral Order: Explorations in Cultural Analysis.* Berkeley: U of California P, 1987.

——. *Sharing the Journey: Support Groups and America's New Quest for Community.* New York: Free, 1994.

IV

Marketing Cultures

Everyone, it seems, is into marketing. Everyone likes to demonstrate that what he/she likes, has, wishes for, is the best in the world and should be shared by everyone else. So everyone is a salesperson. Ultimately the last thing we wish to share—to sell—is stock in Paradise. But before we reach Paradise there are many other more mundane things we wish to sell. Some are political and maybe idealistic, others are less noble. But marketing is justifying one's life and one's actions and attitudes. Sometimes marketing is cheap and tawdry, sometimes nearly obscene. Its power, however, is great and at times obsessive, as the Japanese cult currently being stopped in Japan. One of the cautions against marketing might well be the rule of thumb of carpenters, "measure twice, cut once." In marketing, the caveat is hold on to your pocketbook and think three times. It is imperative then that we understand marketing.

The Big Chiliasm,
or, Julian West, Meet the Genitorturers

Jack B. Moore

Julian West, the protagonist of Edward Bellamy's *Looking Backward 2000–1887*, never had to deal with Gen, the lead female performer of the contemporary sado-masoch-rock group the Genitorturers. When Julian wakes up in the year 2000 after sleeping mesmerized more than a century during which time his vital functions, we are told, are suspended with no waste of tissues, he is greeted by lovely Edith Leete, who combines "feminine softness and delicacy. . . with an appearance of health and abounding physical vitality" (46). Gen on the contrary has clearly been doing aerobics lately so her body looks pretty hard though not Madonna hard. But what is really striking about her is that within or near so many of her orifices (ears, mouth, nares, navel, labia) lurk bits of metal (I guess) or maybe plastic, rings, loops, bars, that she has stuck into or through her skin, through lips and lip-like flesh, tongue, into cartilage, nipples, nose flares, available lobes, some quite obvious, some—at least in Bellamy's time—private. She's dressed like a dominatrix. I don't think she stipples her insides and outsides with all the ornaments in her arsenal at any one time, but even during relatively minimalist performances her range of attachments would make St. Sebastian jealous. She is pretty impressive—or depressing if your mind works like Julian West's or his mentor in meliorism, Edith's father, Doctor Leete.

Another woman performing with the Genitorturers is also dressed in bondage regalia but she doesn't sing as Gen does. She just mainly stalks around the stage brandishing a whip. During their set, sometimes while singing, Gen and the Genitorturers usually tie somebody to a portable rack they've set up, either a volunteer from the audience or a member of their troupe of strolling players, and whip him, and usually they locate a willing guy, whose scrotum Gen pierces absolutely free of charge, just like an ear lobe, and puts a ring through. Another high moment comes when Gen nails some stooge's penis—actually this part is simulated, using a realistic dildo (so far)—to the floorboards. After the show (and it's not easy with performance art to say when the show ends)

155

she sometimes pierces whatever part of themselves men and women hold out or expose to her. Gen and the Genitorturers are what is happening now. They have a contract with "a leading recording company." Really. Keep Gen in mind. We will return to her.

Julian's imaginary trip into the next century coming up after the one just a few years ahead of him, distant enough to grant the world time to change radically into a place of near perfection, is a manifestation of secularized millennialism. Bellamy's father, Rufus, was a Baptist minister and there were other clergymen on both sides of his family lines. His mother was apparently a particularly stern Calvinist (unlike the gentler father) whose zeal for working to achieve a better world Bellamy greatly admired and possibly inherited. But with Bellamy the salvation religion might offer humanity or selected members of the elect, seemed far less alluring than the ways people might save each other and society if only they used the better self everyone possessed. A saved world would not be achieved by Christ but by us. We could do it. Julian, who brings to us the message of what that saved world might be like, was after all born December 26, the day *after* Christmas: close, but no celestially lighted cigar.

Bellamy's revealed world was achievable, he felt, because of what he called the religion of solidarity. Essentially, he said, we humans possess centrifugal and centripetal forces within us. The centrifugal forces lead to most of the bad things we do to each other and ultimately cause us as individuals great misery, so even though they might bring short-term profit or advantage they are ultimately counterproductive. When we cheat, patronize, exploit, enslave, harm each other, we are being centrifugal. When we act harmoniously with others for the good of all and for ourselves—so that we don't fight wars for more markets or we don't squeeze the last drop of labor from workers and then pay them only a pittance, we are behaving centripetally. We enable others to live well, secure, with a range of various opportunities, and we ensure that is the way we will live also—fully, richly, happily. Centripetally.

There is far more to Bellamy's thought and book than this simple resume, and when I teach graduate students *Looking Backward*, usually along with several early 20th-century visions of the future such as Jack London's *The Iron Heel* (1908) and Charlotte Perkins Gilman's *Herland* (1915), we investigate more of the details of Bellamy's dream. Of the three works, Bellamy's undoubtedly made the greatest impact upon contemporary readers (and voters: about a hundred and a half clubs inspired by Bellamy's ideas were formed within two years of the novel's publication). *Looking Backward* is invariably the most—I could not even say disliked, particularly—irrelevant to the mainly 20- and 30-year-old students.

Here we are, in 1990-something, on the brink of not simply another hundred-year cycle but a thousand-year turn, a time when anxiety could enter the popular consciousness through the inescapable contemplation such a symbolic moment demands. And a monument of the past scrutinizing where-oh-where-we-might-be-now-if-we-had-done-things-better seems utterly displaced even as a misleading signpost worth correcting as an exercise in venerating nostalgia. *The Iron Heel*, despite its macho posturing (someone said reading it is like watching London cheer a parade of himself marching by) wins a few advocates and general appreciation for its emphasis on apocalyptic violence. A few hardliners—heavy metal adherents possibly—even applaud the fiery destruction it heralds by predicting the triumph not of nerds but of powerful underdogs. Its view of city-wide, almost block-by-block slaughter is recognized as a distinct possibility since it has been a usual historic occurrence on several continents in our day. Mutual murder has no place in Bellamy's 2000. So even though London's hero is ludicrously enough named Ernest Everhard (is the price of male politics eternally sincere erection?), *The Iron Heel* keeps my gender sensitive students awake.

Sometimes students complain that *Herland* is another version of the pastoral, similar to what the all too heterosexual inhabitants of Hawthorne's Blithedale failed miserably to set up, a country of eternal but unlustful spring. But the book's revelation of the sexual stereotypes that dominated Gilman's premillennial day and that are still common in our own, is so charming, and related with such cunning humor, that her parthogenic matriarchy seems as unthreatening as Bambi's forest before the fire. The book has a New Age allure to it: feminist Muzak from the hearts of space.

In our time, a work like *Looking Backward* lacks appeal as prototype or antitype of the possibilities of new existence. Why is that? Intellectuals once read and studied it carefully, chanticleered its glories or sometimes flayed it mercilessly, but at least some of the best and brightest (together with not a few of the worst and dimmest) dealt with it. Lenin's wife read it assiduously, Tolstoy made certain it was translated into Russian literate serfs and kulaks could study, both Charles Beard and John Dewey listed it as second only to *Das Kapital* in its prophetic significance. Bernard Shaw and the Fabians discussed it. John Dos Passos who had little use for many progressives of his day and the past placed a heartfelt if not completely accurate resume of its plot in the mouth of one of his most admired, rebellious characters in *The 42nd*

Parallel: "It's about a galoot that goes to sleep an' wakes up in the year two thousand and the social revolution's all happened and everything's socialistic [Bellamy would have cringed at this allegation] an' there's no jails or poverty and nobody works for themselves an' there's no way anybody can get to be a rich bondholder or capitalist and life's pretty slick for the working class" (62). For many students Dos Passos still provides a revelation, but not Bellamy.

My focus here is not on Bellamy and certainly not on Gen (for she is eminently replaceable) but on the culture that has produced Gen as a regular part of its popular art, really part of the mainstream of the world I and my students inhabit, whether we go to see her or not. She is there or others like her are there—here. She is unimportant in herself and in a society where performers peak and are thrown away very quickly, where momentarily vibrant cultural symbols are trashed daily, her brief local fame may be over before my words see print or this book is remaindered. My focus is on the change that has occurred in American society that is manifest in the apparent facts that somebody like Gen can be very relevant to whatever the future holds for us, and as far as so many Americans are concerned, somebody like Bellamy can be so irrelevant.

Bellamy's vision was far from perfect. He pretty much ignored the country's ethnic and racial problems and was not nearly as radical in his view of woman's rightfully equal place in society as he was in, say, seeing how ruthless capitalism led to grotesque imbalances of income and opportunity. He completely failed to realize the dangers of entrenched bureaucracies no matter how benevolently intended their construction. So there are lots of possible flaws in the kind of world he imagined as an antidote to the really frightening conditions he has Julian West of 2000 dream about, thinking he is back in an 1887 world of squalor and greed and perverse advertising, a mad world that finally makes him exclaim in a rare religious outcry that cries for a day of reckoning "I have been in Golgotha. . . . I have seen Humanity hanging on a cross!" (215). This past world was of course the real world of Bellamy's own day, and in a sense he could be saying, "Here, look, maybe you don't like all the dimensions of the promised land I've pointed out to you, but isn't it vastly preferable to what you've got? And it's attainable!" That is the real power of Bellamy's project, that so many thought something like it could be achieved. Why?

It was reasonable and optimistic. Or, it *seemed* reasonable and optimistic. Henry George called it "a castle in the air, with clouds for its foundations" and so it may appear now. But at the time and many years after, Bellamy's millennial revelation was for hundreds of thousands of disciples quite convincing in the contours of its possibilities. One could imagine sitting down with Bellamy and saying, "Now see here Edward, you've pretty much forgotten about farmers" and Bellamy, a reasonable man, would say, "You're quite right. What shall we do with them? Ah yes," and off he'd go to work something generous out. Or somebody would tell him he had underestimated the ability of science to create as many problems as it seemed to solve, and he would agree, and ponder *that* for a time, but surely the best minds thinking together could resolve the difficulties. Bellamy's panacea plan was the kind that did not have to be swallowed whole. It captivated or was capable of captivating (for the great majority of Americans never read or probably even heard of the book) vast audiences, because it was a fleshed out image of what humanity could accomplish with its own intellectual resources. It asserted—tapped the feeling or idea—that humanity *could* accomplish such a job. It was, I believe, the last American work to offer such a powerfully compelling and positive picture of things to come.

That phrase reminds me—I am using myself here as an example of the old audience that found if not comfort at least hope in promises such as Bellamy's—of the wonderful British film *Things to Come*—which along with Buster Crabbe's splendid "Flash Gordon" serials provided me with visual representations of the perhaps attainable future. Rockets to paradise! William Cameron Menzies's 1936 film was inspirational in its intent and more emotionally appealing than Bellamy's cerebral book. It dramatized the fight to win a chance to create a better new world symbolized by the clean white city of tomorrow, which resembles something Richard Neutra might have built, part Chicago World's Fair (1933–34) Century of Progress pavilion, part classical modernism, part international style, part Busby Berkeley set awaiting a spinning column of lovely, white chorus girls dressed like harps and singing chipmunk soprano. Run by prophetic engineers and architectocrats (led by Raymond Massey performing with the solemnity of Zeus), the world of tomorrow depicted in Menzies's semidocumentary style film does not finally clash with Bellamy's more stolid, Yankee Boston Beantown of the future, since both share the same rational and optimistic outlook. There are important differences in the two works that I record as differences in the ways magnetically beautiful futures could be imagined in Bellamy's time and in the 1930s, making each a fable appropriate to its day, which was still not our day, but heading for our day. We are slouching toward the Genitorturers.

Raymond Massey's character in *Things to Come,* though a human being, is a savior figure who literally descends from the sky (like a god or later, Michael Rennie in 1951's *The Day the Earth Stood Still,* another save-the-warring-earth-from-self-destructing science fiction motion picture). He acts as an ambassador from a consortium of highly intelligent earthlings and seems, compared to his troglodyte antagonist played by a leering, weird-eyed Ralph Richardson, an incarnation of some superior race or even species. With the zeal of a mystic and the assuredness of an Old Testament doomsayer, he is a quasi-religious *übermensch* who heralds the humane, advanced society we can achieve through struggle, unlike Dr. Leete, Julian's professorial lecturer, who seems more like a kindly, respected tutor or possibly senior fellow. The unearthly quality Massey could project is well utilized here, suggesting that the kind of spontaneous, sensible shift toward harmonious existence that Bellamy made an element of the plausibility of his scheme was no longer possible. Ultimately Massey triumphs because the technology of his society is infinitely more powerful than Richardson's blunderbuss weaponry: hovering aircraft lob sleep bombs on Richardson's unkempt yahoos and render his scatterbrain force somnolent. So *Things to Come* posits an elite set of strong masters or teachers who must either educate or force the masses to realize the splendor of the future that will rise from the rubble of the past, while *Looking Backward* relies on mass (if heavily managerial) awareness of cutthroat social Darwinism's inefficiency and cruelty. In *Things to Come* the social millennium is reached through war—first a cataclysmically disruptive worldwide near-death struggle, and then a kind of soft war won by men of good will with powerful but not always deadly armament. Both works rely heavily upon reason and are optimistic, though somehow *Things to Come* with its quaintly futuristic sets and distinguished, inspirational music by Arthur Bliss, seems more like wishful thinking, perhaps because between Bellamy's time and Menzies's (or H.G. Wells's, for he received credit for the script) the idea of countries organized rationally in peaceful and mutually beneficial coexistence had become a more remote possibility.

Although *Things to Come* set no box office records, it was fairly widely distributed in the United States. I saw it in re-release sometime in the early 1940s at an inexpensive small-town theater specializing in reruns, and charging only 12 cents for a double feature matinee if you arrived before noon. I also saw films such as *Scarface* (1932) and *42nd Street* (1933) there in revivals. I mention this not as irrelevant autobiography but to suggest the film's relative popularity, though it had nothing like the historically verifiable impact upon American audiences that Bellamy's novel produced. Popularity aside, more important is that these fables represent general outlooks and attitudes. They are stories that embody what many people felt about future possibilities, whether they read or viewed the artifacts themselves or not.

In addition to being rational and optimistic, *Looking Backward* and *Things to Come* are typical glimpses of the great day coming mañana, in that they are created and dominated by adults. The same is true of such dystopian works as *Brave New World* and *1984*. An artifact such as Stanley Kubrick's 1971 recreation of Anthony Burgess's 1962 novel *A Clockwork Orange* is not. Kubrick's film centers on young adults barely more than children, and it is brutally pessimistic. When my classes discuss what they think Bellamy failed to anticipate in the world at a time that is now only a few years away, I am always surprised that they do not mention how childless his world is. That may be because the great centrality of childhood and young adulthood in our own society, the tremendous power young people (who are also terribly abused) wield in our culture, or have wielded for them as they are manipulated by older entrepreneurs—all of that cultural weightiness belonging to childhood and young adulthood is so much a part of their experience they do not always recognize its significance. They grew up under conditions determining that radio, to choose only one cultural example, formerly a medium targeted at popular older-adult tastes (low enough often!), would be almost totally dominated by the programming desires of young adults, or older adults who never moved far from their more youthful tastes.

The young louts led by Alex (played with considerable, sometimes attractive, verve by Malcolm McDowell) in Kubrick's film are clearly part of a strong youth constituency to be reckoned with in the world of *A Clockwork Orange*. They have not yet taken over society but prey about on its fringes, sometimes scrapping with other youth groups, once assaulting a decadent, wealthy older couple in a vicious, rapine attack. These young people are hardly the hope of the future. They seem mindless in the violence they commit, which gives them little pleasure beyond the momentary satisfaction of delivering pain to other people. But if they are cruel and irrational, their opponents, who control the part of society that is controllable, seem equally cruel and devious, though still quite rational. The plan of punishment determined by the state after it has captured Alex is quite scientific, in the same sense that many of the tortures instituted in modern totalitarian states such as Hitler's or Stalin's are rational, or much as the fire bombing of Tokyo was based on a rational plan. Part of *A Clockwork Orange*'s special pessimism, part of the nihilistically bleak vision of the future it provides, is that in its world both rationalism and irrationalism seem destructive and murderous. At the very least the distinction between rational and irrational is wickedly muddled. For a time McDowell and his gang are out of control, but then so is the political force that is *in* control of *A Clockwork Orange*'s world.

The film embodies the idea that the future is no longer imaginable as a place where some possible, plausible, or miraculous state of benevolently harmonious existence can be seriously considered. It is a very influential film among the young, one that has drawn my students—mainly intellectuals, mainly liberals—to it, but also one that has attracted a surprising following among what seem to me nonintellectual or anti-intellectual and certainly nonliberal youth who identify with the glamorous (to them) violence committed by the apparently seductive figures of Alex and his droogs, his gang. Several years ago, while doing research for a book I was writing about a racial murder, I found that the central figure in a group of local (Tampa Bay area) skinheads, together with his skinhead gang, frequently viewed and greatly enjoyed a tape of Kubrick's movie. This skinhead leader took Alex for his mentor, even twirling a stick sometimes used like a bludgeon, as Alex does. As a gang member stated, he "always tried to model his life after the guy [Alex], the way I saw it. He just thought it was cool the way the guy, you know, he was so violent, and uh, you know, the movie more or less makes it look cool. He liked to dress up in big boots and go out, you know, and cause trouble. And he used to say, you know, 'let's go out,' you know, 'for an evening of the old ultra-violence.'" On one such evening, the Alex-impersonator and his younger brother—a boy the same age Alex is in Anthony Burgess's book, 15—were implicated in the murder of a black man. The younger brother also admitted that he liked *A Clockwork Orange* a great deal, but that he thought what the state had then done to Alex messed him up, causing his old buddies like Dim to treat him badly. This boy, who was in fact convicted for the racial murder, hoped his friends—his "brothers"—did not treat him like that. Interestingly, he referred to the state in Kubrick's film as "ZOG," the hated Zionist Occupational Government claimed as the enemy by so many loonie hate groups, which shows how far the film he saw had drifted from the film Kubrick probably thought he was making.

What is so grand about *A Clockwork Orange* is how highly compelling it is to so many disparate audiences as a symbolic statement about the future. But what is so terrifying about its popularity is how hopeless a vision it is. The Anti-Defamation League's archives contain a leaflet distributed in Minneapolis around 1988 declaring "Don't become a Clockwork Skinhead," which is good advice, but just as sound would be "Don't participate in a Clockwork state." Between the violent disorder of Alex and his anarchic, murderous droogs, and the violent order of the state that seems capable of systematically executing a holocaust, there seems no functioning alternative. By 1971 when the film came out, older audiences who could at one time have been warmed by the possibilities of *Looking Backward* or even the maybes of *Things to Come* had observed a great deal of history suggesting that (after our time here, of course) if the millennium offered no more than a clean sweep of existence, it might be a good thing. By the end of the 1970s both art and history had conditioned many Americans not to expect much good from any form of a modern millennium. Some, I suppose, had at least dreams from the past that provided memories of hope, giving Bellamy's title an ironic twist: looking backward didn't seem such a bad idea, for things to come no longer had such great mass appeal in the United States. Remember the two Easy Riders looking for the great country that once was America? Remember George McGovern, wasn't it, or who was it then, didn't somebody run for President, who wanted America to come back?

But you can't have a millennium by going in reverse, and anyway, readers of revisionist history know that the old America people were looking for, that they wanted to come back, never existed. It hadn't been the land of the free, or a melting pot. Some claimed it had been more like a crematorium. Look at African-Americans. Look at American Indians. Look at how America won the good war ending at Hiroshima and Nagasaki.

Most of my students grew up in the aftermath of the 1960s decade (which included the early years of the 1970s). For them a work such as *A Clockwork Orange* is a model for the secular millennium, not something approximating *Looking Backward*. A first-year woman student (not a graduate scholar in training) characterized the 1960s in class recently as a sellout, and none of her classmates disagreed with her. We had been discussing the future of her generation, particularly in light of the year 2000 coming up, and how this young group of students might relate their ideas about what could happen to society in their time to what previous generations might have expected. The idealism that I thought I saw operating sometimes in the 1960s had been a failure, I was assured. Civil rights had not led to civil harmony or civil equality but uncivil squabbling; greater ethnic self-determination had led to fragmentation; sexual freedom had somehow led to the disruption of the family and worse, AIDS. Little good, it seemed, had come from the attempt to do good (if it *was* an honest attempt). I did not need Arthur Schlesinger to tell me America was no longer marked by the spirit of optimism. One student even said he read that his was the "first generation in America who didn't expect to live better than our parents." I believe I first read that several decades ago. But I never read it when I was growing up.

Not every young person in America believes the sentiment. Not every older person who enjoyed Mama Cass singing "Make Your Own Kind of Music" or who was ever truly entranced by the idea however faint that a golden day might be discovered lurking around some corner of time in the future, in ten or a hundred or a thousand years, now accepts that America is just another country that has always systematically trashed its chances to become a decent democracy.

Still, today, as a symbol of what we might expect at that great day that's coming, somebody like Gen sometimes seems more potent than somebody like Julian West or Dr. Leete. As a real person in history she is as trivial as most rock performers; she might disappear tomorrow to be replaced by someone else as trivial and as ordinary and so as important to deal with in establishing what's out there. What she represents to me is a response to futility and frustration, which is what many millennia are. She's not for me a good response, she's a solipsistic and not a transcendent response, but then she's not my response. Rather, she's someone who manifests the responses of others whose experience of life has not been like that of people like me who grew up in that other world.

She dramatizes victimization, either performing victimizing acts upon herself or offering them to others. She and her subjects appear to delight in these acts. Particularly since the 1960s, plenty of popular culture heroes have been presented as victims of one sort or another: James Dean, Marilyn Monroe, John F. Kennedy, Martin Luther King, Jim Morrison, Janis Joplin, Malcolm X, John Lennon, Anita Hill, Clarence Thomas. Some were images of victimization through parental indifference, some were truly assassinated, some were harassed by middle-class or sexual hostility, one was called a high-tech lynchee. All—and the list is truncated—shared victimization. Entire groups and classes of people now have demonstrated (a few have only claimed) victimization as a major if unfortunate and to-be-remedied element of their constituent identity.

Christ was of course a victim, and yearning for his second arrival and the rebirth it would bring has inspired much religious fervor among zealots of the past who presumably sought a new, good, spiritually sound life. But in more secular, hopeless, unresurrective times, although decorations of stigmata and the adoption of stigmatization may possess allure or gain sympathy, acts imitating Christ's martyrdom, reproducing the mutilation or even death new life frequently demands at least in myth (not simply Christian myth), can also be interpreted as a search for dead-end self-sacrifice. As our world slouches like an old, impoverished relative or a teenager with poor posture toward its third thousand years since the calculated birth of Christ, a recent, perhaps only momentary culture hero has turned out to be the suicide lead singer of Nirvana (it's impossible to miss the implication of that name), Kurt Cobain, who may not last as a dead god, but just be remembered faintly as another celebrity burnout. One of Cobain's albums, *Nevermind*, has sold over 10 million copies, showing how far supposedly alternative (like rap once was) "grunge" rock has penetrated into the culture—and not just youth culture—mainstream. Most of the victim heroes mentioned above were famous for their maverick feistiness, but not Cobain. *Time* in its April 18, 1994, obituary article offered, as it so often does, the standard comment on Cobain: born to be a victim. *Time* quoted Cobain joking about his image as a "prissy, complaining, freaked-out schizophrenic who wants to kill himself all the time," but apparently that is who he was and a source of his sick glamour. As an anguished outcast, he was in fashion. Claiming "the traumatic split" of his parents when he was eight "fueled the anguish in Nirvana's music," Cobain is said to have retreated from the presumably popular "jocks and moron dudes" at his high school, "suffered the usual torments of the underground poet moving into the mainstream," and used heroin, according to *Time,* "in search of . . . psychic equilibrium." All his music "communicated anger, maybe loathing. . . . His subject was . . . perennial, youthful fury . . . youthful nihilism." One of his last songs was titled "I Hate Myself and Want to Die."

Time's perspective was replicated, I suspect, all over the country by local rock commentators, aware of the temporary, perhaps fleeting magnitude of what Cobain's death meant since he was so popular a figure. A local reviewer for the April 2, 1994, *Tampa Tribune*, Philip Booth, noted that although "the public pain and lost-boy angst that rode the sound and fury of the once-omnipresent 'Smells Like Teen Spirit'. . . might have been taken as simply pumped-up posing," it was not. "Cobain . . . was the disquieting voice of a rootless generation facing bleak job prospects and a kind of spiritual malaise." In an April 16 column Booth claimed that in songs such as "Lithium," where Cobain pleads that it's OK he's so ugly because so are his listeners, his fans, Cobain spoke "for outcasts everywhere, particularly to a generation whose lives have been shaped by dysfunctional families, sex that equals death," and in case you missed Booth's first article, "shrinking job opportunities, a palpable spiritual malaise and a certain rootlessness." Cobain entranced "millions with a personally anguished, powerful, albeit bleak, vision of the rotting world he saw around him." To paraphrase a Chuck Berry song, roll over Julian West.

Gen is alive, no great shock, only a slight jolt, a do-it-yourself crucifier to many of my students, the people who will live into the millennium approaching, and discover its secrets, who already live in a world Bellamy would rebel against and the masterminds of *Things to Come* find an abomination. Soon she will be only a mild buzz, I suspect. In our time, in our world, the aberrant, if we admit it exists, is average.

In that world, the notorious Sex Pistols, scandalously untalented musically and revered for precisely that skill and for their obnoxious attitude, sang in their anthem song, "Anarchy in the U.K.," over and over, three and four times without interruption, that there's no future, a lyric whose phrase is so common it seems obligatory *not* to place it in quotation marks.

In that world David Bowie portrayed Ziggie Stardust as an alien whose great discovery about the future is that there isn't any, and sings that he has heard mothers sighing that the world had only five years of lamentation left, and after that the earth would die. Ziggie's lyric repeats itself as monotonously as the Sex Pistols' screamed moan "five years is all we have, all we've got."

Five years isn't much of a future, but who would want to extend the present since, according to another Bowie song, "All the Madmen" in his album *The Man Who Sold the World*, our life is so crazy that the sane are either in institutions or underground, and there's no indication they'll ever get out or up. The once-popular group Devo accepted as the theory underlying their music that humanity was not evolving but devolving, thus their name. In albums such as *Duty Now for the Future* and *Q: Are We Not Men? A: We Are Devo!* we are instructed in degeneration. The song "Jocko Homo" asserts that though we think we no longer have tails and that we evolved from snails, this isn't so, that's just a lot of wind. "We are Devo," not whole beings, we're just "pinheads." Devo insists we should accept their message. Their album *Freedom of Choice* claims that men don't like this freedom and seek instead freedom *from* choice.

It isn't always easy to decipher the lyrics of punk or new music or post-punk, post-new-music songs, maybe because outsiders to the new visions aren't welcome and initiates are expected to know the codes. The drift isn't hard to catch, though. The enlightened managerial style of *Looking Backwards* and the advanced technology controlled by benevolent professionals that promises great *Things to Come* are bitterly suspect. In "Headcleaner" from the album *Tabula Rasa*, the German group *Einstürzende Neubauten* appears to cry out over a background of jackhammer sounds that the wonderful new world is a horrible place in which humanity is undergoing headcleaning, the wiping clean of their brains. This process seems unaccompanied by any future reillumination. The song titles of the Canadian progressive heavy-metal band Voivod—an organization heavily influenced by William Gibson's cyberpunk novels—would alone be enough to send Julian West back to sleep for another century: "Chaos Mongers," "The Lost Machine," and "Ravenous Medicine." Typically their concept albums such as *Nothingface* present a malevolent and leaderless future where machines seem to have taken over and according to the ambiguously titled song "Killing Technology" computers are in control of the future, not humans or gods. The world they imagine is one of electronic alienation, where children are traded for robots and the disappearance of old people is awaited.

Prophets of any epoch who imagine a far better future, who dream of a world bright with promise, who look for a resurrection of the human spirit, must feel great pain at the present condition of their society, must recognize the awful gap between what is and what could be. I hate to conclude with the words of the tenderhearted young singer Tori Amos, for she is certainly destined at the crack of doom to be an infinitesimally minuscule footnote figure in the chiliastic history of today who only Michael Wigglesworth's relentlessly omniscient God would be able to locate, but hey! maybe Plato and Nietzsche are not the appropriate philosophers for our particular premillennial age. Amos was quoted in that most reliable of sources, a wire-services sound-byte gossip column, saying of her generation, "It loves to complain and not really change. Because if it does change it won't have anything to complain about. I think our generation loves our pain, and if you dare take it away from us, we're going to kill you. We like our pain. And we're selling it."

Just like Gen. Me? I think I'll wait for 3000. This millennium's not for me.

Note

I owe a great debt to Sean Moore, music critic for *Mouth* and *Atlanta 30306* and former member of Triple XXX Girls and the Impotent Sea Snakes, for some needed information on recent music and groups. All opinions and errors are my own.

Works Cited

Bellamy, Edward. *Looking Backward.* New York: Signet Classic, New American Library, 1960.

Dos Passos, John. *The 42nd Parallel* (in *U.S.A.*). New York: Modern Library, 1937.

Marketing the Apocalypse:
The Direct-Mail Ministry of Jack Van Impe

Stephen J. Stein

National multimedia ministries have been an integral part of the religious scene in America for several decades. The religious and cultural impact of these independent organizations, often grouped under the category of the "electronic church" or "televangelism," has been the frequent subject of widespread speculation by religious, political, and cultural observers who, not surprisingly, have failed to reach a consensus on the matter. Much of the attention directed to these large-scale enterprises has focused on the biographies of the leaders of these ministries, the scandals in which they have become embroiled, and the large amounts of money handled by their organizations.[1] Considerably less research has been done on the actual workings of these religious institutions. This essay is an attempt to take seriously some of those procedures, to set aside all impulses to indict the principals on one charge or another, and to discover in what ways the communication strategies chosen by these organizations contribute to their success. In addition, it is an effort to highlight the centrality of apocalyptic in one prominent ministry and to suggest its likely increasing role in such enterprises as the new millennium looms on the horizon.

In a highly instructive essay dealing with the American Tract Society in the 19th century, David Paul Nord demonstrates how that national organization capitalized on the market revolution, harnessing new print technologies on behalf of the reform program of Protestant evangelicals. The American Tract Society organized every aspect of its operations, from the printing to the distribution of their publications. The application of "systematic management" techniques by that organization contributed substantially to the achievement of their religious and cultural goals.[2] In a parallel study, Peter J. Wosh describes the evolution of the American Bible Society in the 19th century, documenting its change from a reform agency to a nonprofit corporate bureaucracy.[3] Similarly, it is clear that effective utilization of the cybernetics revolution of the late 20th century is one of the principal factors contributing to the continued existence and success of national, independent, multimedia ministries today.⁴ This essay explores one of those successful enterprises.

The undated letter that arrived in the mail began as follows: "Dear Mr. Stein: I am so thrilled that you contacted us recently. Since God has a plan for every life and makes no mistakes, He made our paths cross." In the next short paragraph, following the citation of Galatians 6:2 from the King James Version of the Bible ("Bear ye one another's burdens, and so fulfill the law of Christ."), Jack Van Impe asked, "Could we enter into a relationship of bearing one another's burdens?" That invitation in a "personalized," computer-generated letter from the Jack Van Impe Ministries (JVI) has occasioned these observations on the marketing techniques used to sell an apocalyptic version of conservative Protestant Christianity.

In his letter of introduction, Jack Van Impe became highly solicitous. "I long to be your friend, your shepherd . . . ministering to you. If you have a problem or a question . . . or there is a Bible truth that puzzles you, please let me know. Rexella [Van Impe's wife] and I are ready to help and comfort you." He then continued, "So please drop us a note letting us know about some burden you bear, some question you have, or on the other hand, some blessing you have just experienced." Enclosed with his letter was a response sheet with blank spaces for prayer requests and for the notation of blessings received—the print equivalent of a friendly smile, a warm handshake, a caring glance.

To seal this potential new friendship, Van Impe reported that he had arranged for me "to begin receiving" his ministry's magazine, *Perhaps Today*—a full-color publication published every other month. He described it as "a gift of love from my heart to you." He also promised to send a copy of JVI's catalog, filled with "books, cassettes and videotapes" available on various subjects. Van Impe added, "When you order our materials, you not only receive food for your own soul but also allow us to get the message of life to millions via radio and television." Although no plea for money accompanied this missive, there was one short line on the response sheet: "Enclosed is my gift of _____."

In the same initial letter, Van Impe provided a cursory account of his credentials and a brief summary of his ministry. He wrote, "For forty years we have ministered the Word of God to ten million souls in ball parks, arenas and colliseums [*sic*]. Seven hundred thousand (700,000) have received Jesus as personal Saviour. During this time I have spent six to seven hours daily in God's Book. Oh, how I love His Word." Van Impe's letter underscored the importance of the public proclamation of a message of salvation in Jesus and of the authority of the Bible in his ministry. These themes, plus the offer of assistance through prayer, create the impression of a concerned pastor who wants to establish a personal friendship. (The word *love* appears five times in the letter and the accompanying response sheet.) Van Impe's first mailing closed with this postscript: "You are being added to our regular mailing list."[5]

When I received this first letter from Jack Van Impe Ministries, I had no idea what the closing postscript meant. Since then I have come to understand that I became part of a modern, direct-mail ministry. Nearly every week, the postal service delivers at least one piece of mail from JVI. Long ago a large three-ring binder proved unable to accommodate the continuing stream of letters, postcards, catalogs, and issues of *Perhaps Today.*

This mail from JVI was triggered by one purchase I made early in 1993. In preparation for teaching a course entitled "Prophecy, Apocalyptic, and the End Times in America," I regularly watched religious programs on television. On one occasion while viewing "Jack Van Impe Presents," an advertisement for a video cassette entitled "A.D. 2000 The End?" caught my attention. I ordered that cassette by telephone, and my Visa account was charged $22.95. That one order has been responsible for an unbroken flow of JVI printed materials sent through the mails from which this examination and analysis of Van Impe's evangelistic strategies is drawn.

The central tenet of Jack Van Impe's direct-mail ministry is summarized aptly in the title of *Perhaps Today.* In response to the question "How much time is left for the world?" Van Impe writes, "I have always preached imminence, that Jesus could come at any moment, and I believe that we are in the windup now."[6] The impending end of the present order, of the world and time as we know it, dominates every piece of printed material received from JVI. Van Impe concentrates the reader's attention on evidences or signs that confirm his persistent apocalyptic message. "Warning the world about coming end time events!" is a self-description used frequently by the Jack Van Impe Ministries.[7]

In a letter sent near the close of 1993, for example, Van Impe itemized pivotal developments during the past year and spoke of the "spiritual tingle of excitement" that he felt as he both looked back and thought ahead. He singled out five items as especially significant: the resurgence of the Common Market movement in Europe, the outburst of ethnic violence in various locales, the continuing interest in "one world order" by prominent individuals, the warnings about apostasy delivered by the Pope, and the peace negotiations in the Near East. "Each of these phenomena clearly point to the coming of our Lord Jesus Christ in the clouds of glory," he wrote. A sense of "deep urgency" motivated Van Impe to declare, "We must move quickly; time is short. We must do even more in 1994 than we did in 1993, to reach the lost, to declare the truth of the Gospel to a confused and dying world and to warn the world that it's 11:59 on God's prophetic clock!"[8] This "eleventh-hour mentality" dominates the message of JVI.

Eschatology is at the heart of Jack Van Impe's direct-mail ministry. Week after week his letters and printed materials explore the themes derived from "Bible prophecy." Contemporary events are correlated with scriptural passages, creating what for many may seem like a grab bag stuffed to overflowing with unconnected apocalyptic items, but what in the mind of Van Impe constitutes as clear and coherent an urgent message as ancient handwriting on the wall. Van Impe stands squarely in the tradition of apocalyptic interpretation that has thrived in America. The same scriptural figures and images that attracted the commentary of colonial divines, such as John Cotton, Cotton Mather, and Jonathan Edwards, as well as 19th-century preachers as diverse as William Miller and Dwight L. Moody, and 20th-century popularizers of this genre, including most notably Hal Lindsey, are the center of Van Impe's ruminations.[9] The visionary materials in the biblical books of Daniel and Revelation provide the foundation for much of his apocalyptic reflection. He casts himself in the role of a contemporary prophet, exhorting those who will listen to recognize the nearness of the end, and warning of evil that will come on those who do not heed the call of the impending return of Christ.

The apocalyptic message proclaimed by the JVI Ministries contains little that is new or distinctive. In his recent study, *When Time Shall Be No More: Prophecy Belief in Modern American Culture*, Paul Boyer has correctly described Van Impe as a leading spokesperson for the contemporary tradition of apocalyptic belief.[10] Van Impe shares with others of similar outlook an abiding preoccupation with eschatology, an uncritical confidence that God has a specific plan for the close of history that has been revealed in biblical texts, and a resolute conviction that the present moment is tied inescapably to that end-time scenario. According to him, it is the task of contemporary Bible students to open the closed pages of Scripture, to read the sealed messages, and then to proclaim the "day of the Lord."[11]

The direct-mail ministry of Jack Van Impe invites close examination as we seek to understand its function within the larger enterprise of JVI Ministries. His ministry through the mails utilizes an identifiable communication strategy. It combines an apocalyptic message with other elements that contribute to its success.

The principal vehicle of Van Impe's direct-mail ministry is a four-page, multicolor letter, arriving almost weekly. It is addressed in such a manner as to assume a shared perspective on Christianity, eschatology, and current events. Typical salutations include "Beloved believer in Christ's imminent return," "Beloved followers of God's prophetic plan," and "Beloved fellow-laborer in Christ's end-time harvest." Sometimes the letters begin simply with "Dear Friend" or "Dearly beloved in Christ Jesus." The letters convey a sense of friendship and pastoral concern. Each is carefully crafted to draw the reader into the circle of the ministry by identifying some problem or issue that has high visibility in the contemporary world or that is the source of deep curiosity for devout religious persons. These letters are intended for believers, not for skeptics, agnostics, or those inclined to ridicule the apocalyptic preoccupation of Van Impe.[12]

The letters are artfully designed, from the outside of the envelope to the multiple enclosures. "Teasers" in bold print on the envelopes and at the top of the opening page of the letters draw attention to the topic of the week. One, for example, in bold red type surrounded by a gray background and black border reads, "If today a mysterious finger wrote a cryptic message on an Oval Office wall, what would President Clinton do?" Another exclaims, "RACING TOWARD THE RAPTURE . . . STORMING TOWARD ARMAGEDDON! *BE READY!*" Still another banner declares, "OPEN GRAVES! DISAPPEARING BODIES! UNPRECEDENTED CATASTROPHES!"[13] The envelopes scream for attention, alerting the recipient to the weekly focus: "THE MASTER PLAN, THE MESSIAH'S COMING: Jews—Yearning, Christians—Yawning," or "SECRET NEW PROPHECIES! Everybody's talkin' about heaven but nobody wants to die. . . ."[14] These phrases shock and intrigue, thereby inviting the recipient to tear open the letter and read the latest word on the topic at hand.

Each week a different color scheme visually coordinates the printed items, tying the whole mailing together and giving it an eye-catching, professional appearance. The style of the writing is journalistic, featuring brief declarative sentences and short paragraphs. Rarely are the latter longer than seven or eight lines. Sometimes ten or more paragraphs fill a single page. The visual coordination of each letter packet includes the liberal use of underlining to emphasize and feature particular words, phrases, or whole sentences on the page. This colored highlighting appears to be done by hand, not by computer, creating the sense of having been handled personally by Van Impe. From the color-coordinated logo at the top of the first page to the nearly standard closing, "Yours in world evangelism," or "Yours in End-time Evangelism," followed by Jack Van Impe's signature in the same color ink, the letters are visually appealing and easy to read, thereby drawing the reader into conversation with the ministry.

But the content of the letters forms the most important component in the direct-mail ministry. The JVI letter dated "March 5, 1994," provides an example of this effective strategy. The envelope bears an artfully designed banner of brown, black, and white block letters, "Paradise—On Earth—Ten Years or Less?" Addressed to the "Beloved believer in Christ's soon return," the letter speaks directly to the central themes of JVI Ministries, namely, the impending return of Christ at the inauguration of the millennium. After asking why "unbelievers and backsliders" have been so critical of his eschatological views, Van Impe speculates that fear and shame drive them, for all must meet Christ "face to face." By contrast, he declares, "joy and peace" will be the lot of believers who "love His appearing." This sharp contrast frames the fundamental question of the letter, "When He sets up his Kingdom, what will life be like during the one thousand year reign of Christ?"[15]

Van Impe asserts "unhesitatingly" that life during the millennium will be "wonderful." Human bodies will be "incorruptible," Satan's influence will be "dramatically reduced," and "a completely new way of life" will prevail. And there is more. A host of questions that can be asked about the millennium, Van Impe announces, are addressed in a "fascinating" and "instructive" book entitled *Life in the Millennium: God's New World Order* by Mona Johnian, who is described as "an outstanding Bible teacher." In the book Johnian is said to paint "a vivid, scripturally accurate picture of the end times—including—the Rapture—Christ's return with heaven's armies—Christ's reign as King of kings and Lord of lords—and Christ's millennial paradise on earth." Van Impe guarantees his reader that believers will find the prospect of life in the millennium "thrilling," although at the same time he warns them that in the meantime Satan will continue to deceive the world. He also declares that "dozens of events" are currently taking place "in mind boggling fashion" that are to precede the millennium.[16]

Van Impe closes his letter with the desire that his reader understand these end time events, and he promises to send a copy of Johnian's *Life in the Millennium* for a gift of $15 or more to the ministry, or two copies for $25 or more. He adds, "If the Lord burdens your heart to send additional support, above the cost of the books, Rexella and I would be very grateful." Such gifts, he reminds the reader, make possible the television, radio, video, and print ministry. "Thank you from the bottom of our hearts for being our friend and partner in the work. May God bless you. Please write to me today, tomorrow or very soon." A matching insert in the letter contains an additional pitch for the book and an order form. A return envelope, bar-coded and addressed to the headquarters of the JVI Ministries in Troy, Michigan, is included with each letter.[17]

The eschatological preoccupation of the steady stream of letters is reinforced by the arrival of *Perhaps Today*, a glossy, 8 1/2-by-11 inch magazine that describes Jack Van Impe Ministries on its masthead as "Lighting New Fires of Revival, Redemption, and Reconciliation."[18] This attractive, five-color publication typically contains a lead column or short introductory message from Jack Van Impe himself, a second feature article also signed by him dealing with some aspect of eschatological interpretation, an essay by Rexella which may vary in nature from devotional musings on biblical texts to personal recollections or inspirational experiences, a section of testimonies entitled "Letters We Love" in the form of signed excerpts from correspondence received by the ministry, a 3- to 5-page Weekly Television Log identifying the locations, call-letters, and channels of the television stations that carry "Jack Van Impe Presents" as well as the day and time of the telecasts, and numerous full-page, illustrated advertisements for books, videotapes, audio cassettes, records, and maps. Each issue also has stapled into its center a separate order form with an addressed and bar-coded envelope attached to it. The largest percentage of each issue is devoted to advertising.[19]

This summary of a typical issue of *Perhaps Today* does not do justice to its substance. In fact, it unfairly trivializes the contents. An examination of one particular issue, that of March/April 1994, provides more insight into the character of this publication and the potential response of its readers. A traditional painting of the crucified Christ suspended on a wooden cross graces the cover of the issue with the following caption imposed on it: "At this season as we remember His death, burial and resurrection, 20th Century pagans have changed little." Near the bottom of the framed picture, following the line "INSIDE THIS ISSUE," is the title of Van Impe's lead essay, "Twentieth Century Antagonism Toward Christ."[20] As readers open the magazine, on the right-hand page they confront a thorn-crowned Jesus set opposite the smiling face of Van Impe. The initial essay begins with biblical citations describing those who scorned Christ. Three pages of contemporary examples of "antagonism" toward Jesus then follow, including press clippings from diverse sources, such as the *Detroit Free Press*, telling of the American Civil Liberties Union's efforts to remove a picture of Jesus from a high school classroom, reporting the skeptical conclusions of the Jesus Seminar, discussing the debate among Christians concerning the resurrection of Christ, and summarizing Supreme Court decisions on religious discourse in the public schools and on profanity on the airwaves. Van Impe's four-page article closes with a summary judgment in large letters: "America will pay for its mockery of Jesus and clergy. Order my video 'America in Prophecy' for complete details."[21]

In this same issue Van Impe has a second essay three pages in length entitled "Religious Tyranny vs. Christian Love" in which he sharply criticizes "Christians" and other religious persons "who propagate prejudice and hatred." He suggests that denominationalism is a leading cause of this hostility and tyranny. The unity of the "one body of Jesus Christ composed of all born-again believers" has been clouded by the claims of particular denominations. The most strident voices working against unity, he declares, are often "the so-called orthodox defenders of the faith."[22]

Rexella Van Impe's essay in this issue, "I'm Looking, But Which Way?" is a chatty conversational piece that exploits the notion of the eye as "the window of the soul." Her portrait, framed in boudoir fashion by fine, sparkling crystal and flowers, all reflecting light from some unidentified source, greets readers at the upper corner of the page. Below on the same page is a photograph of three young boys, bright-eyed and spotlessly clean, posed as pals in a winsome and friendly way, inviting to every eye. In her essay Rexella draws on biblical passages that speak of the eyes as she moves toward the identification of three possible lines of sight: "(1) Backward, to be discouraged; (2) outward, to be disheartened; and (3) upward, to be delighted." It is the third option that she links to biblical counsel. Rexella writes, "God can be counted on to give a silver lining to our dark clouds if we'll begin looking forward." The closing paragraph cites Psalm 121:1, "I will lift up mine eyes unto the hills," and is followed by a half-page photograph of the sun's rays breaking over an horizon formed by the silhouette of dark mountain tops.[23]

This issue of *Perhaps Today* also includes three pages of "Letters We Love," testimonies of "Souls won" through the JVI Ministries, of diverse individuals "touched by the truth," and of supporters from "around the world." For example, "R.B." of Akron, Ohio, was "enlightened" and "accepted Jesus" as a result of the ministry. A Catholic priest, a Baptist professor of theology, and a Jewish rabbi all testified to the positive impact of JVI Ministries. Individuals from Italy, Grenada, and the Philippines also wrote of their favorable reactions.[24]

The direct-mail portion of JVI Ministries cannot be separated completely from the larger enterprise which includes the television program "Jack Van Impe Presents." Yet the ministry through the mails has an integrity of its own that accounts in part for its success. Its foundation is Van Impe's explicit commitment to the authority of the Bible, with special weight being given to apocalyptic texts. On that basis he identifies contemporary issues and problems that can be understood or solved only by his interpretive skills as a reader of biblical prophecy. Through this means he demonstrates the relevance of the Bible for the world today. Through their letters and publications Jack and Rexella Van Impe project a friendly, caring, pastoral image that creates a feeling of trust and confidence among their readers. That personal relationship, in turn, provides an ideal climate for effective marketing. These four elements—biblical authority, contemporary relevance, personal relationship, and marketability—form the essential core in the communication strategy of Van Impe's direct-mail ministry.

The ultimate credential Jack Van Impe claims for his ministry is the authority of the Bible. In this respect the print ministry is one with the telecasts. "Jack Van Impe Presents" utilizes the format of a news team with Rexella and Jack seated side by side, speaking directly over a desk to the camera, or the audience behind the camera. Rexella "serves up" questions or data requiring comment, and Jack Van Impe typically answers the questions with unbroken chains of Bible passages and/or interpretive commentary punctuated with scriptural texts. Rexella's role is secondary to that of her husband. He is cast as a master teacher, a modern, learned "rabbi," who opens the scripture. She plays the part of the faithful disciple who listens, nods, affirms with an occasional exclamation, and expresses delight and astonishment with his understanding and insight.

In the direct-mail ministry, Jack Van Impe boasts of his command of the King James Version of the Bible. He does possess an unusual capacity to cite passages at will from memory. In his letter of July 9, 1993, Van Impe writes, "In the past 45 years, . . . I have memorized over 14,000 verses of Scripture." In another letter he suggests that he has logged over 70,000 hours of Bible study, the equivalent of eight years of 24-hour days of his life.[25] His mastery of the text of Scripture helps to explain his normal pattern of argumentation, which is prooftexting; that is, he strings together verses from the Bible that speak of similar topics or contain the same words or phrases without a great deal of concern for their original literary contexts. His interpretive mode might be described as catenary, for he constructs chains of meaning by linking biblical texts. Van Impe is a walking concordance.[26]

This pattern of appeal to biblical authority is standard also in the weekly letters that arrive from JVI Ministries. It is common for those letters to focus on some specific scriptural passage, or to draw indirectly on several such texts, and in the course of the letters to cite yet other prooftexts. For example, Van Impe's letter dated January 25, 1994, begins with Philippians 1:21, "To die is gain," printed in large letters at the top of the opening page. Then Van Impe discusses the biblical description of heaven (which, he points out, is mentioned 559 times in the Bible). He and Rexella have "worked on a detailed study of what the Bible says about heaven," drawing on all kinds of sources. They have also produced a video entitled "Heaven: An Out-of-Body Adventure" which provides "commentary and authoritative answers" about heaven based on his "years of research and study." Finally, he devotes several paragraphs of the letter to the citation of parallel texts from other biblical books, all of which, he asserts, describe aspects of life in heaven.

For Christians who value the witness of Scripture or who read the Bible regularly, Van Impe's letters are likely to possess considerable appeal. He has carefully cultivated his image as a Bible "scholar." That is his principal, self-chosen role on the telecasts; he does little else. He makes no effort to package his presentation in other ways. He assumes the posture of a teacher, lecturing to his disciples. There is little charisma or showmanship in his manner of speaking. His letters, likewise, display little artistic or literary flourish. But what he lacks in glitter or technical sophistication, he makes up in sincerity, intensity, and simple mastery of the text. Religious persons who prize the principle of scriptural authority and who share the fascination with apocalyptic are likely to consider Van Impe a champion of their cause.

But the biblical principle alone cannot sustain the direct-mail ministry of Jack Van Impe. A second element figures prominently in its staying power. Van Impe is an inveterate historicist who seeks to correlate the eschatological texts in the Bible with events in the contemporary world. His concern with current events guarantees that his commentary will attract attention. Van Impe takes the headlines of today and links them to ancient prophecy. He moves with apparent equal ease among political, social, and religious topics. It makes no difference to him whether the events occur on the national or the international scene. He is just as quick to integrate positive developments into his apocalyptic scheme as he is tragedies. In his telecasts Rexella often reads newspaper and magazine clippings that provide him an opportunity to offer eschatologically oriented commentary.

The direct-mail ministry utilizes the same device. Headlines from across the world allow Jack Van Impe an occasion to interpret their meaning in terms of Bible prophecy. Many of the letters from JVI Ministries over the past year and a half employ some version of this formula. Conflicts in the Middle East and Bosnia, the fiery conclusion to the standoff with the followers of David Koresh, the new currency of the European Community, the growth of the New Age movement, Satanism, the promiscuity of Magic Johnson, talk about a New World Order, the rise of Zhirinovsky in Russian politics, debate about gay rights, the expansion of cults—these and other "news" items become the subject of Van Impe's eschatological commentary. There appears to be nothing that cannot be incorporated into his apocalyptic framework. He does not ask the question of consistency among his various judgments. What is consistent is his confidence in asserting his interpretations as well as his belief that individually and collectively they point to the nearness of the end times. Van Impe never wavers in his convictions.

The juxtaposition of eschatology and current events is a powerful and attractive combination for those interested in one or the other. Van Impe exploits that appeal in every possible way. For instance, as part of the standard repertoire of apocalyptic commentators, no eschatological image has attracted more attention and speculation than the Antichrist. Through the centuries exegetes have linked that figure with a host of different political or religious leaders. Each age seeks its own Antichrist. In his June 22, 1994, letter, Jack Van Impe addresses himself to this age-old conundrum. Though he is unwilling to assert an absolute judgment because he maintains "that the identity of the Antichrist will not be revealed to the World until after the Rapture of the Church," yet he asserts that there are "hints" of his identity. According to Van Impe, the fact "that every end time sign is in place" leads him to accept the judgments of Charles Taylor, author of *The Antichrist King—Juan Carlos*, that the reigning king of Spain "stands at the exact point where every prophecy about the Antichrist converges." Every detail concerning the Antichrist in the Bible, he writes, has been "painstakingly cross-referenced" by Taylor to fit "the life, the background, the words, and the plans" of the king. "The evidence is chilling," declares Van Impe. Knowing this, it is the task of JVI Ministries to "warn our friends, our relatives, our loved ones. We must sound the alarm."

Many of the readers of the June 22 letter will count themselves among the "friends" of Jack and Rexella Van Impe. It is that perceived relationship that constitutes a third major element in the communication strategy of their direct-mail ministry. The letters that arrive weekly strive to create a sense of extended family. The issues of *Perhaps Today* reinforce that feeling. Jack and Rexella become close friends who disclose the deepest thoughts of their hearts and who want to share the burdens of their readers, too.

The visual image projected by Jack and Rexella Van Impe plays a part in this larger strategy. Again the telecast and the direct-mail ministry mirror each other. The public image of the two principals in the ministry is carefully styled. In all of the materials received through the mail Jack Van Impe never appears in any informal setting. He is always meticulously attired, wearing a dark suit, white dress shirt, and fashionable tie. His carefully groomed hair and fixed smile give no impression of changing moods. He presents himself as a proper "man of God" (or a corporate executive). If he ever wears any other clothing or engages in casual activities, photographs of the same are not shared with his readers. The only other poses Van Impe strikes in the publications apart from formal portraits show him holding an open Bible or sitting at a library desk.

Jack and Rexella frequently appear together in portraits. The standard photograph depicts a prosperous couple. (It is admittedly difficult to imagine that they have been married for more than 40 years, given the youthful appearance of Rexella.) She is fashionably, flawlessly attired in suits and dresses, complemented often with a tasteful strand of pearls, or gold earrings. Rexella conveys the impression of health, wealth, and beauty. She is always smiling, always cheerful, almost to a flaw on the telecasts. She is a delightful visual contrast to her husband's dark, more staid image. It is difficult not to compare her with other figures from the entertainment industry. At times she comes across as the "Vanna White" of the apocalyptic circuit—charming and graceful, friendly and poised. She never assumes a terribly intellectual stance. In fact, her role is that of "the innocent," a natural subject for instruction by her husband. She also assumes a thoroughly traditional role as the loving and caring spouse.

Jack and Rexella Van Impe build the sense of intimacy with their readers by sharing information about themselves. Jack Van Impe describes his marriage to Rexella as "wonderful," stating that they have "learned to weather financial storms" together even though they have known the "crushing load of debt" in earlier years.[27] Months after the death of his father in February 1993, Van Impe wrote a featured article entitled "Prayer Warrior Promoted" in which he spoke of his father's religious convictions, his practice of praying five hours every day, and his final illness, and he thanked his father for the "holy example" he set.[28] In a letter six months later he confessed, "I really miss this great prayer warrior immensely. What a joy to know he is in his eternal home, enjoying every fact of eternal life. . . ."[29] Readers learn of the daily habits of Van Impe who reads one book a day.[30] He often rises at night to study or pray "when the Spirit of God either burdens [his] heart . . . or enlightens [his] mind."[31] He speaks explicitly of the love he and Rexella have for their readers and that they pray "consistently" for them.[32] Readers are even told that Jack has a fondness for chocolate.[33]

The direct-mail publications reveal even more about Rexella through her essays in *Perhaps Today*. She appears the more accessible of the two in the ministry. In one essay recalling a recent trip to Israel, Rexella wrote of her impressions of the land and its people, from Israel's president to "innocent children" with whom she sang and played.[34] Even more revealing is Rexella's two-page feature that she wrote about her cat, Fenica, who was taken in as a stray and whose given name included a suffix meaning "precious, or beloved." In time Fenica became the regular companion of the Van Impes in their world-wide travels. "It was just like having 'family' on the road with us," Rexella stated. After 18 years, when Fenica died, Rexella reported that their "hearts were broken." But, she asserted, "One day we will see her again," a belief she explained on the basis of Jack Van Impe's declaration that there will be animals on earth during the millennium and the saints in heaven will be able to request the resurrection of their beloved pets. Rexella's story ends with arrival of Fenica II, a stray selected from the Humane Society.[35]

The success of JVI Ministries in establishing the sense of an extended spiritual family creates a favorable climate for the marketing aspect of their communication strategy. No successful, national, multimedia ministry can long endure on the strength of ideas, relevance, or friendship alone. Fund-raising is a necessary component for continued existence. Large amounts of money are needed for every aspect of the enterprise. JVI Ministries must persuade its viewers and readers to support the ministry. Jack Van Impe takes great pride in pointing out that no direct solicitation of funds occurs on television or radio, a contrast with almost every other national electronic ministry.[36] That does not mean, however, that he does not work hard at the task of raising money.

In his direct-mail letters, Van Impe regularly presents the financial needs of JVI Ministries. The following paragraph is typical.

Although we keep our costs as low as possible, it's tremendously expensive to buy television and radio airtime in order to beam "Jack Van Impe Presents" via satellite throughout the U.S., Canada, and to 160 nations of the world monthly. Your gifts and prayers helps us stay on our strict pay-as-we-go basis without appealing for financial support on the air. Because of this policy, we have received multiplied letters expressing appreciation for a television ministry that refuses to use tricks, gimmicks, or begging sessions that hinder and harden the unsaved. I will not change this policy. God will meet our needs.[37]

Although Van Impe requests gifts *and* prayers, the amount of space he allots to the two concerns in his letters is not equal. It is common, for example, to devote the closing page to the ways the recipient can participate in the ministry by "giving."

The printed materials sent by the JVI Ministries describe a structured set of options for contributing money to the ministry. Every letter describes a "premium" (JVI also calls it an "appreciation gift") which can be received by the individual who sends a specified monetary gift. On the initial level the organization expresses its appreciation to the giver by sending the designated premium—a book, videotape, audiocassette, or whatever. In all likelihood, JVI Ministries realizes only a minimal financial return from the sale of premiums. The more important return for the organization is the name and address of the person sending the gift. That information adds a new potential partner to the mailing list and identifies a possible fellow-believer.

The premiums offered in the weekly letters illustrate the eschatological focus of JVI Ministries. Typical "appreciation gifts" include *The Handwriting on the Wall: Secrets from the Prophecies of Daniel*, a book by David Jeremiah with C.C. Carlson, offered for a $15 gift or more; *Kept From the Hour: Biblical Evidence of the Pretribulational Return of Christ*, a book by Gerald B. Stanton, for a $15 gift or more; *Everything You Always Wanted to Know About Prophecy But Didn't Know Who to Ask!*, a book and video by JVI for a $25 gift or more; and *Prince of Darkness: Antichrist and the New World Order*, a book by Grant R. Jeffrey, for a $20 gift or more. An order form enclosed with each letter includes several payment options by which the weekly premium may be obtained. There is also a line for enclosing a "monthly PLEDGE gift."

The reverse side of the order form contains an even more important component in the fund-raising strategy of JVI Ministries. It is called the "Decade of Destiny Partnership" and is described as Van Impe's "Master Plan for World Evangelism." This is the logical complement to the note that was struck in the initial letter sent to a new participant in the ministry. In that first exchange Van Impe offered to share the recipients' burdens; now he asks that they become partners with JVI Ministries and share his burden. He asks them to pledge "monthly support to help . . . reach millions for Christ through international TV evangelism."[38]

Three different levels of partnership are available. "JVI Partners" pledge $20 or more each month, for which they receive a "JVI Partner wallet card, wall certificate, Dr. Van Impe's Bible memorization plan, *Encounters* and *That Mystery Called Life* from Rexella, and the Van Impes' special edition "Prophecy Library" on audio cassette." On the next level, "JVI Inner Circle Partners" pledge $50 or more each month, for which they receive all of the premiums, or "appreciation gifts," listed above, plus regular issues of the "Inner Circle Report," a second bi-monthly newsletter described as a way for "regular supporters to keep abreast of the very latest news interpreted in the light of Bible prophecy by Dr. Van Impe and in a unique way keep in touch with the heart of Mrs. Van Impe."[39] On the highest level, "Presidential Council Partners" contribute $100 or more each month, for which they receive all the premiums described in the two lower levels, plus unspecified "gifts of special spiritual growth materials throughout the year." The bottom portion of the partnership sheet is a tear-off form for setting up an "Automatic Giving Plan Request" by which partners may establish a regular monthly gift processed through a credit card (MasterCard, Visa, or Discover Card) or by direct payment from a bank checking account.[40]

The fund-raising strategy of JVI Ministries involves a layered set of "giving" options. Individuals are drawn into the circle of the ministry by means of the premiums offered in the weekly letters and through advertisements for other items that can be purchased. After the initial contact, the stream of printed materials begins. As the letters, magazines, and other items pile up, a sense of obligation grows. The recipient is asked constantly to become a partner in the task, to accept the challenge of assisting with the burden of spreading the message. Each order form carries a short statement of commitment that begs for affirmation.[41]

It appears that the primary function of the direct-mail ministry of Jack Van Impe is to raise funds for JVI Ministries. Jack Van Impe distinguishes his television show from that of other televangelists by not soliciting funds on the air. He has, in turn, created a very successful method of generating financial support by means of his ministry through the mails. His success is apparent in several ways, not the least of which is his own statement of growth and expansion. In February 1994 he wrote, "Our growth has been phenomenal—500% in 40 months."[42] JVI Ministries has learned well how to take advantage of the cybernetics revolution.[43]

This description of the communication strategy of the Van Impe direct-mail ministry leads to several observations about the future prospects of JVI Ministries and other organizations focused on similar issues. On the one hand, the rapid approach of the end of the millennium is certain to feed the interest in apocalyptic, even among scoffers, and therefore Van Impe's message is likely to attract more attention over the next few years than at present. There is no sign that Americans have a lost any of their curiosity about the future or their willingness to consult individuals who claim to be able to open the future. In addition, JVI Ministries is operating in a religious context that has witnessed increasing strength among conservative, Bible-believing Christians, which serves well Van Impe's religious and social program.

But JVI Ministries is not alone in giving increased attention to apocalyptic. Eschatology is a staple with many of the leading televangelists. Paul Boyer has documented the astonishing expansion of interest in such matters among Protestants in America in the years following the Second World War. Preachers, novelists, and political commentators have each in different ways capitalized on popular concern for the future. Boyer cites such prominent and influential conservative religious leaders as Pat Robertson, Jerry Falwell, and Jimmy Swaggart as representatives of the prevailing tendency to interpret contemporary events in the light of biblical prophecy. Political and economic crises, scandals involving celebrities or public figures, conflicts between nations, threats from disease or technology—each of these invites and attracts apocalyptic commentary. There is little inclination to abandon this traditional way of interpreting events as we prepare to enter the 21st century. On the contrary, Boyer writes, "From pulpits, cassette tapes, orbiting communications satellites, and the pages of millions of paperbacks, the ancient cry rings out as it has for hundreds of years, 'He Is Coming Soon.' "[44]

It is more difficult to explain this continuing fascination for apocalyptic. Stephen D. O'Leary's recent effort to do precisely that comprises a rhetorical theory of apocalypticism. He attempts to sort through the claims of apocalyptic interpreters, to unravel the intricacies of their arguments, and to make sense of the logic that informs their judgments. Like Boyer, O'Leary is confident that this ancient practice will retain immense appeal well into the future because many find the apocalyptic arguments marshaled by these interpreters and commentators genuinely persuasive. In particular, the symbolism involved with apocalyptic provides a way of dealing with problems of good and evil and with questions of purpose in history. These are persisting issues for persons in every age. As O'Leary states, "It seems safe to predict that humanity's passage beyond the year 2000 will be imagined, celebrated, and memorialized in literally thousands of ways during the next decades."[45] In other words, it is important to situate Jack Van Impe within the larger context of surging interests in eschatology. Little seems likely to change as we enter the next century.

Yet it must be noted that JVI Ministries is different from many of the independent, national, multimedia ministries in one particular way, a factor that does not bode so well for its long-term success in the new century. Jack Van Impe has no apparent successor, no public heir apparent (genetic or intellectual) standing in the wings being groomed to take over his organization. This fact may be the most striking evidence of his belief that the end is imminent. In 1993 when asked by an interviewer if he might consider retiring soon, Van Impe replied, "God said, 'I've called you to warn the world and let them know Jesus is coming!' So I can't retire. There's no way out for me—except the Rapture!"[46]

Notes

1. E.g., Ben Armstrong, *The Electric Church* (Nashville: Nelson, 1979); David Harrell, *Pat Robertson: A Personal, Religious, and Political Portrait* (New York: Harper, 1987); Larry Martz and Ginny Carroll, *Ministry of Greed: The Inside Story of the Televangelists and Their Holy Wars* (New York: Weidenfeld, 1988); Jeffrey Hadden and Anson Shupe, *Televangelism, Power, and Politics on God's Frontier* (New York: Holt, 1988); and Bobby Chris Alexander, *Televangelism Reconsidered* (Atlanta: Scholars, 1994).

2. David Paul Nord, "Systematic Benevolence: Religious Publishing and the Marketplace in Early Nineteenth-Century America," in *Communication and Change in American Religious History*, ed. Leonard I. Sweet (Grand Rapids: Eerdmans, 1993) 239-69.

3. Peter J. Wosh, *Spreading the Word: The Bible Business in Nineteenth-Century America* (Ithaca, NY: Cornell UP, 1994).

4. For an instructive survey of the ways in which religion has been responsive to market forces over a period of more than 200 years, see R. Laurence Moore, *Selling God: American Religion in the Marketplace of Culture* (New York: Oxford UP, 1994).

5. Jack Van Impe to Stephen Stein, undated letter, in possession of the author.

6. *Perhaps Today*, May/June 1993: 16.

7. Order form enclosed with Jack Van Impe letter of Mar. 21, 1994.

8. Undated "Speed Mail" letter from Jack Van Impe, received at the end of 1993.

9. For a brief but useful summary of this tradition, see Charles H. Lippy, "Millennialism and Adventism," in *Encyclopedia of the American Religious Experience: Studies of Traditions and Movements*, Charles H. Lippy and Peter W. Williams, eds. (3 vols., New York: Scribner, 1988) 2: 831-44.

10. Paul Boyer, *When Time Shall Be No More: Prophecy Belief in Modern American Culture* (Cambridge: Belknap Press of Harvard UP, 1992) 305. Although Boyer writes principally about the period after World War II, he also has a helpful survey of the apocalyptic tradition, extending back to biblical times.

11. For a brief biographical entry on Jack Van Impe, see J. Gordon Melton, *Religious Leaders of America: A Biographical Guide to Founders and*

Leaders of Religious Bodies, Churches, and Spiritual Groups (Detroit: Gale, 1991) 980.

12. This is my judgment, not that of JVI Ministries. Van Impe speaks often of the large numbers of persons brought to Christianity by his programs and materials. It seems more likely that the principal audience for the programs and those likely to correspond with JVI have self-selected because of a favorable predisposition toward the content and/or orientation of the ministry.

13. All three of these banners are found on undated letters from Jack Van Impe received in 1993.

14. These envelopes accompanied letters from Jack Van Impe dated respectively, Jan. 7 and 25, 1994.

15. Envelope and letter from Jack Van Impe, Mar. 5, 1994.

16. Letter from Jack Van Impe, Mar. 5, 1994.

17. Letter from Jack Van Impe, Mar. 5, 1994; enclosed order form; and return envelope.

18. E.g., cover of *Perhaps Today*, Sept./Oct. 1993.

19. See *Perhaps Today*, May/June 1993; and May/June 1994.

20. *Perhaps Today*, Mar./Apr. 1994, cover.

21. *Perhaps Today*, Mar./Apr. 1994, 3-6.

22. *Perhaps Today*, Mar./Apr. 1994, 10-12.

23. *Perhaps Today*, Mar./Apr. 1994, 16-18.

24. *Perhaps Today*, Mar./Apr. 1994, 20-22.

25. Undated letter from Jack Van Impe, received in 1993, with this heading: "IN THESE DANGEROUS TIMES, A GOOD BIBLE FOUNDATION IS THE BEST PROTECTION AGAINST DECEPTION!"

26. Van Impe has been called "The Walking Bible" in his own promotional literature. See Boyer, *When Time Shall Be No More*, 432, note 32; and *Perhaps Today*, May/June 1993, 16. See also Roger F. Campbell, *They Call Him the Walking Bible: The Story of Dr. Jack Van Impe* (Nashville: Action, 1977).

27. Undated letter from Jack Van Impe with the heading, "50 PERCENT OF TODAY'S MARRIAGES END IN DIVORCE."

28. *Perhaps Today*, July/Aug. 1993: 3.

29. Jack Van Impe letter, Jan. 25, 1994.

30. Jack Van Impe letter, May 24, 1994.

31. Jack Van Impe letter, Dec. 31, 1993.

32. Jack Van Impe letters, Aug. 8, 1993, and Jan. 7, 1994.

33. *Perhaps Today*, Sept./Oct. 1993, 17.

34. *Perhaps Today*, May/June 1993, 10-11.

35. *Perhaps Today*, July/Aug. 1993, 14-15.

36 Jack Van Impe letter, June 22, 1994.

37. Undated letter from Jack Van Impe, received 1993, with heading, "RACING TOWARD THE RAPTURE."

38. This language is found on the reverse side of every order form for JVI Ministries.

39. A personalized letter from John R. Lang to Stephen Stein, Sept. 9, 1993, included a copy of *Lighting New Fires: Inner Circle Report*, Aug. 1993, with a special request to become a partner in the ministry.

40. The information in this paragraph is presented on the reverse side of every order form.

41. Order form enclosed with Jack Van Impe letter, July 7, 1994.

42. Jack Van Impe letter, Feb. 7, 1994.

43. Over a period of 22 months in 1993–94, I received at least 74 separate mailings from JVI Ministries as a result of ordering one videotape. With three exceptions, all were sent by bulk mail, costing the organization approximately 9.5 cents or less per item for postage. The fact that my name has not been purged from the computer mailing list is striking testimony to the confidence of the organization that I have self-selected appropriately and that in time my retention will be validated. The computer cannot separate the believer from the nonbeliever.

44. *When Time Shall Be No More*, 339.

45. Stephen D. O'Leary, *Arguing the Apocalypse: A Theory of Millennial Rhetoric* (New York: Oxford UP, 1994), 3.

46. *Perhaps Today*, May/June 1993, 15.

Jock Evangelism:
Defining and Degrading American Christianity
for Future Generations

Ken Baker

Christianity, a nearly 2,000-year-old religious tradition based on even more ancient scriptures, lacks relevance for many contemporary Americans. But the apparatus of popular sports culture—namely the celebrity heroes of professional athletics—captivates millions, who pour money and emotion into the near-biblical clashes of good and evil played out before them on television and in stadiums packed with frenzied fans.

Christians, hoping to tap into the nation's ever-growing worshipful obsession with sports, have piggybacked on top of sports to preach their centuries-old gospel. These sports-minded Christians call their outreach "sports evangelism," one of the most common forms of popular evangelism being practiced in the wake of the late-1980s scandals that precipitated the demise of sports evangelism's popular predecessor: televangelism.

Despite using different celebrities, jock evangelism and tele-vangelism share the same architects—evangelical Christians—and an equally heavy reliance on image over substance. Thus these conversion-seeking "athletevangelical" Christians, like their televangelistic counterparts, in the 21st century likely will project an image of Christianity as a religion that need not be taken seriously.

This sports-centered crusade is not so much about glorifying God as it is about selling God. Thus the evangelical takeover of big-time college and professional sports symbolizes the shameless marketing that many 20th-century Christians have employed in their struggle to remain relevant in an increasingly secular culture. In fact, the evangelization of modern sports is the result of a ministerial effort as well-funded and slick as a corporate advertising campaign. Evangelical Christians' eagerness to entice potential converts with the allure of athletic competition reveals the inability of traditional Christian doctrine to reach a generation whose primary sources of meaning are largely secular— advanced technology, science, New Age religions, and sports itself, in

189

which humanity is celebrated through the exercise of mind, body and spirit.

This convergence of the sacred and profane is destined to confront both religious and secular Americans into the 21st century, an era in which many born-again Christians believe Judgment Day, the second coming of Jesus Christ, will occur.

Indeed, American Christianity faces an enduring conflict: Whether or not—or, rather, to what degree—should it accept secular values held by those it seeks to recruit.

The largest single sports evangelism event occurred in 1994. "Up for the Cup" was coordinated by Sports Outreach America (SOA), a non-denominational consortium of nearly 100 denominations and sports ministries. Members of SOA form the core of the sports evangelism empire.

Christian groups in each of the nine World Cup soccer tournament sites administered evangelistic sports clinics, tournaments, literature distribution and block parties. The effort was the first of several nationwide crusades that will, according to SOA literature, "piggyback evangelism campaigns on top of major secular sporting events."

SOA was founded in 1989, after the television evangelism empires of Jimmy Swaggart and Jim Bakker crumbled amid allegations of corruption. SOA representatives say sports evangelism will be as effective on a large scale as the televangelism was before it fell into disrepute.

"There's definitely a void," says Steve Quatro, SOA's Los Angeles representative. Quatro adds that after the retirement of the world-renowned Rev. Billy Graham, who is 75, sports ministry will replace him as the most recognizable public face of Christianity. "Billy Graham had the unique gift that he could bring people from all denominations together," he says. "We can use sports to unite people."[1]

SOA has already begun planning for the sports event that is expected to be the group's most ambitious attempt to win souls for Christ: The 1996 summer Olympics in Atlanta. Quest Atlanta '96, a coalition of 400 churches and organizations, as well as area leaders such as former mayor of Atlanta Andrew Young, will conduct outreach using the Olympics as a galvanizing theme.

But Christians already have begun to mobilize around sporting events. Thousands of "prayer warriors," as FCA pamphlets describe its members, attend rallies each year to hear popular sports figures speak about how God gives them the power to score touchdowns, steal bases and slam-dunk.

Others purchase video cassettes featuring the testimonials of Christian athletes and coaches that they play for friends during halftime at Super Bowl parties. The first such video evangelism occurred during the 1993 Super Bowl. The program, produced by Pat Robertson's Christian Broadcast Network and narrated by former Dallas Cowboys coach Tom Landry (a former FCA chairman dubbed "God's Coach," who named his squad "God's Team") was distributed to more than 2,000 churches. It was to be used as a substitute for the Michael Jackson halftime show seen by most viewers.

Tens of thousands of people of all faiths also purchase books—such as the recent autobiographies of Landry, former New York Jets player Dennis Byrd, and retired baseball player Dave Dravecky—to marvel at the achievements these American sports heroes have made through faith in God.

Not all Americans' brush with sports evangelism is voluntary, however. Athletes' postgame God-thanking has become so trite that a former *Sports Illustrated* editor once told me he omitted such prophecy from stories.

Then there are the seemingly omnipresent biblical signs, on which chapter and verse numbers are displayed, that find their way into camera's view at major sporting events, an effort coordinated by a small band of Christian sports fans. The most common biblical citation painted on these cardboard signs is John 3:16, which states: "For God so loved the world, that He gave His only begotten Son, that whoever believes in Him should not perish, but have eternal life."

Team prayers are a common athletic ritual witnessed by the public. Millions of American TV viewers watched Michael Jordan and the Chicago Bulls kneel in prayer after winning the 1991 National Basketball Association Championship; upon winning the world heavyweight championship in November 1994, preacher-boxer George Foreman immediately knelt and prayed; and at most every NFL game you can spot a believer on the field deep in prayer. Such incessant imagery has forged a unification of God and sports in the minds of many Americans.

Equally compelling was the Academy Award–winning movie "Chariots of Fire," which dealt with an athlete's dilemma over whether or not to violate the Sabbath and run in the 1924 Olympics. The runner, Eric Lidell, decided God was more important than country and refused to compete—a decision most athletes today do not make.

Some affiliations between Christianity and sports are so deeply embedded in American culture that few people take notice anymore. Mormon Brigham Young University and Catholic Notre Dame have become virtually synonymous with athletic excellence. Other Catholic institutions such as Villanova, St. John's University and Boston College also have evolved into sports citadels.

Notre Dame folklore consists more of championship coaches such as Lou Holtz, Digger Phelps and Knute Rockne, as well as the legendary player George "the Gipper" Gipp, than its holy priests. And the painting most commonly associated with the school is not *The Last Supper*. Rather, it is a 132-foot-high stone mosaic on Memorial Library depicting Jesus standing above his apostles and an assembly of saints. Because the mosaic—which can be seen from inside the school's football stadium—displays Jesus with his arms raised in a position similar to that of a referee signaling a touchdown, students have nicknamed it "Touchdown Jesus."

The president of Liberty University, Rev. Jerry Falwell, seeks to build an evangelical rival to Brigham Young and Notre Dame. Falwell, who was the religious point man for the Reagan Revolution and founder of the defunct conservative political group Moral Majority, hopes his "spiritual boot camp" will—as Notre Dame's and Brigham Young's athletic success has—culturally legitimate previously marginalized fundamentalists.

"Every kid in the world is interested in two things: sports and music," says Falwell, who founded Liberty in 1974. "They might not know Billy Graham but they know Michael Jordan, Larry Bird and Michael Jackson."[2]

Whereas sports ministries seek to convert wayward souls, Falwell says he just wants to lead by example. When the National Collegiate Athletic Association (NCAA) said Liberty's football team could no longer inscribe Bible verses on towels, their coach got around it by putting biblical decals on helmets. Players wear T-shirts under their uniforms reading: "His pain, Our gain."

Although many Christians' behavior—such as football's end-zone genuflection and prayer circles—have become commonplace, one newly created combination of sports and Christianity recently drew criticism. Many Christians voiced opposition in 1992 when the International Bible Society published a sports New Testament, in which Christ's teachings were juxtaposed with quotes from popular athletes and color photos of them in action.

The prominence of sports in Christianity is also evidenced by the long list of sports ministries: Athletes in Action, Baseball Chapel, Missionary Athletes International, Pro-Basketball Fellowship, Sportsworld Ministries, Hockey Ministries International, and Pro-Athletes Outreach are only a few of the more than 100 sports-based ministries nationwide. Many of these ministries train community church leaders in methods by which churches can use sports to recruit children.

There are even several ministries focused exclusively on less-popular sports such as rodeo. The largest of them, Rodeo Cowboys for Christ, has recently expanded to Canada.

The aptly named founder of the Texas-based group Christian Cowboys, Ronny Christian, boasts of his success. "I usually hold service behind the bucking chutes," says Christian. "And it's not only people getting saved back there. I've seen horses healed."[3]

The remarks of the director of Dallas's World Cup evangelism efforts, Jim Riley, reflect the significant role sports play in Christianity: "Sports will be to evangelism in the twenty-first century what the Sunday school was to Christian education in this century.[4]

Every National Football League (NFL) and major league baseball team and all but two NBA squads have a full-time team chaplain who leads a prayer service at home and away games. One baseball team, the New York Mets, has six chaplains.

In the NFL, in recent years chaplains' efforts have expanded beyond mere spiritual counseling. Many actually have begun teaching players how best to communicate their faith through the media. Essentially, players receive lessons from their Christian elders in how to articulate beliefs in the form of 10-second sound bites.

I have interviewed players and chaplains about their gridiron evangelism. As I will describe in subsequent pages, I have found the NFL's rampant sports evangelism reveals how much influence sports have had on Christian outreach efforts and how these efforts glorify jocks more than Jesus.

It would be an opportunity to sell God to America. The New York Giants and the San Francisco 49ers, each with an impressive 10-1 record, represented the NFL's top two teams. For many football fans, the game would mark the highlight of the 1991 regular season.

Adding to the game's significance was that it would be waged before a national TV audience. Indeed, in less than a week, roughly 30 million Americans would witness the spectacle on ABC's *Monday Night Football*.

Some of the greatest players of the modern football era—Lawrence Taylor, Phil Simms, Jerry Rice and Joe Montana—would block, tackle, pass, kick and wrestle on the grassy turf of San Francisco's Candlestick Park.

But Pat Ritchie didn't care much about who would win the game. Instead, Ritchie, the 49ers team chaplain, felt that God had placed his team in the national spotlight for one reason: to spread the gospel.

Following through on what he viewed as God's game plan, a week prior to the game Ritchie phoned the Giants team chaplain, Dave Bratton who reported: "Ritchie called me up and said, 'There's so much interest in this game. What can we do to show these guys are more than physical specimens?'" Bratton recounted in an interview three-and-a-half years later.[5]

Bratton didn't realize it at the time of his conversation with Ritchie, but his response would initiate a new form of Christian worship that eventually would spread throughout the league.

Bratton suggested they arrange for Christian players on either team to join hands and recite an on-the-field prayer. The fellow evangelical Protestant chaplains agreed to hold a brief session at midfield immediately following the end of the game. That way TV cameras— before cutting away to a commercial break—could beam the prayer huddle to viewers across the country. "He talked to his guys, me mine, and we did it," said Bratton.[6]

On that December 3 night cameras captured the sweaty group of Christians, heads bowed, kneeling at the 40-yard line. And with that display, a nearly 20-year evolution of the relationship between football and Christianity reached a historic point.

Starting in the 1970s, team by team, chaplains entered onto the NFL scene. They offered a spiritual refuge in the high-pressured professional sports environment. Christian players banded together, meeting for Bible study sessions and Sunday-morning chapel services. Public testimonials of their faith in Jesus Christ soon followed. Upon the urging—and in most cases the direction—of their chaplains, players offered locker room God-thankings after victories. End-zone genuflections gradually became as common as hot-shot touchdown celebrations.

Football's evangelical wave crested on that misty San Francisco night. Millions watched as the holy warriors huddled. At that moment, sports—after rock music, politics and television culture itself—became the final secular institution, formerly branded as demonic, to be embraced by evangelical Christians for the purpose of mass-scale religious marketing.

But while the display marked the end of conservative Christians' abstention from secular pursuits, it also forged a beginning. In the four years since the Giants–49ers huddle, the postgame prayer ritual has become a fixture at nearly every NFL game.

But that's just the public face of a larger movement occurring within professional sports: the explosion of the sports evangelism industry. Videos, magazines and TV shows promoting Christian athletes—most notably football players—now bombard the public.

NFL players and coaches frequently are interviewed on religious broadcaster Pat Robertson's 700 Club. The Christian book publishing industry also has cashed in on the increased popularity of Christian football figures. Here are a few of the books to come out since 1990:

- *Rise and Walk*: The story of how former New York Jets player Dennis Byrd—who broke his neck during a 1992 game—used his Christian faith to overcome paralysis and walk again.
- *Fourth and One*: Born-again Christian and former Washington Redskins Coach Joe Gibbs's spiritual autobiography.
- *Tom Landry, an Autobiography*: The legendary retired head coach of the Dallas Cowboys recounts how Christian principles placed his teams a cut above the rest of the league.

The marriage between Christianity and professional football seems incompatible given the violence and materialism of the sport. Still, the use of football as a promotional tool for Christianity continues.

Football is violent. Leg bones snap like matchsticks under the force of high-speed collisions. And when helmets crunch, greater damage often results. The NFL commissioner's office reported in 1994 that a player receives a concussion every 3.5 games. That's nearly four each weekend league-wide. And head injuries are nothing new for the NFL. In fact, ironically enough, one of the most famous Christian players of all time, Dallas Cowboys quarterback Roger Staubach, was forced to retire after experiencing four "dingers," as concussions are termed in NFL parlance.

But the statistic apparently keeping evangelicals piggybacked on top of the NFL machine is the millions of people who flock to stadiums each season to witness the barbaric matches. About 14 million people packed into NFL stadiums in the 1994 season—an all-time attendance record. And that's not including the millions of TV viewers who worship their remotes throughout the fall and winter.

But while the growing sports evangelism faction of Christianity concerns itself with reaching non-Christians, most have failed to recognize the mixed message associated with such shameless religious marketing. For the intermingling of the sacred values of religion with the often profane values exhibited in the NFL has blurred the distinction between the religious and nonreligious.

The NFL's first high-profile born-again Christian coach Tom Landry cautioned Christians about the perils of sports-centered evangelism before football developed into the born-again sport it is today. Landry's warning to his fellow evangelicals, however, was not heeded.

Landry distinguishes acts of religious proclamation from those of salesmanship. As head coach of the hugely successful Dallas Cowboys teams of the 1970s and '80s, Landry, clad in his ever-present fedora, attempted to infuse the spirit of Jesus Christ into his coaching like no other previous NFL coach. "I never tried to hide what I believed," Landry wrote in his 1990 autobiography. "I regularly shared appropriate Bible verses in talks during team meetings. And every year at training camp when I met with incoming rookies for the first time, I would share the story of my own spiritual pilgrimage."[7]

While Landry certainly was not the first professional football coach to invoke religious messages in pep talks, he was the first to publicly preach a muscular gospel of Jesus Christ. In that sense, Landry, who is now 70, was a pioneer in the field of sports evangelism—privately, at least.

Yet Landry's reluctance to convert nonbelievers from his coaching pulpit vastly differs from the philosophy of many current Christian coaches and players.

The revered coach says he always was careful not to "push my own beliefs down the throats of my players." Although Landry says he appointed Christian players to lead voluntary chapel services on Sundays, he generally implored players to keep their faith private.

Due to his strong faith, many Christian sports ministries have tried to recruit Landry. Though he briefly served as chairman of the Fellowship of Christian Athletes in the 1970s, he has resisted the temptation to use his fame as a mechanism for non-Christians' spiritual conversion. In fact, Landry voices contempt for popular athletes and coaches who use football as a preaching platform.

He criticizes Christian players for inappropriate displays of faith on the playing field, saying, "I have to admit that I'm troubled a little and have very mixed reactions when I see a football player kneel down in the end zone and thank God after a touchdown.

"Don't get me wrong," he has written. "I think an athlete should feel gratitude for his God-given abilities. I think we all ought to give thanks to our Creator for our blessings, our opportunities, for life itself. But I'm afraid these little 'God helped me score a touchdown' and 'God helps me be a winner' testimonials mislead people and belittle God."[8]

Fred Raines couldn't disagree more. Raines, who serves as chaplain for the Buffalo Bills, encourages his team's more than 25 born-again players to use their fame for evangelism. "I make sure they get training, so they can give testimonies in a concise way," explains Raines, who has served as chaplain since 1984.

The successful ministry Raines has built over the past 10 years (from about 5 to currently 25 players) reflects the Christianization of most NFL teams. But while Raines's experience with the Bills illustrates the increasing impact of born-again Christianity on football, it also reveals the inevitable perils that arise from such a motley marriage.

Anyone who watched the Bills in recent years witnessed the fruits of Raines's ministry: an increasing number of players had begun publicly praising the Lord. From brief moments of prayer in the end zone following touchdowns, to year-round speaking engagements at churches and schools, to postgame prayer huddles (ever since that historic Monday night game in 1990), religious symbols had become synonymous with the Buffalo Bills. And since the team had gained national attention—thanks to four straight Super Bowl appearances—NFL fans everywhere witnessed the Bills' Christian influence. The Christian presence was so pervasive that some members of the media nicknamed them, "The God Squad." My job as a reporter was to find out what exactly Raines was doing to ignite the team's evangelical fervor.

Raines agreed to meet me at the Bills practice field during one of the team's Wednesday afternoon workouts at Fredonia State College. It was just one week into the team's training camp at the flat, sprawling campus located about 40 miles south of Buffalo. The smacking of hard plastic shoulder pads and helmets echoed across the fenced-in field, where the team's 80 or so players ran through various drills.

As I approached the sidelines, I had difficulty spotting the 45-year-old Raines. I saw the team's diminutive head coach, Marv Levy, standing with a clipboard in his hand, intensely observing his players. Surrounding Levy was his cast of assistant coaches and trainers. The coaching staff paced, barking out orders to the grunting players.

A TV reporter, standing amid a throng of cameras and microphones, pointed Raines out for me. A white golf shirt with a red Bills helmet stitched on the right chest was tucked into black polyester shorts that clung to his trim body. A cool breeze, tossing his sandy-brown hair, swept across the field from nearby Lake Erie. Behind the players stood about a hundred fans amassed at the west end of the field.

Arms crossed, Raines peered through his mirrored sun glasses at the players. When I spotted him, I scribbled a quick physical description of Raines. At the end of the list, I scrawled, "looks like a coach." Through subsequent interviews, I learned that he more than just looks the part.

"I've been around longer than most everybody," he said, noting this was his eleventh training camp. Like every other NFL chaplain, Raines is not paid by the Bills. Private donations from players and local churches support his efforts.

Officially, Raines serves as a missionary with the nondenominational sports ministry Athletes in Action, which also supports roughly 20 other NFL chaplains. Raines provides more than prayers. According to current and former players, he has saved marriages from seemingly imminent divorce, weaned players off drugs and instilled confidence in those who, once deemed average, now enjoy all-star status and lucrative contracts.

Following the hour-long training camp workout, Raines chatted with some players. I walked down the sideline to where Coach Levy was holding an impromptu press conference. Afterward, as Levy headed for the locker room, I asked the silver-haired coach about his team's much-talked-about Christian revival.

Levy, who is Jewish, seemed fairly surprised by question, which followed 10 minutes of football-oriented inquiries by sports reporters. "I stay away from the spiritual side. That's an individual thing," he said, walking briskly. "We provide chapel but we leave it up to the players."

"Is Raines, in part, responsible for the team's recent success?" I asked.

"I'd say he's definitely a team asset," Levy curtly replied, before heading for the locker room.

While Levy does not meddle in the religious lives of his players, there's much evidence the team's on-the-field performance has improved as a result of Raines's presence.

Raines conducts a 30-minute chapel service on Sunday mornings before every home game. When the team plays out of town, Raines arranges for the opposing team's chaplain to conduct a service. The only exception has been the Bills' four Super Bowl appearances, which the team paid for Raines and his wife to attend.

The Sunday-morning gathering, which is usually attended by about 25 players and coaches and held in a banquet room at the hotel the team stays in before home games, features a guest speaker and a brief Bible-based message from Raines. Raines delivers sports-related sermons for players, providing a last-minute spiritual boost.

Raines's ministry runs seven days a week. On Mondays during the season, Raines, who attends a Wesleyan church, meets with the team's Christian "leadership group." Comprised of a five or six veteran players hand picked by Raines, they discuss the Bible and how it relates to their lives and, as he says, "help them grow in their faith." The weekly team Bible study is held on Thursday evenings and is attended by single players and married couples.

For the few Catholics on the team, a local priest celebrates Mass on Sunday morning just a few doors down the hotel hallway from Raines's packed Protestant gathering. Players deny that there's tension between the two groups. But Raines's attendees definitely practice a more Bible-based brand of Christianity compared to their Catholic teammates, most of whom simply attend the Sunday service, according to players.

Receiver Steve Tasker, a United Methodist, eats lunch with Raines once a week for prayer and discussion. Unlike the rigid, professional relationship he shares with football coaches, he talks openly about his personal life with the Bills' spiritual coach. "He's a real friend, someone you can really talk to," says Tasker. "He gives us guidance, direction."

Raines has witnessed many changes. Two head coaches, four consecutive losing seasons and Super Bowl losses have since faded. And except for team owner Ralph Wilson, veteran defensive player Daryl Talley and a few members of the team's training staff, Raines has been associated with the team longer than any other person. In short, Raines holds clout.

Until the 1994 season, the Bills had enjoyed a winning record all 10 seasons with Raines as chaplain. The team finished 8–8 in 1984, Raines's first year. It was a drastic improvement over the consecutive 2–14 outings of the previous two years. Moreover, the team won four consecutive American Football Conference championships from 1991 to 1994. Raines said he doesn't care about wins and losses, though he says winning has been a nice byproduct of his spiritual counseling. "The success of this team has paralleled the growth and spiritual maturity of the Christians on the team," he boasts.[9]

Former Bills tight end Mark Brammer helped recruit Raines to Buffalo in 1984. Brammer, who now owns a construction company headquartered near Buffalo, recalls the days prior to the mid-'80s, when most NFL teams still were not served by a full-time chaplain. "Players were reluctant to proclaim their faith," says the 36-year-old Brammer.[10]

Brammer, and a few other devoted Christian players, invited Raines, who was working as missionary in Central Illinois with Campus Crusade for Christ, to establish a team ministry. Brammer compares Raines's ability to motivate players to that of a good coach. "You can have guys who say they're Christian," says Brammer. "But if they don't have a committed chaplain they're probably not going to grow spiritually."[11]

Raines says Christian players, because of their fame, have responsibility that transcends winning football games. The men of faith are obligated to use their exalted status to spread the good news of Christianity, he says. "It's not even a choice," says Raines, citing Mathew 28:19 as evidence of Christians' responsibility to spread Jesus' teaching. "From my perspective, it's something that's expected. God has placed them in their high-profile position for a reason. . . . Jesus said, 'Go therefore and make disciples of all nations.' He commanded us to share our faith with others."[12]

Raines teaches players that one of the most effective ways to proclaim their faith is in the form of 10-second soundbites.

"I tell them not to spend fifty-five minutes on all the things you used to do before you were a Christian, and then finish by saying you asked Christ into your life and now you're fine," he explains. "You know, that wouldn't communicate a whole lot."

That's where Raines's ministry has gone from counseling to coaching. Before players speak about their faith publicly, Raines says, "I make sure their testimonies have four parts: What their life was like before Christ, how they became a Christian . . . and some of the differences that he made in their life. Then they should share a Bible verse that means a lot to them. And I get them to do that in ten to fifteen minutes."[13]

Raines's disciples have executed their leader's game plan. Backup quarterback Frank Reich has been the team's most outspoken Christian. He made headlines during the 1993 playoffs when, after engineering a 32-point come-from-behind victory against the Houston Oilers, he referred to his success as "a miracle of God."[14]

That comment put Reich on the defensive. Letters from fans published in the *Buffalo News* of January 28, 1994 lambasted Reich for suggesting that God cares about the outcome of sporting events. But the lanky Christian quarterback refused to back down from his statements, and, in fact, used the attention to proclaim his faith with even more gusto.

"People might call you a hypocrite. But whenever you stand for something you can be called a hypocrite," he told me in an interview at the '94 training camp. "You're gonna get shot down. But they can shoot us down all they want. The fact is that we have a risen savior in Jesus Christ. He defeated death. That's what sets Christianity apart from any other religion: He has risen."

If the Bills were a Catholic church, the Bible-thumping Reich would be Raines's favorite altar boy. Handsome and congenial, he sounds like a religious bully but rarely offends—the type of Christian who can tell you that you are going to straight to hell as a wide smile stretches across his face.

With Raines's help, the articulate Christian has perfected his sermon. As a result, Reich has become one of the most prominent Christian stars showcased by the sports evangelism industry.

Sports Spectrum, the monthly magazine of the Fellowship of Christian Athletes, featured Reich on its cover in 1993, in the wake of his celebrated comeback victory against the Oilers. The glossy FCA magazine—the *Sports Illustrated* of Christian sports magazines—in 1994 also published a question-and-answer article titled, "I Can Overcome Anything."[15]

Reich's explanation for why he feels obligated to spread the gospel on and around the gridiron reflects more than a strong religious faith. Reich earns more than $1 million a year for his football-throwing exploits. His comments show how he uses faith in Christ to give him a psychological edge, which, in turn, keeps millionaire Reich at the top of his game:

My Christian faith has made me a better athlete because I don't feel I have to be controlled by my circumstances or the environment around me. It's in my faith in Jesus and the strength and hope that I find in him that I can overcome anything, on or off the field. Sometimes that means overcoming a 32-point deficit. But sometimes that means coming back from the devastation of defeat, as we experienced in the Super Bowl only a couple games after the great comeback. Through my relationship with Jesus I can have victory in every situation.[16]

Many Christians proclaim how their faith empowers them in their daily lives. So it's not so strange to hear a football player speak of the psychologically transformative powers of faith. The difference is that while, say, a plumber feels God gives him strength to carry on his daily work in obscurity for relatively meager wages, a professional athlete plays games and gets paid hundreds of thousands of dollars per game to do it. Moreover, the Christian player—unlike a plumber who quietly goes about his work—injures his fellow men with punishing tackles and body blows. Then, the player justifies his violent vocation by claiming it's all for God's glory. The plumber, however, just does his job without any pretense that God wants him to be an evangelist. But who is exalted by the public and sports-minded ministers? The millionaire athlete.

That is why Christian players who use their high-profile status to proselytize nonbelievers engage in little more than fraudulent marketing.

Reich and other players have the right to exercise their freedom of religion, but to equate their athletic pursuits with a monastic lifestyle is foolish and a misapplication of Christian doctrine. It is a slap in the face to priests, nuns, missionaries and all devout followers of the religion.

Despite the contradiction between Christ's message of love and football's brutality—which commonly causes dislocated shoulders, broken bones and twisted knees—most Christian players I've interviewed view their play as pious. "You don't have to go to seminary and be a priest," reasons Washington Redskins defensive back Pat Eilers. "You can go to an NFL camp and be a football player."[17]

Eilers's rationale has been shaped by Redskins chaplain Lee Corder, who ministers to a core group of 15 to 20 players.

My requests to attend several NFL teams' chapel services were denied by chaplains concerned about players' privacy. But Corder agreed to let me observe his weekly prayer meeting with players.

It was the last week of November 1994 and the team was amid a disappointing 2–10 season. I met Corder in the lobby of the Marriott Hotel, a low-rise building bordering Dulles Airport in the Northern Virginia suburb of Chantilly. Players and coaches stay at the hotel the night before home games. The 45-minute chapel service consists of prayer, a sermon from Corder and usually a speech by a Christian who has been successful in sports, business or politics.

The 44-year-old Corder has served the Redskins since 1987, when he was recruited by former head coach and professed Christian Joe Gibbs. The evangelical Protestant Corder, a lanky 6-foot-4-inch former high school basketball player, also directs the Harrisonburg, Virginia–based Young Life Ministries, from which he receives a salary. Like other NFL chaplains, he is not paid by the team he serves.

Corder's friendly demeanor and broad frame are an effective ministerial tool with the muscular players. After greeting me in the lobby, he escorted me downstairs to a ballroom that serves as the team's makeshift sanctuary on Saturday nights. Maroon curtains were drawn across the wall of windows on one side of the room, as about 20 players and coaches filed through two wide doors opening to a carpeted hallway.

Burgundy and gold sweat suits, blue jeans, high-top sneakers and "I love Jesus" T-shirts were among their uniforms, leather-bound Bibles resting on top of team playbooks, their equipment. The hulking players did not look like the average church congregation. But, then again, this wasn't a typical worship service. To the drone of an air conditioner, the players, along with four coaches, bowed their heads and joined silently in an opening prayer recited by Corder. "Lord Jesus, we thank you for the beauty of the day," began Corder, softly. "And we thank you for purpose in our life, for the values, the encouragement to be all that you've made us to be."

About 22 hours later, the football players would battle their foes, the New York Giants, on a muddy RFK Stadium field. But for now, the fine physical specimens would focus on getting God on their side.

Since no Jew or Muslim has ever played for the Redskins with Corder as chaplain and there are only about five Catholic players on the roughly 45-man team, the prayer meeting effectively represents the players' primary worship service.

On this night, the featured guest speaker was Douglas Holladay, a former investment banker with Goldman, Sachs & Company and a White House aide for Ronald Reagan. Holladay offered the players advice on how to cope with the pressures of their job. "When you have a lot of notoriety, you don't have privacy," he said. "And when you have wealth, you can lose it. The Bible says pride comes before a fall. God can wipe us out in quite a hurry."

Holladay encouraged players to stay strong in their faith, because they will need it to guide them through tough times. "You're not always going to be professional coaches or football players. Try to base your life on something that'll last. . . . When you're young and vigorous you seem invulnerable. But, as it says in the book of Hebrews, our success is going to come and go, fame is fleeting, but the person of Christ is everlasting."

The well-spoken Oxford graduate enjoyed the undivided attention of the assembled players. They listened quietly to his 30-minute homily. While most of Holladay's message focused on the theme of eternal salvation, he closed with a prayer sounding very much like a request for a win. "I pray that you'll give them amazing faith tomorrow," Holladay implored God at the end of a brief prayer. "I wish you guys tremendous success tomorrow. I know you'll do great."

Like Raines with the Bills, Corder outlines a two-fold purpose for Redskins players: Use your faith to guide your personal life and use your celebrity status to spread Christ's message. "Given the unique nature of the game—the public access—players have a unique opportunity to share their faith and values," he says.

Eilers, 28, is a defender noted for his toughness on the field. When the 5-foot-11, 197-pounder steps onto the field, he says he becomes a "sports evangelist."

But Eilers, who is Catholic and a graduate of Notre Dame University, sees no conflict between his practicing a peaceful, Christ-loving faith and crunching enemy players. "You can minister to God using the talents and the abilities God has given you," he said.

Corder, however, recognizes the contradictory values of sports and Christianity. He admits that it is often difficult to reconcile football's brutality with Christianity's love-thy-neighbor message. "I stand on the sidelines sometimes and wish it were less violent," he says.

Corder is particularly troubled by players who desire to, as he says, "get out there and rip heads off for Jesus." But he believes players should gather in on-the-field prayer huddles and pray for the cameras because they can reach a wider audience than the average preacher. "I have no great love or commitment to football," he adds, "but we live in a culture that holds it with great value."[18]

The Redskins lost the game against the Giants the day following the chapel service I observed. But perhaps God does play favorites. Keep in mind that the Bible says he parted the Red Sea for Moses, then closed it on the Egyptian army. But such logic clearly breaks down. Who does God side with when both teams pray equally hard? This divine dilemma may have occurred at the end of the 1990 Bills–Giants Super Bowl game.

The Bills' inconsistent place kicker Scott Norwood could have won the game with a last-minute field goal. As more than 100 million Americans watched the cliffhanger at home on television, players for both teams knelt, held hands and prayed.

Coach Levy nervously clasped hands with players, many of whom never participated Raines's pregame chapel services. A similar scene appeared on the Giants sideline.

Norwood, a Christian active in Raines's Bible study, missed the field goal—wide right—and the Giants won. But for those tense few seconds preceding the kick, cameras panned the competing prayer huddles.

Characteristically, Christian sports ministry leaders, instead of deploring the misguided requests for victory, viewed it as a powerful display of faith. (Even though God may have more important miracles to deliver than blowing a gust of wind so a football sails wide of a goal post.)

One Christian sportswriter defended the prayer huddles. "Remember the Super Bowl a couple of years ago, when several of the Giants' players prayed along the sidelines, as Buffalo attempted a last-minute field goal?" wrote *Sports Spectrum* writer Gordon Thiessen, who also directs a Christian sports publishing business. "Some think Christians have gone too far. What's the real issue? For Christians it seems to be one of obedience. After all, God has told us to reach the world with the gospel (which includes sports fans)."

What if those fans—who pay upwards of $60 a game to see football, not Christian worship—don't want Christianity forced on them? By not forbidding such displays, the NFL does not seem too concerned about offending non-Christians. What if Jewish players decided to glue yarmulkes on top of their helmets? Or Muslim players carried prayer rugs, which, after scoring a touchdown, they would kneel on and pray facing Mecca? Maybe then the NFL would be forced to place restrictions on acts of religious worship during games.

Whether Christians continue using sports to preach the gospel depends on how critically and honestly they assess their theologically dubious evangelistic endeavor. But whatever may be the outcome of their introspection, locker room preaching continues today with the enthusiastic approval of more than 100 of the nation's largest churches and ministries—from the Billy Graham Evangelistic Association to the Southern Baptist Convention, the nation's largest Christian denomination. The affiliation between conversion-seeking Christians and NFL players likely will continue because it's a relationship based on utility. Christianity gets promoted; players get exalted. And it's an alliance forged with every NFL team.

The impact of sports evangelism on professional football is secondary to that on Christianity, however. The parasitic attachment to professional athletes and sports teams exposes Christianity's contemporary challenge: staying relevant in an increasingly secular American society.

Although relying on popular culture icons such as coaches and players to promote a 2,000-year-old religious tradition makes sense from a marketing perspective, theologically it substantiates many sociologists' theories that sport is America's great new religion. It's as if American sports fans—as well as conversion-seeking evangelicals—view athletes as a collective messiah, who will rescue them from their mundane lives, someone who can lead them to victory, glory and power.

Christianity already centers on a messiah theology. Has Jesus Christ, and his teachings described in the Bible, lost relevance to average Americans to such a degree that Christians embrace non-religious cultural phenomena like sports to evoke a sexy image? I believe this is the case. And the evidence is found in the NFL and most every other popular American sport.

A 1991 article by Rick Reilly that appeared in *Sports Illustrated* following the Bills-Giants competing Super Bowl prayer huddles, borrowed a historical analogy to illustrate the dangers of Christians' piggybacking on top of sports: "Just because you rant and rave about how tight you are with God, doesn't necessarily mean it's true. I'm reminded that in World War II, German soldiers had a phrase inscribed on their belt buckle: *Gott mit uns*. The translation: 'God is with us.'"[19]

To Christ, one of the most dangerous aspects of ancient society was the practice of pagan religion, which worshiped many gods. Jesus warned that polytheism's idolatry compromised Christians' loyalty to the almighty God of monotheism. Sports, with the deification of its multimillionaire athletes, resemble pagan religions of biblical times. Yet sports evangelists fail to recognize the inherent contradictions of their actions.

Not only have many Christians failed to learn from past errors committed while exploiting the apparatus of pop culture to win souls for Christ, but they have deviated from principles outlined in the Bible. It's a sorry exhibition of popular religion being witnessed by yet another generation of children, whose current perceptions will determine the future of Christianity in America.

Notes

1. Steve Quatro, personal interview, Atlanta, GA, 30 Apr. 1994.

2. Bud Shaw, "The Mission: Football," *Cleveland Plain Dealer* 10 Oct. 1993: 1d.

3. Ronny Christian, phone interview, 1 Mar. 1994.

4. Jim Riley, personal interview, Atlanta, GA, 30 Apr. 1994.

5. Dave Bratton, phone interview, 30 Aug. 1994.

6. Bratton interview.

7. Tom Landry, *Tom Landry: An Autobiography* (Grand Rapids: Zondervan, 1990) 173.

8. Landry, 293.

9. Fred Raines, personal interview, Fredonia, NY, 29 July 1994.

10. Mark Brammer, phone interview, 29 July 1994.

11. Brammer interview, 29 July 1994.

12. Raines interview, 29 July 1994.

13. Fred Raines, personal interview, Hamburg, NY, 7 Sept. 1994.

14. "I Can Overcome Anything," *Sports Spectrum*, Jan. 1994, 9.

15. "I Can Overcome Anything."

16. "I Can Overcome Anything."

17. Pat Eilers, personal interview, Chantilly, VA, 26 Nov. 1994.

18. Lee Corder, personal interview, Chantilly, VA, 26 Nov. 1994.

19. "Save your prayers, please," *Sports Illustrated*, 4 Feb. 1991, 86.

V

Extension or Circularity?

With the concept or development of a new technology, the future always looks more promising. Now, with the rapid saturation of our means of communication with the computer and its generated outreaches, many people sense that the conquest of space and time and our human problems may have been achieved. Other people, however, feel that the compression of space, time and the human community into a tighter ball may have exacerbated our many problems. Certainly the new Paradise has not yet been reached. Richard Jensen, in "Internet 2001 and the Future," cautions that more than electricity and computers may be needed to guide us through the next thousand years, and Winfred Barton's dark brow in "Millennium" suggests that the new period may be merely an extension of the present one with no problems automatically solved by the calendar.

Internet 2001 and the Future

Richard Jensen

Railroads provided a spectacular increase in the freedom of 19th-century Americans. At low cost the network transported them, and their products and their needs, from anywhere to anywhere else. It broke the isolation of rural America, it opened the West, it created great inland cities and stimulated old ports. The railroad built 19th-century America, and quickly cities, businesses, financiers, and government adjusted to the Railway Age. Psychologically, railroads provided the freedom to travel, to tour, to explore. Of course, the railroad patrons had to accommodate themselves to an impersonal agency that set rates and schedules in arbitrary fashion. Only a few very rich men had private railway cars and could design their own itinerary. For the 20th-century American, the automobile was the next stage. Although somewhat more expensive than railroads to use, they provided much greater freedom, exhilaration, and control over schedules and actions. Automobiles promoted not only gas stations and suburbs but individualism as well—a sense of personal control free of the mandates of an impersonal bureaucracy. Promptly, society, the economy, the popular culture, and the government again readjusted to the new technology.

The question is whether computers and the Internet will comprise by 2001 a technological system comparable in impact and importance to the railway and the automobile. The computerized changes that swept America after the introduction of the IBM Model 360 in 1965 rivaled the impact of railroads. Computers reorganized people's lives, and made the economy, the government and education more productive, but they were not easily accessible to ordinary mortals. Mainframes were multimillion-dollar installations operated by a priesthood of white-coated technicians. Their liturgical language was not Latin but FORTRAN and COBOL. They set the schedules and the routes that everyone had to use. When personal computers began arriving in quantity in the 1980s, the old Mainframe Establishment tried to stop, impede, or control the shift toward decentralized computing. It was no use, for by the early 1990s personal computers packed more power than giant mainframes of a decade earlier, cost 1/1000 as much, and featured software that was as easy to learn as driving a Model T. Word processing meant that people could enter and control their own words, without the intervention of a secretarial staff. Spreadsheets meant that junior staffers could analyze complex data sets and build models of the sort that previously cost tens or hundreds of thousands of dollars to handle.

A valuable breakthrough came in the program Notes by Lotus (which became part of IBM in 1995). Notes allowed work teams to share textual information in an intuitive fashion, and the team could be geographically dispersed. Text no longer had to be filtered through faxes (or "smail"), and the delay factor implicit in collaborative work was strikingly lessened. The limitation of the PC came in terms of connectivity. In bureaucracies, the PCs were connected to local servers, which contained only the information and programs selected by management. PCs in the academic world were generally not controlled by managers, thus allowing for a much greater "freedom." Most students used the freedom to play complex games, of course, while a few created programs that made them millionaires before graduation.

The Internet was created in 1969 by the U.S. Defense Department but was taken over by the National Science Foundation, which supervised it until 1995. The Internet was originally designed for easy communication among research scientists and engineers. By the early 1990s, its e-mail functions gave it broad popularity among academics with modems. E-mail proved a fast, free, highly convenient communications mechanism. (Smaller schools set up a rival system called Bitnet that performed much the same e-mail role. Bitnet faded away after 1994.) The Internet is free—or at least it appears that way to users. The economics depends on the availability of very cheap band width. In the 1980s the telephone industry recabled America, and most other industrialized countries, with fiber-optic cable, which consists of thin strands of glass that carry not electricity but flashes of light. The flashes can be encoded as digital signals, and the fiber optic can thus replace copper wires because they are much cheaper. The carrying capacity ("bandwidth") of fiber-optic cable is so large that the telephone companies sold the excess capacity very cheaply. College computer centers formed regional cooperatives. These coops, like NYSERNET (New York), SURANET (South), and CICNET (Midwest), used dues from colleges to purchase large blocks of bandwidth. The dues were low—perhaps $50,000 a year for a major university—and provided virtually unlimited message capacity. The cost of e-mail messages fell to less than one penny per hundred messages—virtually free, and certainly less than the cost of hiring the technical people at the computer centers who handled Internet chores and wrote software. True to its co-op origins, the computer centers donated the software they wrote for free distribution. For example, the University of Minnesota developed and gave away "gopher" programs that allowed easy, menu-driven access to files stored on a mainframe. CERN (the European Laboratory for Particle Physics in Switzerland) wrote and gave away the World Wide Web software in 1991; the Supercomputer Center at the University of Illinois donated Mosaic in 1994.

By the mid-1990s, NSF pulled out of the Internet business and numerous commercial providers moved in. Tens of thousands of commercial accounts were established, as business began exploring a new marketing frontier. With most information and software "free" it was not immediately obvious how people were making money on the Internet. The answer was that communications giants (telephone and cable utilities, computer companies, and publishers) were pouring millions into the system in order to establish a presence. The first major service on Internet was person-to-person e-mail. It was like having free telegrams. But if messages could be sent to one address free, then why not to many addresses at once? Eric Thomas created Listserv software for Bitnet that provided a simple, reliable e-mail publications system. A "list" could be created on a mainframe, and people subscribe via e-mail. The subscribers could post and answer messages to each other. Thousands of e-mail lists formed, each narrowly focused. The tendency in science and scholarship throughout the century has been to greater specialization. College professors were not just teachers on a particular campus; they were also research scholars operating in a national and international Republic of Letters. They established occasional newsletters, annual conferences and technical journals to support their specialty, and they seized upon the "lists" as a simple, cheap, fast communications medium run by and for their specialty.

H-Net as Humanities On-Line

H-Net announced itself to the world in December 1992 as a project to create and operate specialty lists for historians (and, soon, other humanists too). By June 1993, it had three lists in operation with 500 pioneer subscribers. By July 1994 it had 28 public lists that reached over 12,500 subscribers in 50 countries, with about one million messages a month. H-Net met the growth challenge by adding new lists in specialty areas, new editors, and a few nonmoderating staff. Most were college professors at smaller schools from every part of the United States, plus Canada, Australia, Britain, Italy, and Japan. The editors were all volunteers who contributed their time out of a sense that they were shaping the new communications system in academe. The editors ran

H-Net, electing officers and obtaining grants to cover expenses. The original H-Net goal was to support 25-35 electronic discussion lists for 5,000 historians by the year 1997. By mid-1995 it operated 49 lists reaching over 30,000 people in 60 countries—scholars, professors, graduate students, librarians, archivists, journalists, and teachers, plus a few undergraduates. Growth continued at 10 percent a month. At that rate, by 2000, every person in the world would be an H-Net subscriber, so the expectation is that this innovation will stabilize well before then. The dramatic technological advantages of Internet publication included prompt publication within hours, not months, and no printing or postage costs—and thus no artificial length limitations. Add to this the eagerness of publishers to become involved in the Information Highway, and H-Net had the formula for a highly innovative book review program. Each of its lists began commissioning book reviews, in fashion similar to paper journals. H-Net reviews were timely—they appeared as soon as their viewer finished them, and did not have to wait in a queue that was often one or two years long. Its reviews were more numerous and three times longer than the average for paper journals, and subscribers immediately reacted with comments, questions and rebuttals. The reviews were stored permanently on-line, and could be searched electronically.

To look behind the scene, consider H-Net's second-largest list, H-AmStdy. In March 1995 it had 1,250 subscribers representing all 50 states and DC, plus 140 others from 35 foreign countries. Among the subscribers were the directors of American Studies programs at 60 colleges, 80 full professors, 130 associate professors, and 408 assistant professors. (Computer users tend to be younger scholars.) Subscribers came from 620 different institutions, with strong representation from the large graduate programs. Two out of three were faculty or graduate students in an American Studies program, with the rest drawn from English, history, and numerous other departments, libraries, and museums. They received an average of 44 messages a week, every week of the year. In 1994 this one list posted about 500 research-related queries and 280 calls for papers. Its threads ranged from "Advice on Developing New American Studies Programs" and "Antiheroes in Oppositional Cultures" to "Wrestling in the 1950s" and "Zines." Many threads involved dozens of contributions, such as those on Disney history, historical consciousness, multiculturalism, and postmodernism, the relationship of American Studies to the social sciences, and homefront culture during World War II. All subscribers discussed their own background, teaching, and research in entries in an alphabetical "white pages" assembled by the editors. At a deeper level, however,

H-AmStdy was a revolt against the official print culture, against the established journals in American Studies, and, indeed, regularly questioned the notion that America was either unique or worthy.

The H-Net lists became one of the major communications media for humanities scholars, with notable impact on teaching, research, and community involvement. They had by far their greatest impact on people at the periphery of academe—graduate students, independent scholars, professors at smaller colleges, professors in other disciplines for whom history is a secondary interest. The lists have these people talking to one another, and discovering that they too were part of the Republic of Letters, that their ideas counted, that their teaching innovations and problems were of national interest, that scholarship no longer was a monopoly of famous graduate schools.

World Wide Web

After e-mail the second breakthrough in Internet connectivity was the creation of the World Wide Web and easy-to-use web browsers, especially Mosaic (invented at the University of Illinois-Urbana in 1993) and Netscape. Free software enabled anyone with academic or commercial Internet connections to become their own publisher by starting up a "home page." As folk art, the home page has its niche, especially as high-powered multimedia editors become available (in the late 1990s) to enable people to easily combine text, video, and sound. While a one-megabyte file is enough to contain the complete text of two scholarly books in ascii format, it suffices for only two or three seconds of video. To use multimedia for more than a minute or so, users will either turn to stand-alone CD-ROMS which can be sent through the mail, or they will use vast amounts of Internet bandwidth.

In 1995 it was hotly debated which way academe would go, as both CD-ROMS and Internet had advocates who stressed the relative advantages. One important advantage of CD-ROMS is that they can be sold—they are not free. Whether the Internet will develop financing mechanisms to keep itself alive remains an open question. Commercial providers, like America On-Line, Compuserve and Prodigy, with several million paying subscribers each, discovered that World Wide Web and Internet access was a major selling point. One key attraction of the World Wide Web is its unpredictability. The Web in 1995 contained far less information that the typical, under-utilized local public library, but it was new, exciting, unexplored. No one knew what would turn up around the next corner. Pornography, especially the hard-core variety not easily found in most places, was easy enough for teenagers to find, stirring up concerns about controls and censorship. The cartoons showed the father asking his son for help setting up an intercept program to limit access by the boy.

Academe started moving into the World Wide Web in 1994–95, but no one knew quite what to make of it. Librarians already had their card catalogs on-line; now they began uploading large textual data bases, such as guides to archives. Some libraries and historical societies began plans for putting photographic collections and historical documents on-line. Technologically the World Wide Web was much cheaper and easier to use than "distance learning" technology, suggesting that colleges could start offering courses on-line at low cost. With administrations eager to use high tech to lower instructional costs, it was likely that significant efforts would be made, especially in fields that depend heavily on text and images, like the humanities, rather than laboratory work.

Conclusion

Perhaps we should go back earlier than the new transportation systems, the automobile and railroad, for our analysis. Frederick Jackson Turner in 1893 propounded the "frontier thesis" to explain the evolution of American character. The prerailroad era was based on agriculture; most families lived by farming. In Europe, the good farm land was controlled by great lords and gentry, who built powerful governments, established churches, and a standing army. Individualism on the part of common people—peasants—was not fostered. Turner emphasized the easy availability of nearly "free" land in America, enabling the vast majority of white settlers to acquire economic independence. As each wave of settlers moved westward, they were further removed from the influences of Europe, and they discarded one after another of the European establishments. The further society moved west the more individualistic it became, the less tolerant of government or establishments, the more masculine. It became freer, more individualistic, less "cultured" (in European terms), more anarchistic, more violent, more American. The frontier—the periphery—decisively shaped American character. The economy is no longer based on farmland, or manufacturing. People who control vast acreages, or big factories, are no longer privileged and powerful. Instead the economy will be based on information and communication, and people who have information and communication will be privileged. That is a heady future, especially for academics who never felt fully comfortable in the agricultural or industrial stages of American society. But will free bandwidth have the same psychological and social impact on the American psyche as Turnerian free land? Will scholars on the periphery wrest control of their disciplines from the old core establishment? Will Info-Americans become more individualistic, more equalitarian, less respectful of academic hierarchies and established scholarly organizations? The flareup of "flame wars" and vigilante episodes suggest that the e-frontier will be anarchistic and violent. Will it create a new culture or merely manage to trash the print culture?

Bibliography

December, John, ed. *The World Wide Web Unleashed.* Indianapolis: SAMS, 1995.

Krol, Ed. *The Whole Internet User's Guide & Catalogue.* Sebastopol, CA: O'Reilly & Associates, 1994.

Millennium

Winfred E. Barton

I have been asked to present my thoughts about the term millennium . . . and rather than avoid the possibility of becoming sucked into philosophic quicksand maybe I can jump over the quagmire.

Predictability—second only to the discovery of the fountain of youth for humankind ever since we learned to reason, make fire, create excuses, and pass water without sitting in it. And now as we near the year 2k (at least by our most common calendar), will a major time juncture be at 2004–07, or will the millennium actually start in 1995–96? Maybe it really occurred in 1993! Even 1995 doesn't look all that promising at the moment.

These are the questions of humankind, this is the demand for predictability. Where we like to dwell in our discussions of intellect and merit is really upon probability under which guise humankind is often "predicted" to behave in a particular manner—especially in reaction to certain triggers of the ego system. Consider too that there is an absolute state of human positivity. Given time and good food people will become spoiled and arrogant, overbearing, self-serving, czarist, despotic communist, and ironhanded. Take away the food and pleasures and humans in their group form will simply become animalistic and mean. Beaten, whipped, starved, beheaded, and humiliated we become creatures of the spirit—people of prayer—apologist all. Purged of all evil we begin to accept our limitations (for a time), and the need to know the future increases exponentially. The multipliers increase again if we add the X factors of color, creed, race, and gender—or preferences for certain food groups. Then there is the great supercharger, the nova explosion—differing political opinions.

So everyone wants to know about the (a) millennium? Inject here the usual definitions:

1. Any span of 1000 years
2. A 1000-year span of holiness
3. The hoped-for period of happiness, justice, and prosperity (worldwide, that is).
4. Jesus' rule of 1000 years (after which the devil is released).

217

Item 3 above certainly does in a number of socio-politico-religiosity blurbs I've heard lately.

If you are not a Christian believer how is it that you are concerned about when, or even if there will be such an occurrence? Or, if you are a believer how is it that you worry about if or when the millennium will come—and go? Does the doubt come from the believer or nonbeliever? For one it will happen, and for the other it will not happen if there is an ending of time for humankind on this earth. If there is a great ending, does either win? If no end comes, can anyone win the game of predictability?

It would do much more for our state of humanity to concern ourselves with a transfer of our energies from indignance, arrogance, hate, and deceit to compassion, friendship and responsibility, work, honesty, loyalty and faith.

I don't have to predict the probability that self-discipline will be lacking and courage will fail many at lesser confrontations than a millennium would bring about.

Me, I'm a believer; and I fully accept that I know "neither the day nor the hour" and make no presumptions beyond my own behavior. "A wicked and adulterous generation looks for miraculous sign, but none will be given it except the sign of Jonah."

Did you say that the fountain of youth still hasn't been found either? . . . .

Contributors

Ken Baker is currently a reporter for the *Daily News* in Newport News, Virginia. He received his M.S. in journalism from Columbia University and his B.A. in geology from Colgate University, where he played on the varsity ice hockey team. Baker's religion writing has appeared in the *Washington Post, Charisma* magazine, and the *Buffalo (N.Y.) News* and is available to subscribers of the nationally syndicated Religion News Service. As a reporter and columnist, he frequently writes about popular culture issues. Baker, who considers himself a "nondenominational, nontraditional believer in God," lives in Hampton, Virginia.

Winfred E. Barton is the Manager of Classroom Audiovisual Services at Virginia Polytechnic Institute and State University, Blacksburg, Virginia. He and his wife, Sue, are parents of a daughter and two sons. A scholar of politics and the behavior of mankind, and a descendant of the earliest settlers in the Blue Ridge and New River areas of Virginia, Barton has a great interest in history and pursues an active evaluation of human attitudes. Prior to his work at Virginia Tech, he was employed in corporate research and development.

Ray B. Browne is Chairman Emeritus of the Popular Culture Department at Bowling Green State University. With Marshall Fishwick, he founded the Popular Culture Association/American Culture Association, the *Journal of Popular Culture*, and the *Journal of American Culture*. He is the author and editor of more than 50 books on various aspects of American and world cultures.

James Combs has written extensively on politics and popular culture including, most recently, *Phony Culture, Film Propaganda and American Politics*, and *The Comedy of Democracy*. He is currently at work on "The Global Political Village," shamelessly ripping off McLuhan's famous phrase. He hopes to keep studying popular culture, and live long enough in the new century to delight if it is a garden, and disappear quietly if it is a desert.

Marshall Fishwick, a founder and past president of the Popular Culture Association, is Professor of Humanities and Communication Studies at

Virginia Tech. He serves on the Advisory Board of the *Journal of Popular Culture* and the *Journal of American Culture*, and has held Fulbright grants to Denmark, Germany, Italy, India, Russia, Poland, Bangladesh, and Korea. He joined the staff of the Salzburg Seminar in Austria in 1995 for lectures on "American Popular Culture." Recent books include *Great Awakenings: Popular Religion and Popular Culture* and *Go and Catch a Falling Star: Pursuing Popular Culture.*

Gerald Graff is George M. Pullman Professor of English and Education at the University of Chicago. He is the author of *Professing Literature* and *Beyond the Culture Wars.*

H. Theodore Groat is a Professor of Sociology at Bowling Green State University, where he teaches community, social demography, and social stratification. Much of his research has been funded by various government agencies, including the Center for Population Research (NIH) and the Violence and Traumatic Stress Branch of NIMH. Currently, he is collaborating on a longitudinal project that is examining the life-career paths of young adults who, as adolescents, were serious juvenile offenders.

John A. Hague, a Yale Ph.D. in American Studies, taught at Yale from 1950 until 1955 and at Stetson from 1955 until his retirement in 1992. In 1979 he received the award for outstanding teaching at Stetson, and in 1992 was named Florida Professor of the year by the Council for the Advancement and Support of Education. In 1989 he received the Bode-Pearson prize for distinguished contributions to the national American Studies Association. He has edited two books dealing with American Culture, and is now writing a book titled "Search for Identities in Contemporary America." Currently Dr. Hague is serving as an advisor to the American Studies Center in Salzburg, Austria. That Center is in the process of establishing an International American Studies and English Language Faculty.

Richard Jensen, Professor of History at the University of Illinois-Chicago, is the Executive Director of H-Net. He is a specialist in historiography and American political history.

Jack B. Moore is a Professor of English and American Studies at the University of South Florida. His books include studies of W.E.B. Du Bois, Joe DiMaggio, and the culture of American skinheads. Along with his social worker wife, Judith Moore, the parent of five children, he has long been a concerned observer of the passing contemporary music scene in its manifold incarnations, and one of his favorite female singers is still Doris Day.

Arthur G. Neal, a Distinguished University Professor of Sociology at Bowling Green State University, recently retired and is currently living in Portland, Oregon. His research interests over the years have been focused on the forms, antecedents, and consequences of alienation within community-wide populations. His present research is on individual and collective responses to the major national traumas of the twentieth century. Attention is directed toward the place of trauma in shaping national identity as well as toward the variety of ways that traumatic events become embedded in collective memories.

Gerry O'Connor broke in with Toledo in '70, got called up to the Bigs by veteran skipper Ray Browne in '71. Ray was managing in East Lansing that year, the same year that the phenom from Brooklyn, Dick Powers, broke in. Since then, O'Connor has caught some of the greatest pitchers in PCA history: the legendary Tom Towers, the immortal Rich Shereikis, the fabled Peter Lennon, the late great Don Hausdorff. And others like Dan Fuller, Josie Campbell, Jim Ferreira, Lew Carlson. O'Connor is Professor Emeritus of the English Department at the University of Massachusetts, at Lowell.

Richard Gid Powers has been trying for a quarter of a century to stop Ray Browne from destroying those few remaining standards that keep mankind from slipping back into the muck. During those infrequent interludes when Ray is temporarily distracted from his impious schemes, Powers manages to write things like *G-Men: Hoover's FBI in American Popular Culture; Secrecy and Power: The Life of J. Edgar Hoover;* and *Not Without Honor: The History of American Anticommunism* and teaches in the History Department at the College of Staten Island and the Graduate Center of CUNY.

Stephen J. Stein is Chancellor's Professor of Religious Studies, Adjunct Professor of History, and Chair of the Department of Religious Studies, Indiana University, Bloomington. His publications include volume 5 entitled *Apocalyptic Writings,* in *The Works of Jonathan Edwards* and *The Shaker Experience in America: A History of the United Society of Believers.* He is a past president of the American Society of Church History.

Carol Traynor Williams is Chair of the Travel Culture sections for the Popular Culture Association national conferences, and is compiling an anthology of papers written for these conferences in 1995 and 1996. She is Professor of Humanities at Roosevelt University and author of *"It's Time for My Story": Soap Opera Sources, Structure, and Response; The Dream Beside Me: The Movies and the Children of the Forties;* and articles on television, literature, women's studies, rhetoric, and adult education.